CADOGAN GUIDES

"Entertaining companion, with sharp insights, local gossip and far more of a feeling of a living author ... The series has received plaudits worldwide for intelligence, originality and a slightly irreverent sense of fun."
—*Daily Telegraph*

"The most attractive of all general guides series published in recent years. The elegant jackets, the literate cultured texts and the balanced practical information make these enlightening companions for the independent traveller and luxury tourist alike."
—*The Bookseller*

"Cadogan Guides' 'Spain' is one of those books you can easily curl up in bed with. It's also full of useful details that other authors omit—the address of the best English bookshops, for example, and a shortlist of the most curious sights of Spain."
—*Costa Blanca News*

"It is difficult to praise the Cadogan Guides series too highly." —*The Independent*

Other titles in the Cadogan Guide series:

AUSTRALIA
BALI
BERLIN
THE CARIBBEAN
GREEK ISLANDS
INDIA
IRELAND
ITALIAN ISLANDS
ITALY
MOROCCO
NEW YORK
NORTHEAST ITALY
NORTHWEST ITALY
PORTUGAL
PRAGUE
ROME
SCOTLAND
SOUTH ITALY

SPAIN
THAILAND & BURMA
TUNISIA
TURKEY
TUSCANY, UMBRIA AND
  THE MARCHES
VENICE

Forthcoming:

AMSTERDAM
CENTRAL AMERICA
CZECHOSLOVAKIA
ECUADOR, COLOMBIA &
  THE GALAPAGOS
GERMANY
MEXICO
MOSCOW & LENINGRAD
SOUTH OF FRANCE

ABOUT THE AUTHORS

Authors of a number of travel guides on the Mediterranean and United States, Michael Pauls and Dana Facaros lived in Granada for a year researching the Cadogan Guide to Spain, visiting its distant corners and seldom-frequented villages, and trying not to eat too many *churros*.

Travellers and teachers Michael Davidson and Brian Walsh have updated all the practical information in this guide, and added to the book immeasurably with research and experience gathered in their travels from their home in Spain. Michael and Brian updated the Cadogan Italy Series; they have a home in Umbria, where they met the authors, and became firm friends.

ACKNOWLEDGEMENTS

This book would not have been possible without Michael and Brian, whose healthy disregard for national boundaries and love of Europe made them well qualified for the job. They were true Europeans long before it became fashionable.

The updaters would like to thank Valerie Moore and Michael Lloyd for free rein on their friendship, home and office; David and Joanne; all the folks at El Faro; Enzo Russi in Torremolinos; Ana Colom and Bertha in Sevilla; Pat and George, Joe of Campo Blanco; James Gaggero and Joshua Gabay of Gibraltar; and all the staff in the tourist offices for their help and patience.

The publishers would particularly like to thank Meg and Stephen Davies for respectively indexing and proof-reading this book.

PLEASE NOTE

Every effort has been made to ensure the accuracy of the information in this book at the time of going to press. However, practical details such as opening hours, travel information, standards in hotels and restaurants and, in particular, prices are liable to change.

We intend to keep this book as up-to-date as possible in the coming years. Please write to us if there is anything you feel should be included in future editions.

CADOGAN GUIDES

SOUTHERN SPAIN

Gibraltar & Andalucía

DANA FACAROS & MICHAEL PAULS

CADOGAN BOOKS
London

THE GLOBE PEQUOT PRESS
Chester, Connecticut

Cadogan Books Ltd
Mercury House, 195 Knightsbridge, London SW7 1RE
Copyright © Dana Facaros & Michael Pauls 1991
Illustrations © Pauline Pears 1987, 1991
Maps © Cadogan Books Ltd 1991,
drawn by Thames Cartographic Services Ltd
Cover design by Keith Pointing
Cover illustration by Povl Webb
Index by Meg Davies
Updaters: Michael Davidson and Brian Walsh
Editor: Victoria Ingle
Series Editors: Rachel Fielding and Paula Levey

Extracted from the Cadogan Guide to Spain (first published 1987,
updated and revised 1989), with amendments and additions.

A catalogue record for this book is available from the British Library.

ISBN 0–947754–28–8

Library of Congress data available.

ISBN 0–87106–187–2

Photoset in Ehrhardt on a Linotron 202
Printed on recycled paper and bound in Great Britain by
Redwood Press Limited, Melksham, Wiltshire

CONTENTS

LIST OF MAPS

INTRODUCTION

There is a story about haughty Queen Isabella, so proud of her conquest of the godless Moors of Andalucía, that sums up the region's sad history...

The Moors, lovers of art and poetry, were also the great architects of water, making the dry hills of the south into lush fields and gardens; Spanish folktales often speak of them almost as sorcerers. During the campaigns against Granada, Isabel found herself lodging at the Alcazar of Córdoba, where an old Moorish waterwheel in the Guadalquivir churned up water for the pools and fountains of the Alcazar gardens. After a few nights Isabel ordered it dismantled—it disturbed her sleep.

The ghost of Islamic al-Andalus still haunts the south; a more graceful and delicate spirit could not be desired. In the gardens and palaces, and in the white villages this great, lost civilization is a separate reality that shines through centuries of Spanish veneer. And what of the new Andalucía, after its centuries of trouble, of oppression and Inquisitions, expulsions, poverty and emigration? It is looking exceedingly well, thank you, with its exuberant life and culture, and a delightful, fun-loving population of sane and friendly people, as much of an attraction as the land itself. Andalucía is a minefield of unexploded stereotypes: sequined matadors and strumming guitars, torrid flamenco and hot-blooded gypsies, orange blossoms and jasmine. They may be hard to avoid, but then again, why try? Few regions of Europe have been blessed with such stereotypes. Visitors never weary of them, and the Andalucíans certainly don't either; they cultivate and polish them with the greatest of care.

Today, with its new green and white flag flying proudly on every public building, autonomous, democratic Andalucía may have the chance to rediscover itself. With a fifth of Spain's population, its biggest tourist industry, and potentially its richest agriculture, it has great promise for the future. And as the part of Spain with the longest and most brilliant artistic heritage—not only from the Moors, but from the troubled, creative, post-Reconquista Andalucía that has given Spain Velázquez, García Lorca and Manuel de Falla—the region may find it still has the resources once more to become the leader in Spain's cultural life.

For its size, Andalucía contains a remarkable diversity of landscapes—from Spain's highest mountains to endless rolling hills covered with olive trees, Europe's biggest marshland preserve and even some patches of desert. And no other part of Spain can offer so many interesting large cities. Andalucía is a world unto itself; it has as many delights to offer as you have time to spend on it.

How This Book is Organized

For convenience, we've divided Andalucía's complicated geography into four parts: Sevilla, Córdoba, and the valley of the Guadalquivir; then the coasts, of which the famous Costa del Sol is only a small part; next come the inimitable white villages of the mountains, between the Guadalquivir and the sea; then Granada and the Sierra Nevada. Finally, we deal with Gibraltar.

THE BEST OF SOUTHERN SPAIN

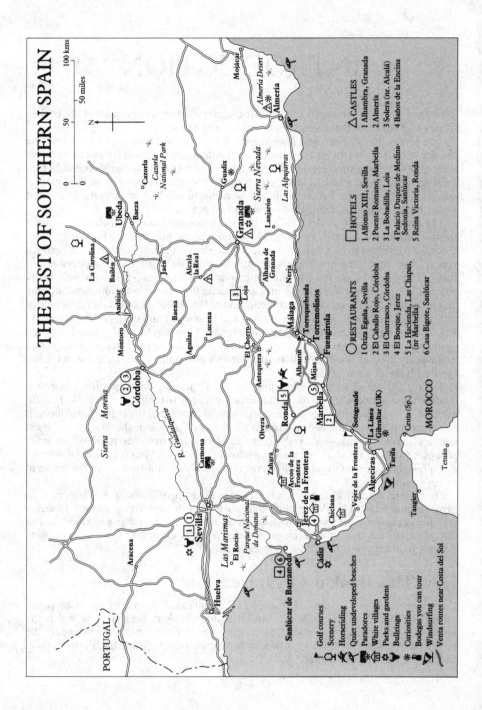

100 kms
50 miles

△ CASTLES
1 Alhambra, Granada
2 Almería
3 Solera (nr. Alcalá)
4 Baños de la Encina

□ HOTELS
1 Alfonso XIII, Sevilla
2 Puente Romano, Marbella
3 La Bobadilla, Loja
4 Palacio Duques de Medina-
Sedonia, Sanlúcar
5 Reina Victoria, Ronda

○ RESTAURANTS
1 Oriza Egaña, Sevilla
2 El Caballo Rojo, Córdoba
3 El Churrasco, Córdoba
4 El Bosque, Jerez
5 La Hacienda, Las Chapas,
(nr Marbella)
6 Casa Bigote, Sanlúcar

PORTUGAL

MOROCCO

Golf courses
Scenery
Horseriding
Quiet undeveloped beaches
Paradores
White villages
Parks and gardens
Bullrings
Curiosities
Bodegas you can tour
Windsurfing
Venta routes near Costa del Sol

The Best of Southern Spain

This selection is admittedly subjective, but it may give you a start in planning your holiday. In no particular order...

Scenery: mountains around Ronda and the Alpujarras (Granada); the Pass of Despeña-perros, and the rugged heights of the Sierra Nevada.

Towns and villages: Arcos, and the picturesque White Villages of Andalucía and their views; Cazorla and Baeza (both near Ubeda), Alhama de Granada, Montoro, Mojacár, Zahara, Nerja (especially for views).

Parks and gardens: the tropical plantlife and trimmed hedges of the Generalife in Granada; the Alameda gardens of Cádiz, and several in Sevilla.

Bullrings: Ronda, Sevilla, Córdoba.

Wild country: Sierra Nevada and Alpujarras (Granada); the marshlands of Las Maris-mas and Coto Doñana National Park (near Huelva); the hiking country of the Sierra de Cazorla (near Ubeda); Almería desert; and the twisted rock formations of El Torcal National Park.

Castles: Alhambra (Granada), Almería, Baños de la Encina (near Bailén), Solera (near Alcalá).

Bodegas you can tour: Alcazaba, La Tasca and Gonzalez Byass in Jerez de la Frontera.

Beaches: many quiet, undeveloped beaches on the windy Costa de la Luz, and sandy coves in Almería.

Curiosities: Gibraltar; cave dwellings in Guadix; mini-Hollywood in Almería.

Restaurants: El Caballo Rojo and El Churrasco (Córdoba), Egaña Oriza (Sevilla), Casa Bigote (Sanlúcar de Barrameda), El Bosque (Jerez de la Frontera), La Hacienda (Las Chapas, nr. Marbella).

Hotels: the 18th-century splendour of the Alfonso XIII (Sevilla); the superb setting and gardens of the Puente Romano (Marbella); the grand but affordable Palacio Duques de Medina Sedonia (Sanlúcar de Barrameda); the old-world charm of the Reina Victoria (Ronda); and the pueblo-style La Bobadilla (Loja).

Paradores: Granada, Carmona, Ubeda.

Golf courses: Torrequebrada (between Torremolinos and Málaga), Sotogrande (near Gibraltar).

Windsurfing: off Tarifa.

Horse trekking/riding: Serrania de Ronda.

Venta routes: through the mountains of Málaga along the old road to Granada, along the Guadalhorce river valley through Churriana, Cartama and Alhaurin; along the road to Ronda from San Pedro de Alcántara; along the road to Ojen from Marbella; the road from Mijas to Alhaurin el Grande.

SOUTHERN SPAIN

Part I

GENERAL INFORMATION

Getting to Spain

By Air

There is an astounding variety of flight options from North America and especially from the UK; even Spain's national airline, **Iberia**, offers tempting discounts—bargain fly-drive deals, as well as an unlimited domestic flight option for purchasers of regular flight tickets. No matter how you go, you can always save by going off-season (15 September–June).

APEX fares, purchased at least two weeks in advance, and for a stay of 7–180 days, offer a discount, especially if you're travelling in the mid-week. Ask, too, about their UK deals: 'Moneysaver' weekend specials, 'Countdown' second-ticket discounts to Almería, Jerez and Málaga, 'Citysaver' reductions on flights to Sevilla, and discounts for children under 12. Discounts are also available for domestic flights, especially if you're flying from North America: inquire about the 'Visit Spain' offer.

Iberia Offices in the UK and Ireland

130 Regent St, London W1R 5FE. Reservations: Mon–Fri, 8–8, Sat and Sun 9–5.30, tel (071) 437 5622. Information: tel (071) 437 9822
15th Floor, The Rotunda Building, New Street, Birmingham B2 4PA. Reservations: Mon–Fri, 9–5.30, tel (021) 643 1953. Information: tel (021) 643 9726
Room 2, Level 5, Manchester Airport, Manchester M22 5PA. Mon–Fri, 9–5.30, tel (061) 436 6444

Stock Exchange House, 7 Nelson Mandela Place, Glasgow G2 1QY. Mon–Fri, 9–5:30, tel (041) 248 6581
54 Dawson St, Dublin 2, tel (010 353 1) 779 846

Iberia Offices in the US and Canada
509 Madison Ave, New York, NY 10022. Tel (212) 644 8843
Suite 1308, 150 South East Second Avenue, Miami, Florida 33131. Tel (305) 381 8301
205 North Michigan Ave, Chicago, Illinois 60601. Tel (312) 819 2900
20 Park Plaza, Boston, Massachusettes 02116. Tel (617) 426 8335
1725 K. Street NW, Washington DC 20006. Tel (202) 293 6970
8111 LBJ Freeway, Suite 941, Dallas. Tel (214) 669 3336
From anywhere in the US, you can use Iberia's toll-free line (800) 221 9741.
102 Bloor St West, Toronto. Tel (416) 964 6625
2020 University St, Montreal H3A 2A5. Tel (514) 849 3352
While most regular flights from the US or Canada are to Madrid or Barcelona, from the UK you can also fly direct from Heathrow to Alicante, Bilbao, Santiago, Málaga, Sevilla or Valencia, or from Manchester direct to Madrid or Barcelona.

Other Airlines
British Airways (from the UK) or **TWA** and **Pan Am** from the US offer many of the same services as Iberia. **GB Airways** has daily flights from London to Gibraltar, and several times a week from Manchester.
British Airways: Serrano 60, Madrid (91) 431 7575
Pan Am: Gran Vía 88, Madrid. Tel (91) 241 4200
TWA: Pl. Colón, 2 Madrid. Tel (91) 410 6012

Charter Flights from the UK
These can be incredibly cheap, and offer the added advantage of departing from local airports. Companies such as **Thomson**, **Air Tours** and **Unijet** offer return flights ranging from £130–220. This theoretically includes *basic* accommodation, but nobody expects you to make use of this facility. Some of the best deals have return dates limited strictly to one week or two; sometimes four, the maximum allowed by law. In many cases, though, a return charter ticket is a big saving over a one-way regular fare—and although it's illegal to sell the return half of your charter ticket, who's going to put you in jail? In London, check it out at your local economy travel agent or bucket shop, or in your local paper or *Time Out*.

Charter Flights from the US
These require a bit more perseverance to find, though you can save considerably on the cost of a regular or APEX flight—currently a charter from New York to Madrid is around $800. You may want to weigh this against the current trans-Atlantic fares to London, where in most cases you can get a low-cost flight to Spain departing within a day or two of your arrival. This is an especially cheap way to go in the off season.

Call the major charter companies and compare prices: **Access**, New York, tel (212) 333 7280, Toll Free No. (800) 333 7280, is often the cheapest, even if you end up flying to Málaga via Morocco sometimes. It is also one of the USA's prototype 'bucket shops',

2

offering good last-minute options on empty charter seats. **Spanish Heritage Association** at 116 West 47 Queens Blvd, Forest Hills, NY 17375, tel (718) 520 1300, makes use of SPANTAX, a Spanish charter firm. They're in New York, tel (718) 520 1300. Also try **TFI**, New York, tel (212) 736 1140, Toll Free No. (800) 223 6363; **DER**, Los Angeles, tel (213) 479 4140, Toll Free No. (800) 782 2424. The Sunday *New York Times* has the most listings.

Get your ticket as early as possible, but be doubly sure of your plans, as there are no refunds for missed flights—most travel agencies sell insurances, so that you don't lose all your money if you become ill. You can also expect delays on charters. Students and anyone under 26 have the additional option of special discount charters, departing from the UK. Most of the big firms have offices in major cities. In London they are **STA Travel**, 6 Wright's Lane, W8, tel (071) 937 9921; **Academic Travel**, 38 Store St, WC1, tel (071) 580 7733; and **USIT**, 52 Grosvenor Gardens, SW1, tel (071) 730 7285.

By Ferry

The last sea link between Spain and Great Britain is the **Plymouth–Santander Ferry**, operated by Brittany Ferries. This is a good way to go if you mean to bring your car or bicycle. Prices for passengers are just a bit less than a charter flight; children from 4–13 go for half price, under 4s free. Prices for vehicles vary on size and season—it's most expensive from 22 July–16 September; one adult (without vehicle) pays £65–74 one way, one adult with vehicle pays £125–200 depending on length and type of vehicle. In the high season, on-board accommodation goes from £5.50 for a simple Pullman seat, to £22 to share a four-berth cabin, finishing at £105 for a deluxe twin-berth cabin. There are also 8-day return specials, where one adult plus car comes to £180–270. The 24-hour crossing is made twice a week. For more information, contact your travel agent or Brittany Ferries in Plymouth, Milbay Docks, Plymouth PL1 3EF, tel (0752) 221321. In Santander the address is the Estación Marítima, tel (942) 21 45 00.

By Train

From London to Andalucía takes at least a day and a half and requires a change of trains in Paris and Madrid or Barcelona. A two-month return, London–Madrid costs £163; London–Sevilla, £175. Students, those under 26 and holders of a Senior Citizen's Railcard can get reductions.

If you've been a resident in Europe for the past 6 months and are under 26, you can take advantage of the **InterRail Pass**, available at British Rail or any travel agent's, giving you a month's rail travel for £175, as well as half-price discounts on Channel crossings and ferries to Morocco, where the pass is also valid. The American **EurRail Pass**, which must be purchased before you leave the States, is a good deal only if you plan to use the trains every day in Spain and elsewhere—though it's not valid in Great Britain, Morocco or Eastern Europe. A month of travel is around $460 for those under 26; those over 26 can get a 15-day pass for $550 or a month for $630. In Spain you'll have to pay supplements for any kind of express train. Note that neither InterRail nor EurRail passes are valid on Spain's numerous narrow-gauge (FEVE) lines. Rail tickets to Spain from

3

England, or vice versa, can be obtained from: British Rail Continental Ltd, Ticket and Information Office, PO Box 29, Victoria Station, London SW1V 1JX, tel (071) 834 2345. Tickets for local Spanish services can be obtained from certain UK travel agents, but bookings must be made weeks in advance. For *couchette* and sleeper reservations in France, contact French Railways, 179 Piccadilly, London W1, tel (071) 409 3518.

By Bus or Coach

One major company, Eurolines, tel (071) 730 0202, offers departures several times a week from London to Spain, along the east coast as far as Alicante, or to Algeciras via San Sebastián, Burgos, Madrid, Córdoba, and Málaga. Buses take nearly two days, a couple of hours longer than the train. An adult single costs £75–80, return £135–140. Within the British Isles, National Express and Caledonian Express connect with the continental bus service. There's a special deal which will get you as far as Alicante for about £50, from where buses leave regularly for destinations further south. In the summer the coach is the best bargain for anyone over 26; off-season you'll probably find a cheaper charter flight. Details of all UK–Spain bus services can be obtained from the Spanish Tourist Office in London.

By Car

From the UK via France you have a choice of routes. Ferries from Portsmouth cross to Cherbourg, Caen, Le Havre and St Malo. From any of these ports the most direct route takes you to Bordeaux, down the western coast of France to the border at Irun, and on to San Sebastián, Burgos and Madrid, from where you can choose your entry point into Andalucía. An alternative route is Paris to Perpignan, crossing the border at the Mediterranean side of the Pyrenees, then along the coast to Barcelona, where the E15 will take you south. Both routes take an average of two days' steady driving. You may find it more convenient and less tiring to try the ferry from Plymouth to Santander, which cuts out driving through France and saves expensive *autoroute* tolls. For the scenery, opt for one of the routes over the Pyrenees, through Puigcerdà and Somport-Canfranc or Andorra, but expect heavy traffic; if you're not in a hurry, take the classic route through Roncevalles, Vall d'Aran, or through Tarbes and Aragnouet through the tunnel to Parzán.

Passports, Customs and Visas

Holders of British, Irish, US or Canadian passports can enter Spain for up to 3 months without a visa; holders of Australian or New Zealand passports need a visa, available from any Spanish consulate. You can also enter Spain with a 'British Visitor's Card'. If you fly to Gibraltar you'll have no trouble getting into Spain.

If you are a British citizen or EEC national residing in the UK and want to stay in Spain for longer than 3 months, you must apply for a residence visa from the Spanish Consulate (20 Draycott Place, London SW3 2RZ) *before you go*. This entitles you to an extended stay of 6 months and costs about £40. For extensions beyond that, or for full-residence permits, once you are in the country you are required to apply to your local

Spanish police station within 90 days of arrival, taking with you your passport, a couple of photographs and evidence that you are financially self-supporting, i.e. you are living on a pension or independent income (£6,000 a year). For full permanent-resident status you must obtain a *visado de residencia* from your nearest Spanish consulate. This entitles you to apply for permanent residence upon arrival in Spain. Note that this does not allow you to seek employment—to obtain a work permit you are obliged to present written proof of an offer of employment.

For Gibraltar there are no extra visa requirements for US citizens, and EEC nationals have the same rights and status as in the UK.

Customs are usually polite and easy to get through—unless you come in through Morocco, where they'll search through everything you own. If coming from the UK or USA, don't bother to pick up any duty-free alcohol—it's cheaper on the supermarket shelves in Spain. It may be worth buying cigarettes if you are fussy about the flavour of your tobacco.

Spanish Consulates in the UK and Ireland
20 Draycott Place, London SW3 2RZ. Tel (071) 581 5924
1 Brooks House, 70 Spring Gardens, Manchester 2. Tel (061) 236 1233
63 North Castle Street, Edinburgh EH3. Tel (031) 220 1483
17a Merlyn Park, Ballsbridge, Dublin 4. Tel (010 353 1) 691 640.

Spanish National Tourist Offices

Before you go, you can get maps, brochures and booklets from the national travel offices listed below:
London: 57–58 St James St, London SW1A ILD. Tel (071) 499 0901
Chicago: 845 North Michigan Ave, Chicago, Illinois 60611. Tel (312) 944 0215
Houston: 4800 The Galleria, 5085 Westheimer, Houston, Texas 77056. Tel (713) 840 7411
New York: 665 Fifth Ave, New York, NY 10022. Tel (212) 759 8822
St Augustine: Casa del Hidalgo, Hipolita and St George Sts, St Augustine, Florida 32084. Tel (904) 829 6460
Toronto: 102 Bloor St West 201, Toronto, Ontario, M4W 388. Tel (416) 961 3131

Getting Around Spain

By Air

Internal flights in Spain are on Iberia or Aviaco. Both carriers are nationally run and almost always share the same office in the cities. In Andalucía you'll find airports in Almería, Córdoba, Granada, Jerez (Cádiz), Málaga, Sevilla, together with Melilla in North Africa.

Prices are inexpensive compared to most of Europe, and if you shop around and are willing to travel at night on slow days you can pick up some bargains, especially if you're going on a round trip. Also, check out the national charters in Spanish travel agencies.

Iberia Offices in Southern Spain
Sevilla: Almirante Lobo 2. Tel (954) 422 8901

Córdoba: Ronda de los Tejares 3. Tel (957) 47 89 28
Granada: Plaza Isabel la Católica 2. Tel (958) 22 75 92
Málaga: Molina Lario 13. Tel (952) 22 76 03
Jerez: Plaza Reyes Católicos 2. Tel (956) 34 40 54
Almería: Paseo de Almería 42. Tel (951) 23 00 34
Gibraltar: Com. Centre, 24 Main St. Tel (350) 77666.

By Car

This is probably the most pleasurable way of getting about, though the convenience is balanced by a considerably greater cost; petrol is as expensive in Spain as anywhere else in Europe, and unlike Italy, there are no petrol concessions or coupons for tourists. In cities, parking is always difficult; another problem is that only a few hotels—the more expensive ones—have garages or any sort of parking. Spain's highway network is adequate and in good repair, and many major cities are now linked by dual carriageways. The government is currently investing trillions of pesetas on a full-scale highway system, but until it is completed, you will often have to be content with the two-lane roads that blanket most of the country. Once you venture off the beaten track, be prepared for a few surprises; some roads in Andalucía wind tortuously up mountainsides, with steep drops into gorges below. Pay particular attention when driving on the notorious N340 between Málaga and Gibraltar, also known as 'mortuary mile'.

To drive in Spain you'll need an **International Driver's Licence**, available through the AA or RAC or any auto club in the US, and a **Green Card** proving limited liability insurance. Americans should not be intimidated by driving in Europe. Learn the international road-sign system (charts available to members from most auto clubs), brush up on your gear-stick shift technique, and get used to the idea of few signals, and traffic constantly converging from all directions. Seat belts are mandatory. The speed limit is 100 km per hour on national highways, unless otherwise marked, and 120 km per hour on motorways. Drive with the utmost care at all times— having an accident will bring you untold headaches, and to make matters worse, many Spaniards drive without insurance.

Renting Cars

This is moderately cheaper than elsewhere in Europe. The big international companies are the most expensive but ATESA, the government-owned Spanish firm, is cheaper. Prices for the smallest cars begin at about £80 ($160) per week with unlimited mileage, insurance extra. Small local firms can sometimes offer a better deal, but these should be treated with some caution. On the Costa del Sol you may find some slightly better deals, but often with a stipulation that you limit your driving to the coastal region between Málaga and Algeciras. Local firms also rent **mopeds** and **bicycles**, especially in tourist areas. **Hitchhiking** involves a long wait anywhere; few Spaniards ever do it.

Ask your travel agent about the 'Tour Spain' package that offers an inclusive price for ATESA car hire and accommodation in any of Spain's *paradores* for seven nights or more. The plan is for a minimum of two people or maximum of four in one car; savings are considerable.

6

By Train

Mister Traveler, take the Spanish Train!
—RENFE brochure

If you're using public transportation, there is usually an even choice between the bus and train. The slight difference in price usually favours the train, while buses are usually a bit faster and run more frequently.

Democracy in Spain has made the trains run on time, but Western Europe's most eccentric railway, **RENFE**, still has a way to go. The problem isn't the trains themselves; they're almost always clean and comfortable, and do their best to keep to the schedules, but the new efficient RENFE remains so phenomenally complex it will foul up your plans at least once if you spend much time in Spain.

To start with, there are no fewer than 13 varieties of train, from the luxury **TEE** (Trans-Europe Express) to the excruciating *semidirecto* and *ferrobús*. Watch out for these; they stop at every conceivable hamlet to deliver mail. The best are the **Talgo** trains, speedy and stylish beasts in gleaming stainless steel, designed and built entirely in Spain; the Spaniards are very proud of them. **TER** trains are almost as good. Note that a majority of lines are still, incredibly, single-track, so whatever train you take, you'll still have to endure delays for trains coming the other way.

Every variety of train has different services and a different price. RENFE ticket people and conductors can't always get them straight, and confusion is rampant. Prices are never consistent. There are discounts for children (under 4 years old, free; 4–12 pay 50 per cent), large families, senior citizens (50 per cent), regular travellers, and 25 per cent discounts on *Días Azules* ('blue days') for *round-trip tickets only*. 'Blue days' are posted in the RENFE calendars in every station—really almost every day is a 'blue day'. Interpretations of the rules for these discounts differ from one ticket-window to the next, and you may care to undertake protracted negotiations over them like the Spaniards do. There is a discount pass for people under 26, the *tarjeta joven*, and BIGE or BIJ youth fares are available from TIVE offices in the large cities.

Every city has a **RENFE travel office** in the centre, and you can make good use of these for information and tickets. Always buy tickets in advance if you can; one of RENFE's little tricks is to close station ticket-windows 10 minutes before your train arrives, and if you show up at the last minute you could be out of luck. Other stations don't open the ticket-windows until the train is a couple of minutes away, causing panic and confusion. Don't rely on the list of trains posted; always ask at the station or travel office. There may well be an earlier train that makes an obscure connection. Fares average 500 pts for every 100 km (63 miles)—750 pts first class—but there are supplements on the faster trains that can raise the price by as much as 80 per cent.

RENFE has plenty of services you'll never hear about—like car transport to all parts of Spain. If you plan to do a lot of riding on the rails, buy the *Guía RENFE*, an indispensable government publication with all the schedules, tariffs, and information, available for a pittance from any station newsagent.

Excursion Trains

Southern Spain's answer to the famous Transcantábrica which operates in NW Spain, is the *Al Andalus Expresso*, a luxury tour taking passengers from Sevilla to Córdoba,

Granada, Málaga and Jerez. Although expensive, the trip is a memorable experience—the carriages are done out in fancy period decor and the cuisine is superb. The trip takes 4–5 days, depending on which 'cruise' you take. For details of RENFE cruises, contact: Marsans Travel, 7a Henrietta Place, London W1M 9AG (tel (071) 493 4934) or the same company in the US: 205 East 42nd St, Suite 1514, New York, NY (tel (212) 661 6565); or RENFE direct.

Local Renfe Offices
Almería (951) 25 11 35
Cádiz (956) 25 43 01
Córdoba (957) 47 87 21
Granada (958) 27 12 72
Huelva (955) 24 66 66
Linares/Baeza (Jaén) (953) 65 01 31
Málaga (952) 31 25 00
Sevilla (954) 41 41 11

By Bus

With literally dozens of companies providing services over southern Spain, expect confusion. Not all cities have bus stations; in some there may be a dozen little offices spread around town for each firm. Like the trains, buses are cheap by northern European standards, but still no bargain; if you're travelling on the cheap you'll find that transportation is your biggest expense. Usually, whether you go by train or bus will depend on simple convenience: in some places the train station is far from the centre, in others the bus station is. Again, sometimes on the inter-city routes, tickets are sold at the last minute.

Small towns and villages can normally be reached by bus only through their provincial capitals. Buses are usually clean, dependable and comfortable, and there's plenty of room for baggage in the compartment underneath. On the more luxurious buses you even get air-conditioning and a movie (Rambo, Kung Fu, sappy Spanish flicks from the Franco era or locally produced rock videos). **Tourist information offices** are the best sources for information.

By Boat

The *Transmediterránea* line operates services from the Spanish mainland to the Balearic Islands, North Africa and the Canary Islands. Full details may be obtained from their agents, Melia Travel, 12 Dover St, London W1LX 4NS (tel (071) 491 3881 and 409 1884).

Left Luggage

Since terrorists began leaving bombs in rail stations, RENFE has closed all of its left-luggage facilities; you'll have about an even chance of finding one in a bus station or small bus company office, and sometimes bars near train or bus stations are willing to let you leave your bags. Ask around; the word in Spanish is *consigna*.

City Buses and Taxis

Every Spanish city has a perfectly adequate system of public transportation. You won't need to make much use of it, though, for in almost every city all attractions are within walking distance of each other. City buses usually cost 65 or 75 pts, and if you intend to use them often there are books of tickets called *abonamientos* or *bono-Bus* or *tarjeta* cards to punch on entry, available at reduced rates from tobacco shops. Bus drivers will give change but don't give them a 1000 pta note. In many cities, the bus's entire route will be displayed on the signs at each stop (*parada*).

Taxis are still cheap enough for the Spaniards to use them regularly on their shopping trips. The average fare for a ride within a city will be 500–700 pts. Taxis are not always metered, but the drivers are usually quite honest; they are entitled to certain surcharges (for luggage, night or holiday trips, to the train or airport, etc.), and if you cross the city limits they usually can charge double the fare shown. It's rarely hard to hail a cab from the street, and there will always be a few around the stations. If you get stuck where there are none, call information for the number of a radio taxi.

Tourist Information

After receiving millions of tourists each year for the last two decades, no country has more information offices, or more helpful ones, or more intelligent brochures and detailed maps. Every city will have an office, and about two-thirds of the time you'll find someone who speaks English. Sometimes they'll be less helpful in the big cities in the summer. More often, though, you'll be surprised at how well they know the details of accommodation and transportation. Hours for most offices are Mon–Fri 9.30–1.30 and 4–7, Saturday mornings only and closed on Sundays. Don't mistake tourist offices for the new **consumer information** booths the Socialist government is setting up everywhere. Many large cities also maintain **municipal tourist offices**, though they're not as well equipped as those run by the Ministry of Tourism, better known as **Turismo**.

Maps

Cartography has been an art in Spain since the 12th-century Catalans charted their Mediterranean Empire in Europe's first great school of map-making. The tourist offices hand out beautifully detailed maps of every town; ask for their *Mapa de Comunicaciones*, an excellent general map of the country. The best large-scale maps are produced by *Almax Editores*. If in London visit Stanfords at 12 Long Acre, WC2.

Money, Communications, Health and Other Concerns

Money

Spanish **currency** comes in notes of 1000, 2000, 5000, 10,000 *pesetas*, all in different colours, and coins of 1, 5, 10, 25, 50, 100, 200 and 500 pts. Don't be surprised to see Generalísimo Franco's scowling mug staring at you from the older coins—but do watch out for the old ornately decorated notes larger than the standard size. These went out of use in 1986. At street markets, and in out-of-the-way places, you may hear prices given in *duros* or *notas*. A *duro* is a 5 pta piece, and a *nota* is a 100 pta.

Exchange rates vary, but until any drastic changes occur £1 is 180 pts, and $1 equivalent to 90 pts. Think of 100 pts as about 55p or $1.10—so those green 1000 pta notes, the most common, are worth about £5.50 or $11. Spain's city centres seem to have a bank on every street corner, and most of them will exchange money; look for the CAMBIO or EXCHANGE signs and the little flags. There is a slight difference in the rates, though usually not enough to make shopping around worthwhile. Most banks are open 8.30–2, and Saturdays (sometimes) 8.30–1. Beware of exchange offices (one chain, called *Exact* charges a hefty 9.5 per cent commission on all transactions). You can sometimes change money at travel agencies, fancy hotels, restaurants or the big department stores. There are 24-hour *cambios* at the big train stations in Barcelona and Madrid. Wiring money from overseas entails no special difficulties; just give yourself two weeks to be on the safe side, and work through one of the larger institutions (Banco Central, Banco de Bilbao, Banco Espanol de Credito, Banco Hispano Americano, Banco de Santander, Banco de Vizcaya). All transactions have to go through Madrid. **Plastic money** will not necessarily be helpful unless you rent cars, fly a lot, or patronize the most expensive hotels and restaurants. If you have credit cards, though, do take them along as they can be lifesavers in emergencies. A Eurocheque card will make your British bank cheques good, though it may not be easy. **Travellers' cheques**, if they are from one of the major companies, will pass at most bank exchanges.

In Gibraltar you can use local currency, UK sterling or pesetas, though you'll lose considerably on the exchange rate with pesetas. Spanish banks in Gibraltar tend to give a better rate of exchange from sterling to pesetas. Banks in Gibraltar are open 9–3.30, weekdays only.

Post Offices

Every city, regardless of size, seems to have one post office (*Correos*) and no more. It will always be crowded, but unless you have packages to mail you may not need ever to visit one. Most tobacco shops sell stamps (*sellos*) and they'll usually know the correct postage for whatever you're sending. Mailboxes are bright yellow and scarce. Send everything air mail (*por aéro*) and don't send postcards unless you don't care when they arrive. The post offices also handle telegrams, which normally take 4 hours to arrive within Europe but are very expensive—a one-word message plus address costs around 2000 pts. There is also, of course, the *poste restante* (general delivery). In Spain this is called *lista de correos*, and it is as chancy as anywhere else. Don't confuse post offices with the *Caja Postal*, the postal savings banks that look just like them. Post Offices in Gibraltar are open 9.30–6, and mail sent from here arrives much faster than from Spain.

Telephones

Spain has long had one of the best telephone systems in Europe. During the Civil War it kept running no matter what; commanders used it to keep in touch with their troops, and called towns on the front during offensives to check if they had fallen to the enemy.

Today, calls within Spain are comparatively cheap (15–25 pts for a short local call), and Spain is one of the few countries where you can make an international call conveniently from a phone booth—within Europe at least. In newer phone booths there are complete instructions (in English) and the phone itself has a little slide on top that holds coins; keep it full of 5 and 25 pts pieces—the newer ones also take 100 pts—and you can gab all day like the Spaniards do. This can be done to the USA too, but take at least 3000 pts in change with you in 100s. Britain costs about 250–350 pts a minute, America substantially more. There are central telephone offices (*Telefónica*) in every big city, where you call from metered booths (and pay a fair percentage more for the comfort); they are indispensable, however, for reversed-charge or collect calls (*cobro revertido*). Telefónicas are generally open from 9–1 and 5–10 pm and closed on Sundays. For international calls, dial 07 followed by the country code. The national code for Britain is 44, for the US and Canada, 1, and for Spain 34. Remember that if you are calling Spain from outside the country, you drop the '9' in the area code. Expect to pay a big surcharge if you do any telephoning from your hotel. Cheap rate is from 10 pm–8 am Monday–Saturday and all day Sunday and public holidays. Telephoning abroad from Gibraltar, dial 00 followed by country and area code.

Official Holidays

The Spaniards, like the Italians, try to have as many as possible. Everything closes on: New Year's Day; 6 January—Epiphany; Holy Thursday and Good Friday; 1 May—Labour Day; Corpus Christi (late May or early June); 25 July—Santiago Apostol (St James' Day); 15 August—Asunción (Assumption); 12 October (Columbus Day); 1 November—Todos los Santos (All Saints Day); 6 December—Constitution Day; 8 December—Immaculate Conception; Christmas.
Be aware that every region, town, and village has at least one of its own holidays as well.

Official Holidays in Gibraltar

New Year's Day; Commonwealth Day (mid-March); Good Friday and Easter Monday; 1 May (May Day); Last Monday in May (Spring Bank Holiday); Queen's Birthday (mid-June); Last Monday in August (late-summer Bank Holiday); Christmas Day and Boxing Day.

Opening Hours and Museums

Spaniards take their main meal at 2, and most shops shut down for 2–3 hours in the afternoon, usually between 1 and 2. In the south, where it's hotter, the siesta can last from 1 to 5. In the evening most establishments stay open until 7 or 8.
Museums and historical sites follow these hours too, though abbreviated in the winter months; nearly all close on Mondays. We have tried to list the hours for the important sights. Seldom-visited ones have a raffish disregard for their official hours, or open only when the mood strikes them. Don't be discouraged; bang on doors and ask around. Most of the less important churches are always closed. Some cities probably have more churches than faithful communicants, and many are unused. If you're determined to see

one, it will never be hard to find the (*sacristán*) or caretaker. Usually they live close by, and would be glad to show you around for a tip. We haven't bothered to list admission prices for museums and sites; usually the sum is trivial. The Alhambra in Granada at 475 pts is the most notable exception; hardly anything will cost more than 200 pts, usually much less. Don't be surprised when cathedrals and famous churches charge admission; just consider the costs of upkeep.

Shops in Gibraltar are generally open 9–7 year round.

Embassies and Consulates

US
Madrid: C. Serrano 75 (tel 91 276 34 00); consular office for passports: Paseo de Castellana 52, around the corner.
Sevilla: Paseo de las Delicias 7 (tel 954 423 18 85)
Fuengirola (Málaga): C/Martinez Catena, Portal 6, Apt 5B, Complejo Sol Playa (tel 952 47 98 91)

Britain
Madrid: Fernando el Santo 16 (tel 419 02 00)
Sevilla: Plaza Nueva 8 (tel 954 22 88 75)
Málaga: Edificio Duquesa, Duquesa de Parcent 8–1 (tel 952 21 75 71)
Algeciras: Avenida de las Fuerzas Armadas 11–1 (tel 956 66 16 00)
Gibraltar: (Vice Consul) 65 Irish Town (tel 350 78 305)

Canada
Madrid: Nuñez de Balboa 35 (tel 91 431 43 00)
Málaga: Plaza de la Malagueta (tel 952 22 33 46)

Australia
Madrid: Paseo de la Castellana 143 (tel 279 85 004). For New Zealand go to either the British or Australian embassy.

Police Business

Crime is not really a big problem in Spain and Spaniards talk about it perhaps more than is warranted. Pickpocketing and robbing parked cars are the specialities; in Sevilla they like to take the whole car. The big cities are the places to be careful, especially Málaga and Sevilla. Crime is also spreading to the tourist areas, particularly the Costa del Sol. Even on the Costa, though, you're probably safer in Spain than you would be at home; the crime rate is roughly a quarter of the British. Note that in Spain less than 8 grams of reefer is legal; anything else may easily earn you the traditional 'six years and a day'.

There are several species of **police**, and their authority varies with the area. Franco's old goon squads, the Policía Armada, have been reformed and relatively demilitarized into the *Policía Nacional*, whom the Spaniards call 'chocolate drops' for their brown uniforms; their duties largely consist of driving around in cars and drinking coffee. They are, however, more highly thought of than the Policía Armada, and their popularity

12

increased when their commander, Lt-General José Antonio Saenz de Santa María, ordered his men to surround the Cortés to foil Téjero's attempted coup in 1981, thereby proving that he and his *Policía Nacional* were strongly on the side of the newly born democracy.

The *Policía Municipal* in some towns do crime control, while in others they are limited to directing traffic. Mostly in rural areas, there's the *Guardia Civil*, with green uniforms, but no longer do they don the black patent-leather tricorn hats. The 'poison dwarfs of Spain', as Laurie Lee called them, may well be one of the most efficient police forces in the world, but after a century-and-a-half of upholding a sick social order in the volatile countryside, they have few friends. They too are being reformed; now they're most conspicuous as a highway patrol, assisting motorists and handing out tickets (ignoring 'no passing' zones is the best way to get one). Most traffic violations are payable on the spot; the traffic cops have a reputation for upright honesty.

Gibraltar has no serious crime to speak of, and given its military status, security is very tight. Gibraltarians like to forget the incident in which members of the armed forces shot dead suspected IRA terrorists in the late 80s. There has been only one murder since the opening of the border with Spain in 1985; other than that there are occasional street scuffles among service men, the odd burglary and a multitude of parking offences.

Electricity

Current is 220 V, the same as most of Europe. Americans will need converters, and the British will need adapters for the different plugs. If you plan to stay in the less expensive *hostales*, it may be better to leave your gadgets at home. Some corners of Spain, even some big cities, have pockets of exotic voltage—150 V for example—guaranteeing a brief display of fireworks. Big hotels always have the standard current.

Photography

Film is quite expensive everywhere; so is developing, but in any city there will be plenty of places—many in optician's shops (*óptica*) or big department stores—where you can get processing done in a hurry. Serious photographers must give some consideration to the strong sunlight and high reflectivity of surfaces (pavements and buildings) in towns.

Toilets

Outside bus and train stations, public facilities are rare in Spain. On the other hand, every bar on every corner has a toilet; don't feel uncomfortable using it without purchasing something—the Spaniards do it all the time. Just ask for '*los servicios*' and take your own paper.

Health

There is now the standard EEC agreement for citizens of EEC countries, entitling you to a certain amount of free medical care, but it's not straightforward. You must complete all the necessary paperwork before you go to Spain, and allow a couple of months to make

13

sure it comes through in time. Ask for a leaflet entitled *Before You Go* from the Department of Health and fill out form E111, which on arrival in Spain you must take to the local office of the *Instituto Nacional de Seguridad Social*, where you'll be issued with a Spanish medical card and some vouchers enabling you to claim free treatment from an *INSS* doctor. At time of writing the government is trying to implement a much easier system. In an emergency, ask to be taken to the nearest *hospital de la seguridad social*. Before resorting to a *médico* (doctor) and his £20 ($40) fee (ask at the tourist office for a list of English-speaking doctors), go to a pharmacy and tell them your woes. Spanish *farmacéuticos* are highly skilled, and if there's a prescription medicine that you know will cure you they'll often supply it without a doctor's note. (*El País* and the other national newspapers list *farmacias* in large cities that stay open all night.)

No inoculations are required to enter Spain, though it never hurts to check that your tetanus jab is up-to-date, as well as some of the more exotic inoculations (typhoid and cholera) if you want to venture on into Morocco. The tap water is safe to drink in Spain, but at the slightest twinge of queasiness, switch to the bottled stuff.

Insurance

You may want to consider travel insurance, available through most travel agents. For a small monthly charge, not only is your health insured, but your bags and money as well, and some even will refund a missed charter flight if you're too ill to catch it. Be sure to save all doctor's receipts (you'll have to pay in cash on the spot), pharmacy receipts, and police documents (if you're reporting a theft).

Women and Children

On the whole, the horror stories of sexual harassment in Spain are a thing of the past—unless you dress provocatively and hang out by the bus station after dark. All Spaniards seem to melt when they see blondes, so if you're fair you're in for a tougher go. Even Spanish women sunbathe topless these days at the international *costa* resorts, but do be discreet elsewhere, especially near small villages.

Spaniards adore children, and they'll welcome yours almost everywhere. Baby foods, etc. are widely available, but don't expect to find babysitters except at the really smart hotels; Spaniards always take their children with them, even if they're up until 4 am. Nor are there many special amusements for children though these are beginning to spring up with Spain's new prosperity, for better or worse; traditionally Spaniards have never thought of their children as separate little creatures who ought to be amused.

Sports, Entertainment and Culture

Football (soccer) is the most popular sport throughout Spain, and the Spaniards play it well: Barcelona (Barca) and Real Madrid are the best teams to watch. **Bullfighting** (see 'Spanish Topics') and **cycling** vie for second place in the Spanish heart and are regularly shown on **television**, which, despite a heavy fare of dubbed American shows, everyone is inordinately fond of watching. Both channels are state-run, but with satellite dishes outnumbering *bodegas*, who watches them anyway? Certainly not the expat coastal residents, who tune into BSkyB, SUPERCHANNEL and even the spectacularly tedious Gibraltar TV network.

If you want to bring your own **bicycle** to Spain, you can make arrangements by ferry or train; by air, you'll almost always have to dismantle it to some extent and pack it in some kind of crate. Each airline seems to have its own policy. The south of Spain would be suicide to bike through in summer, though all right in winter. For more information call the Cycling Federation of Andalucía (in Jerez) (956) 34 88 12; in Fuengirola (952) 47 70 75; in Nerja (952) 52 43 97.

Spain's sierras attract thousands of **hikers** and **mountaineers**. There are paths in the Sierra Nevada above Granada (which also has skiing in the winter) and the Serrania de Ronda. *Refugios* in many places offer mountain shelter (write to the tourist office or the Spanish Mountaineering Federation, Alberto Aguilera 3–4°, Madrid-15, tel (91) 445 13 82, for a list. Some are well equipped and can supply food. Most, however, do not, so take your own sleeping bags, cooking equipment and food with you. Hiking boots are essential, as is a detailed map of the area, obtainable from either Instituto Geográfico Nacional, Calle General Ibañez de Ibero 3, Madrid, tel (91) 233 38 00; or from the bookshop Llibreria Quera, Petritoxl 2, Barcelona, tel (93) 318 07 43.

Many of these same mountains attract **ski** crowds in the winter. An hour from Granada you can be among the Iberian Peninsula's highest peaks and Europe's southernmost ski resorts, whose après-ski life can rival anything in the Alps. The Sierra Nevada will host the **World Alpine Ski Championships** in 1995. In preparation for this, new roads are being laid and new facilities, including artificial snow-making machines, are already in place. In Spain, it's easy to arrange all-inclusive ski packages through a travel agent. A typical deal would include six nights' accommodation in a three- or four-star hotel with half board, unlimited use of ski lift for the week, at a cost of just under 100,000 pts. With instruction fees, count on 10–15,000 pts extra per week. For further information, write to the tourist office or the Spanish Ski Federation, Claudio Coello 32, Madrid 1, tel 275 8943.

Water sports are the most popular activities in the summer. You can rent a windsurf board and learn how to use it at almost any resort; *aficionados* head for Tarifa, Europe's windsurfing mecca and the continent's southernmost tip. If you're bringing your own boat, get the tourist office's literature on marinas before setting out. You have a choice of 30 along the coasts of Andalucía. There's a full calendar of sailing events and races, as well as sailing schools and rentals. A number of reservoirs have become quite popular as well for water sports. For more information, write to the Spanish Sailing Federation, J. Vigón 23, Madrid. Underwater activists flock to the Almería coast in particular for its sparkling water and abundant marine life. Write to the Spanish Sub-Aqua Federation, Santaló 15, Barcelona, tel 200 67 69, for more information, or contact the *Federación Española de Esqui Nautico*, Saino de Arana 30 1–1, Barcelona, tel (93) 330 89 03.

English settlers built Spain's first **golf** course at the Rio Tinto Mines in the 19th century and since the advent of Severiano Ballesteros Spaniards too have gone nuts for the game. The sunny warm winters combined with greens of international tournament standard attract golfing enthusiasts from all over the world throughout the year. Any real estate agent on the coast hoping to sell villas to foreigners, especially Scandinavians and the latest newcomers, the Japanese, stands little chance of closing a deal unless his property is within 10 minutes of a golf course. It's the rage of the Costa del Sol; the

Marbella area alone boasting over a dozen fine courses, some so exclusive that if you manage to get in you could find yourself tee-ing off next to Sean Connery. On the other hand, there is an abundance of humbler clubs where a mere 3000 pts will get you a round. Most places hire out clubs. Inland you'll find courses around the big cities. The tourist office can supply names, or contact the Royal Spanish Golf Federation, Capitan Haya 9–5, Sur, Madrid, tel (91) 455 27 57.

There is equal fervour for **tennis**, also inspired by an international champion—a bubbly 18-year-old, Arantxa Sánchez Vicario, who is ranked alongside Graf, Navratilova and Sabatini. Again, the best clubs are to be found on the coast, and every resort hotel has its own courts; municipal ones are rare or hard to get to. The most famous tennis school in Andalucía lies just behind Fuengirola on the Mijas road, and is owned by Australian Lew Hoad, the Wimbledon favourite of the 50s and 60s. If you're looking for a game in Marbella, call Los Monteros Tennis Club, tel (952) 82 38 46, but expect to pay much more.

Where there are concentrations of British residents, **cricket** has taken root; the MCC plans to set up a cricket school near Mijas. For general information about watching or playing, call the Málaga Cricket Association, tel (952) 82 38 46, and ask for Gordon Samuel. **Rugby** enthusiasts are predictably asked to call a bar for information on their sport—the Micadela Bar, C/Camilio José Cala 4, Marbella, tel (952) 82 92 95, (ask for Danny).

Fishing and **hunting** are long-standing Spanish obsessions, and you'll need to get a licence for both. Freshwater fishing permits (*permiso de pesca* are issued on a fortnightly basis from the municipal ICONA office, or from the Jefatura Provincial del ICONA, Licencia Nacional de Caza y Pesca, Jorge Juan 39, Madrid, tel (91) 225 59 85. For a listing of the best trout streams (there are many), write to the Spanish Fishing Federation, Navas de Tolosa 3, Madrid-13, tel 232 8352, or to the Instituto Andaluz de Reforma Agraria de la Junta de Andalucía, Avenida República Argentina 25, Sevilla, tel (954) 27 00 73. Deep-sea fishermen need to obtain a 5-year licence from the provincial Commandancias de Marina. The Directorate General of Sea Fishing, Subsecretaria de la Marina Mercante, Ministerio de Comercio, C. Ruiz de Alarcón 1, Madrid can supply information on the best areas and boat rentals. You may bring sporting guns to Spain, but you must declare them on arrival, accompanied by a valid firearms certificate with a translation in Spanish. Hunters (boar and deer are the big game, with quail, hare, partridges and pigeons, and ducks and geese along the coasts in the winter) are obliged to get a licence as well (*permiso de caza*) from the local autonomous community, presenting their passports and record of insurance coverage. The Spanish Hunting Federation, Av. Reina Victoria 72, Madrid, tel (91) 253 9017, or the tourist office can supply more information.

Pelota, although a Basque game by origin, has a following in Andalucía. This is a fast, thrilling game, where contestants wearing long basket-like gloves propel a hard ball with great force at high walls; rather like squash. The fast action on the *jai-alai* court is matched by the wagering frenzy of the spectators. Every Spaniard is a gambler, whether it's in the infinite number of lotteries run by the State (the *Lotería Deportiva*), for the blind (ONCE), the Red Cross, or the church, and there are **casinos** in all major resorts and at least one slot machine in every bar, doling out electronic versions of *La Cucaracha* whenever it gets lonely.

16

Horse racing is centred in Madrid, but there is a winter season in Sevilla. Andalucía has some perfect terrain for **horse-riding**, whether exploring the smugglers' trails around Cádiz, the Serrania de Ronda, or following in the hoofprints of Sir John Betjeman's wife, Penelope Chetwoode, who experienced one bosom-heaving emotion after another as she trekked boldly through the Sierra Nevada on horseback in the 1960s, an odyssey so delightfully recorded in her journal *Two Middle Aged Ladies in Andalucía*. There are a number of stables offering organised treks. For further details contact Caminos and Caballos, Duque de Liria 3, Madrid, tel (91) 242 31 25.

Gibraltar has a number of sports clubs and associations, many of them private. For further information ask at the tourist office for details.

Bars and cafés collect much of the Spaniards' leisure time. They are wonderful institutions, where you can eat breakfast or linger over a glass of beer until 4 in the morning. Some have music—jazz, rock or *flamenco*; some have great snacks, or *tapas*, some have games or pinball machines; in any of them you could see an old sailor delicately sipping his camomile tea next to a young mother, baby under her arm, stopping in for a beer break during her shopping. **Discos, night clubs**, etc. are easily found in the big cities and tourist spots; most tend to be expensive. Ask around for the current favourites. Watch out for posters for **concerts, ballets**, and especially for **circuses**. The little travelling Spanish troupes with their family acts, tents, tinsel and names like 'The National Circus of Japan' will charm you; they often gravitate to the major fiestas throughout the summer.

El País, the Socialists' press, is Spain's biggest and best national **newspaper**, though circulation is painfully low; Spaniards just don't read newspapers (the little magazine with television listings and scandals is by far and away the best-selling periodical). *El País* has the best regional **film** listings, indicating where you can see some great films subtitled instead of dubbed. English films are occasionally shown on the Costa del Sol and dozens of shops rent English-language video releases. Films are cheap and Spaniards are great cinema-goers; there are lots of inexpensive outdoor movie theatres in the summer. Look for new films by Carlos Saura, Spain's brightest cinematic light (*Carmen, Blood Wedding, El Dorado*), or Victor Erice, or, most incredibly, Marx Brothers movies dubbed in Spanish.

The other big papers are *Cambio 16* (centrist), *ABC* (conservative, in a bizarre 60s magazine format), and the *Alcazar* (neo-fascist). You can also get the Spanish translation of *Pravda* and a vast selection of other leftist sheets. Major British papers are available in all tourist areas and big cities; the American *Herald Tribune*, the *Wall Street Journal*, and the awful *USA Today* are readily available where Americans go. Most hit the news-stands a day late; issues of *Time* and *Newsweek* often hang about until they find a home. There are also publications in English on the Costa del Sol, notably *Sur*, a translation of a Málaga paper with general items of news; *Lookout*, a glossy monthly general consumer magazine; *The Entertainer*, for local news, events and classified ads; and the *Marbella Times*, another slick mag for expats. All British newspapers are flown daily to Gibraltar.

Shopping

There are some delightful tacky tourist wares (Toledo 'daggers', plastic bulls and flamenco dolls ad nauseam) but there are also some excellent buys of quality items like

leather, most notably from Córdoba and the town of Ubrique, which has been producing leather-work since Roman times. Moorish craftsmen later had a major influence on the method of treating the cured skin for export. While Córdoba is better known for its ornate embossed leather for furniture decoration, and **filigree jewellery**, Ubrique specializes in handmade items such as diaries, suitcases, bags and wallets. If you want an everlasting memory of Andalucía, have your boots made to measure in Valverde del Camino, Huelva province—guaranteed to last a lifetime. Ceramic plates, pottery and colourful *azulejo* tiles are made all over Andalucía; the quality varies enormously, from the shoddy factory-made products adorning tourist shop shelves, to the sophisticated **ceramic ware** of Sevilla. Granada is well known for its **inlaid wood** *taracea* work (chests, chess boards and music boxes). Spanish **woven goods** are reasonably priced; Sevilla produces exquisite *mantillas* and embroidered shawls, and is the centre for the extraordinary designs which adorn the bullfighter's costume. In the Alpujarras a concentrated effort is being made to revive old skills, using the wooden loom particularly, to produce the typical **woollen blankets** and **rugs** which this area had long been known for—a fascinating mixture of ancient Christian and Arab designs. Brightly coloured handwoven blankets are the claim to fame of Grazalema, a village less than 20 km to the west of Ronda. In the province of Almería, the village of Nírjar produces colourful *jarapas*—woven blankets and mats.

To encourage the nation's craftsmen, the government has organized a kind of cooperative, *Artespaña*, with various outlets selling their work located at: Sevilla: Rodríguez Jurado 4; Granada: Corral del Carbón; Marbella: Ricardo Soriano 54. The major **department store** chains in Spain, El Corte Inglés and the Galerias Preciados, often have good selections of crafts. All of the above ship items home. You can also get some good buys at the **weekly markets** where Spaniards do a good deal of their shopping. Local tourist offices will have details.

Good-quality antiques aren't the great finds they once were—Spaniards have learned what they're worth and charge accordingly. Guitars, mandolins and bagpipes, fine wooden furniture and Goya tapestries are some of the bulky, more expensive items you'd like shipped home. Best buys in Gibraltar are brand-name luxury items such as jewellery and clothing (see Gibraltar 'Shopping').

A Little Geography for the Perplexed

Andalucía covers the southern fifth of the Iberian Peninsula, occupying an area slightly more than half of Portugal. Its natural border on the north is the rugged Sierra Morena mountain chain; the wild Atlantic batters its western shores and the timid Mediterranean laps its southern coast. The Sierra Morena mountains, although reaching barely 4000 ft, were for a long time a deterrent to northern foreign invaders. The only natural interruption is the Pass of Despeñaperros, or the 'gateway to Andalucía'. Numerous early travellers spoke with awe of the first time they traversed this pine-clad gorge; the frontier that separated 'the land of men from the land of gods'. Arriving in Andalucía at this point provides a strong contrast indeed from the barren plains of La Mancha to the north. These peaks, rich in minerals, sweep down to the fertile Guadalquivir plain, widening as it proceeds to the western coast to form broad salt marshes and mud flats—including the Doñana National Park, one of the largest bird sanctuaries in

Europe. From here, the coast as far as the Portuguese border is virtually one long sandy beach, its hinterland undulating farming terrain and the gentle mountains of Huelva province. South of the Guadalquivir valley the land rises again to form the craggy, spectacular Serrania de Ronda mountain range, home to bandits and smugglers for centuries; the terrain then descends sharply to meet the balmy palm-lined shores of the Mediterranean, with Tarifa, the furthest south you can go on mainland Europe, and Gibraltar, that geological oddity of a rock, whose outline resembles one of the sentinel lions on guard at the foot of Nelson's column. From the Serrania de Ronda the land dips and rises as it goes east till it joins the heights of the snow-capped Sierra Nevada, the highest peaks in Spain, below which lie long beaches, tiny coves and crystal-clear water.

Dry as it is, Andalucía when properly tended has been the garden of Spain. The soil in most areas, *argiles de montmorillionite*, holds water like a sponge. The Romans first discovered how to irrigate it; the Moors perfected the system, and also introduced the palm and such crops as cotton, rice, oranges and sugar. Today most of the inhabitants of the region live in cities—it's traditionally one of the most urbanized regions in Europe—but its farmers have discovered the modern delights of tractors, and of owning their own land, and unless the Hapsburgs or the Francoists come back the region will have no excuse for not making a good living. Between the towns, spaces seem vast and empty, endless hillsides of olives, vineyards, wheat and sunflowers. Come in the spring, when the almond trees are in blossom, the oranges turn orange and wild flowers surge up along the roadsides—the unforgettable splash of colour that characterises cheerful Andalucía and its warm, vibrant people.

Climate

Andalucía is hot and sunny in the summer, brisk and sunny in the winter—in fact you can count on more sunshine here than anywhere else in Europe. The mild winters in coastal regions give way to pleasant, warm springs with minimal rainfall. Temperatures inland can be considerably lower, especially in the mountainous regions. Autumn weather can pack a few surprises: while normally warm and comfortable, recent years have seen torrential rains, causing land-slides and extensive flooding. On the Atlantic coast, the *Levante* wind can make life uncomfortable, even in summer, when it will not only blow your beach umbrella away, but might even make you a bit kooky.

Gibraltar's climate is of course Mediterranean, but appropriately enough it also manifests that most characteristic feature of British weather—cloud and rain. The easterly wind, the moisture-laden *Levante* that batters Gibraltar's shores is forced up the sheer face of the rock, to condense in the lower temperatures at the top, forming a dense cloud that can be seen for miles, and in winter months letting fall a sometimes relentless shower on all beneath—pack your brolly.

For comfort, spring and autumn are the best times to visit, by far; winter is generally pleasant on the Mediterranean coast, though damp and chill inland. You'll probably feel more uncomfortable inside than out; Spanish homes—and hotel rooms—are not made for the winter.

19

Seasonal Temperatures in °C (°F)

	January		April		July		October	
	High	Low	High	Low	High	Low	High	Low
Sevilla	15(59)	6(43)	23(74)	11(52)	35(95)	21(70)	26(79)	14(58)
Málaga	17(63)	9(49)	21(70)	13(56)	29(84)	21(70)	23(74)	16(61)
Cádiz	15(59)	8(47)	21(70)	12(54)	29(84)	20(68)	23(74)	15(59)

Average monthly rainfall in mm (in.)

	January	April	July	October
Sevilla	99 (4)	80 (3)	0 (0)	37 (2)

Where to Stay

Hotels in Spain are still bargains—though as with prices for other facilities, Spain is gradually catching up with the rest of Europe. One thing you can still count on is a consistent level of quality and service; the Spanish government regulates hotels more intelligently, and more closely, than any country in the Mediterranean. Room prices must be posted in the hotel lobbies and in the rooms, and if there's any problem you can ask for the complaints book, or *Libro de Reclamaciones*. No one ever writes anything in these; any written complaint must be passed on to the authorities immediately. Hotel keepers would always rather correct the problem for you.

No government could resist the chance to insert a little bureaucratic confusion, though, and the wide range of accommodation in Spain is classified in a complex system. **Hotels** (H) are rated with from one to five stars, according to the services they offer, not price. These are the most expensive places, and even a one-star hotel will be a comfortable, middle-range establishment. *Hotel Residencias* (HR) are the same, only without a restaurant. Next come *Hostales* (Hs)and *Pensiones* (P), rated with one to three stars. These are more modest places, often a floor in an apartment block; a three-star *hostal* is roughly equivalent to a one-star hotel. *Pensiones* may require full- or half-board; there aren't many of these establishments, only a few in resort areas. *Hostal Residencias* (HsR), like *hotel residencias*, do not offer meals except breakfast, and not always that.

The bottom of the scale is occupied by the *Fonda* (F) and *Casa de Huéspedes* (CH), little different from a one-star *hostal*, though generally cheaper. Off the scale completely are hundreds of unclassified cheap places, usually rooms in an apartment or over a bar and identified only by a little sign reading *Camas* (beds) or *Habitaciones* (rooms). You can also ask in bars or at the tourist office for unidentified *Casas Particulares*, private houses with a room or two; in many villages these will be the best you can do, but they're usually clean—Spanish women are manic housekeepers.

Look for the **little blue plaques** next to the doors of all hotels, *hostales*, etc. that identify its classification and number of stars.

Paradores
The government, in its plan to develop tourism in the 1950s, started this nationwide chain of classy hotels to draw some attention to little-visited areas. They restored old palaces, castles and monasteries for the purpose, furnished them with antiques and installed fine restaurants featuring local specialities. *Paradores* for many people are one of the best reasons for visiting Spain.

Not all *paradores* are in historical landmarks; especially in resort areas, some are cleanly designed modern buildings, usually in a great location with a pool and some sports facilities. With the *paradores'* success has come some increase in prices; in most cases both the rooms and the restaurant will be the most expensive in town. If you can afford them, though, there are no better places to stay. We've mentioned nearly all of them throughout this book. *Paradores* can be booked in advance from the UK through Keytel International, 402 Edgware Road, London W2 1ED, tel (071) 402 8182; and in the US through Marketing Ahead, 515 Madison Ave, New York, NY, tel (212) 750 8682 or through Marsans Travel, 205 E 42nd St, Suite 1514, New York, NY, tel (212) 661 6565; or in Madrid through the head office at Calle Velázquez 18, tel (91) 435 97 00.

Resort Accommodation

Almost everything along the coasts of Andalucía has been built in the last 25 years, and anonymous high-rise buildings abound. Lately the trend has turned towards low-rise 'villages' or *urbanizaciónes* built around a pool, usually on or near the beach. We've tried to include places that stand out in some way, or that are good bargains for their rating. Most hotels in the big resorts cater for package tours, and may not even answer a request for an individual reservation during the peak season.

In almost all resorts, there's a choice of hotels in every price range. The best bargains, though, are usually in the places where foreigners seldom tread—the Costa de la Luz west of Cádiz, or the small resorts west of Almería. If you intend to spend a couple of weeks on the Costa del Sol, your best bet is to book an all-inclusive package deal from the UK or US. This stretch of coast has some ritzy hotels, particularly down near Marbella, the millionaires' playground. However, all sorts of bargains are to be had, especially if you plan a long-term stay in winter, a practice often followed by cold pensioners from the north. Incidentally, no beaches in Spain are private.

Cheap Accommodation

The best is in small towns and villages, and around universities. Occasionally you'll find a room over a bar, run by somebody's grandmother, that is nicer than a four-star hotel—complete with frilly pillows, lovely old furnishings, and a shrine to the Virgin Mary. The worst are inevitably found in industrial cities or dull modern ones. It always helps to see the room first. In cities, the best places to look are right in the centre, not around the bus and train stations. Most inexpensive establishments will ask you to pay a day in advance. Be warned: small cheap *hostales* in ports (such as Málaga, Cádiz and Algeciras) can be crummy and noisy beyond belief—as you lie there unable to sleep, you can only marvel at the human body's ability to produce such a wealth of unidentifiable sounds, coming through the paper-thin walls of the room next door.

Gibraltar doesn't have the same range of accommodation, and there are no official categories; the only guide to quality is price—unfortunately not an accurate guarantee of standards anywhere. Based on Spanish categories, most hotels would fall into the two- or three-star bracket, with one or two exceptions, but don't expect any bargains—£50 is about average for a double room with bath, and there's little cheaper than that unless you go on a package deal.

Information

If you're travelling around a lot, a good investment would be the government publication *Guía de Hoteles*, a great fat book with every classified hotel and *hostal* in Spain, available

21

for only 750 pts in many bookshops. The government also publishes similar guides to holiday flats (*apartmentos turísticos*) and campsites (*campings*). Local tourist information offices can also give you a complete list for their provinces, and some can be very helpful with finding a room when things are tight.

Price ranges (pts) for a double room with bath
(not including 6% VAT)

Hoteles	high	average	low
*****	40,000	25,000	17,000
****	30,000	16,000	12,000
***	18,000	12,000	8000
**	9000	6000	4000
*	6000	4000	3000

Hostales and Pensiones	high	average	low
***	9000	5000	3500
**	7000	4000	3000
*	4000	3000	2000

Unlisted Fondas, Casas de Huéspedes or camas (without bath)

3000	2000	1400

Prices for single rooms will average about 60 per cent of a double, while triples or an extra bed are around 35 per cent more. Of course, *hostales, fondas*, etc. with one or two stars will often have rooms without private baths at considerable savings. Within the price ranges shown, the most expensive are likely to be in the big cities. In resorts, prices will usually be around the average or below it, while the cheapest places are always provincial towns. On the whole, though prices throughout Andalucía are surprisingly consistent.

One thing to remember is that many of the more expensive hotels have some rooms available at prices lower than those listed. They won't tell you, though; you'll have to ask. Many establishments have discounts in the off-season and higher rates during important festivals. These are supposedly regulated, but in practice hotel-keepers charge whatever they can get for spectacles like Sevilla's Holy Week. If you want to attend any of these big events, always book as far in advance as possible.

Paradores are classed as three- or four-star hotels, and their prices for a double room with bath range from 7000 pts in remote provincial towns to 12,000 pts for the most popular. All stay open all year and offer substantial off-season discounts.

Alternative Accommodation
Youth hostels exist in Spain, but they're usually not worth the trouble. Most are open only in the summer; there are the usual inconveniences and silly rules, and often hostels are in out-of-the-way locations. You'll be better off with the inexpensive *hostales* and *fondas*—sometimes these are even cheaper than youth hostels. There are sometimes

monasteries that will put you up in rural areas; ask at the local tourist office for these and for rooms that might be available in **university dormitories**.

Camping

Campsites are rated with from one to three stars depending on their facilities, and in addition to the ones listed in the official government handbook there are always others, rather primitive, that are unlisted. On the whole camping is a good deal, and most first class sites' facilities include shops, restaurants, bars, laundries, hot showers, first-aid, swimming pools, telephones and occasionally, tennis court. Caravans (campers) and trailers converge into all the more developed sites, but if you just want to pitch your little tent or sleep out in some quiet field, ask around in the bars or at likely farms. Camping is forbidden in many forest areas because of fears of fire, as well as on the beaches (though you can often get close to some quieter shores if you're discreet). If you're doing some hiking, bring a sleeping bag and stay in the free **refugios** along the major trails. (See p. 15).

The Spanish publication *Guía de Campings* can be found in most bookstores. Further details can be obtained from: Federación Española de Campings, Gran Via 88, Grupo 3 10–8, Madrid, tel (91) 242 3168; or Camping and Caravan Club, 11 Lower Grosvenor Place, London, tel (071) 828 1012. Reservations for sites can be made through Federación Española de Empresarios de Camping, Principe de Vergara 85, 2-dcha, Madrid.

Price range for camping per day

Adult	275–420 pts	Caravan	300–650 pts
Child	200–300 pts	Tent	250–650 pts
Car	300–400 pts		

There are no camping facilities in Gibraltar, but plenty on the Spanish side of the border, from where you can make a day-trip. Note that if you are travelling in a camper/caravan, you will not be allowed to take it in, as the streets are narrow and congested with normal traffic at the best of times. You can, of course, leave it on the Spanish side, but mind where you park—you could return to find it displaying a ticket, or clamped, or simply towed away.

Buying Property in Spain

The depressed property markets in northern Europe have predictably affected sales in southern Spain, and real bargains are to be found. A re-sale villa on the coast with two bedrooms can cost as little as £40,000; apartments considerably less. Usually buying property in Spain causes few serious problems, but there are some unpleasant and expensive exceptions, so inform yourself fully, and liaise constantly with your lawyer. For example, if you don't follow the correct legal procedures you could end up with either no house or a demand for payment of back debts existing on the property. This happens when a developer sells off apartments to the public, pockets the cash and neglects to pay the outstanding building taxes to the local authorities. The developer then changes the name of his company and liquidates the old one, thereby *legally* avoiding payment. The tax authorities then come to the new owner, and ensure the debt is paid by putting a lien on the property. This happens with surprising frequency. So, before you sign *anything*

23

get an English-speaking lawyer to do a 'search' on the property, a standard practice in other countries. This will show whether there are any outstanding debts or creditors waiting in the wings. (Unbelievably enough, this legal situation applies equally to cars—pending traffic and parking violations stay with the car, not the owner!) If your lawyer has done his homework, and all goes smoothly, the buyer and seller meet at the notary's office to sign the contract and hand over the loot. After that there is a wait of a couple of months before you receive the *escritura*, or title deeds; needless to say there are numerous administrative costs to cover, based on the sale price. In some cases, if the sale price is suspiciously low, a new value will be agreed and costs worked out accordingly.

If buying an apartment or villa on an *urbanización*, you have to contribute to upkeep costs, pool maintenance, etc. This is done through an administrative *communidad*, voted in by the owners. Usually, once a year a general meeting is held to decide on a budget for the year. Annual costs for a two-bedroom apartment average around £700, including house and contents insurance.

A new law obliges non-residents to pay a wealth tax. Although not a very significant amount, it is designed to stop non-declaration of funds received by owners for real or theoretical holiday rentals in their absence. Now all property owners must obtain a fiscal number, or *NIE*, available from the foreigners department of the local police station. It is used to log all transactions, including the opening of a convertible current account at the bank, which allows you to deposit both pesetas and foreign currencies.

'You and the Law in Spain', by David Baird, published by Lookout Publications, gives in-depth information and advice on all aspects of living (legally) in Spain.

Buying property in Gibraltar presents no special difficulties; you only need plenty of cash—house prices are on a par with England.

Timeshare

In the coastal resorts of the Costa del Sol there lurks a demon that will pounce brazenly in broad daylight—the timeshare tout. This jeans-clad smile-toting charmer of the street has antennae for married couples of 20–65, out for a leisurely morning stroll. These unsuspecting innocents are bundled into taxis and taken off to 'resort clubs', from which many emerge elated with the free gifts of alcohol, bus trips or T-shirts, but thousands of pounds poorer.

The system works like this: the touts sweet-talk the eligible into a 'no obligation' guided tour of a resort development, with the dangled carrot of gifts, or cash. The free taxi-ride delivers them into the claws of the waiting 'closers', guys who persuade the couple to part with a few thousand pounds (contract signed, on the spot) in exchange for two weeks a year, every year for the rest of their lives, in one of the resort's apartments. Whilst in theory the idea of timeshare must appeal to many, what most don't realise is the relatively enormous costs involved. Many timeshare owners, when they arrive back to move into 'their' apartment, find not only that they have been allocated quite a different one, but also that their yearly quota for maintenance fees is astronomical.

Special Interest Holidays

Flamenco: Albeit 'flamenco players are not born, they are made in heaven', you may nevertheless consider a course from the *maestro* himself, Paco Peña. The Peña home is in the Plaza del Potro, in the historic and picturesque centre of Córdoba. Students from as far as Japan and the USA come here for the lectures in classical guitar, flamenco dancing and flamenco guitar. For details write to: Centro Flamenco Paco Peña, Plaza del Potro 15, 14002 Córdoba.

Outdoors: Benamonarda Cooperativa offers nature activity holidays in the Serrania de Ronda; hiking, cycling, horse-trekking, photography. They also have complete programmes for children, starting at three years old. Write to: Benamonarda, C. Postigo 66, 29492 Jubrique, Málaga, or: Jon Bland, 43 Prentis Road, London SW16 1QB.

Andaluz Cuisine: The region's centre for culinary research is housed in a charming renovated old mill on a river near Granada. There is a restaurant offering Andaluz, Moorish and Sephardic dishes, besides the cookery training centre and workshops, conducted in a very practical way. For more information write to: Centro Andaluz de Investigaciones Gastronómicas, Plaza del Carmen 2, 2-b, 18009 Granada, tel (958) 22 71 23.

Spas: In Andalucía there's a spa to cater to every complaint, from allergies to rheumatism. Some addresses in major centres:

Almería: Balneario San Nicolás, Ctra Almería–Granada Km 18, 04400 Alhama de Almería, tel (951) 10 01 58.

Cádiz: Balneario Fuente Amarga, Avda de Fuente Amarga s/n, 11130 Chiclana de la Frontera, tel (956) 40 05 20.

Granada: Balnearios Alhama de Granada, 18120 Alhama de Granada; tel (958) 35 00 11.

Jaén: Balneario de Marmolejo, Ctra Balneario s/n, 23770 Marmolejo, tel (953) 54 01 03 or 54 04 04.

Málaga: Balneario de Carratraca, Baños 1, 29551 Carratraca, tel (952) 45 80 20.

Language and Arts: Specialist centres include:

Sevilla: *Hispalis Center*, Instituto de Lenguas y Cultura Española, Amor de Dios 31–2, 41002 Sevilla.

Granada: *Espalengua*, Calle Nueva de Cartuja 24, 18012 Granada. Tel (958) 20 77 82.

Málaga: *Instituto de Español Picasso*, Plaza de la Merced 20, 29080 Málaga.

Nerja: *Escuela de Idiomas*, Almirante Ferrandiz 73, 29780 Nerja, Málaga.

Courses generally last from 2–12 weeks, beginners to advanced. Course fees average 30,000 pts for 2 weeks, and accommodation can be arranged, whether boarding with families (12–15,000 per week) or sharing an apartment (8–10,000 per week). For more information and complete listings, contact: The Spanish Institute, 120 Eaton Square, London SW1, tel (071) 235 1484.

Escuela de Español de las Alpujarras, Calle Natalio Rivas 1, 18001 Granada. Language courses integrated with activities in the Alpujarras area, including cycling, hiking, horseriding, cooking and flamenco dance.

Specialist Operators
Cox & King's Travel Ltd., St James Court, 45 Buckingham Gate, London SW1E 6AF, tel (071) 834 7472. Wildlife tours in southwest Andalucía.

Aventura, Apartado 21, Orgiva, Granada, tel (958) 78 52 53. Long-distance riding holidays in the Sierra Nevada. Groups of 8–10; accommodation in local inns along the way.

Estudio al Raso, 102 Fairfoot Road, London E3 4EH, tel (071) 515 7773. Painting holidays in the Alpujarras, transport, accommodation and meals included.
Cortijo Romero, 72 Meadowsweet Road, Creekmoor, Poole, Dorset BH1 7XT, tel (0202) 699 581. Personal and spiritual 'growth' vacations in the Alpujarras; yoga, tai-chi, meditation. Vegetarian food.
Allegro Holidays, 15a Church Street, Reigate, Kent RH2 0AA, tel (0737) 244 870.
Parador, 'character' hotel and villa holidays, especially on the Costa del Sol.
Cadogan Travel, 10 Portland Street, Southampton, SO9 1ZP, tel (0703) 332551. Reservations: tel (0703) 332 661. Up-market inclusive holidays in four- and five-star hotels in Gibraltar, Southern Spain and Morocco. Flights included; optional car rental.

Eating Out

Read an old guidebook to Spain, and when the author gets around to the local cooking, expressions like 'eggs in a sea of rancid oil' and 'mysterious pork parts' or 'suffered brain damage through garlic excess' pop up with alarming frequency. One traveller in the 18th century fell ill from a local concoction and was given a purge 'known on the comic stage as angelic water. On top of that followed four hundred catholic pills, and a few days later . . . they gave me *escordero* water, whose efficacy or devilry is of such double effect that the doctors call it ambidexter. From this I suffered agony.'

You'll fare better; in fact, the chances are you'll eat some of the tastiest food you've ever had at half the price you would have paid for it at home. The massive influx of tourists has had its effect on Spanish kitchens, but so has the Spaniards' own increased prosperity and, perhaps most significantly, the new federalism. Each region, each town even, has come to feel a new interest and pride in the things that set it apart, and food is definitely one of those; the best restaurants are almost always those which specialize in regional cooking. The greatest attraction of **Andalucían cuisine** is the use of simple, fresh ingredients. Seafood plays a big role, and marinated or fried fish is a speciality. (The traditional marinade, or *adobo*, is a mixture of water, vinegar, salt, garlic, paprika, cumin and marjoram.) Other specialities include the wholesome broth made with fish, tomato, pepper and paprika, and the famous cured hams of Jabugo and Trevelez. Almost everybody has heard of *gazpacho*; there are literally dozens of varieties, ranging from the *pimentón* of Antequera made with red peppers, to the thick Córdoban version, *salmorejo*. Olives, preserved in cumin, wild marjoram, rosemary, thyme, bay leaves, garlic, savoury fennel and vinegar are a treat, especially the plump green ones generally known as Sevilla olives. In Granada an unappetizing mixture of brains, bulls' testicles, potatoes, peas and red peppers results in a very palatable *tortilla Sacromonte*; and many restaurants in the city work wonders with slices of beef *filet* or loin larded with pork fat and roasted with the juice from the meat and sherry. However, watch out for odd little dishes like *revoltillos*, whose name gives you a fair warning of what flavours to expect in this subtle dish of tripe, rolled and secured with the animal's intestines, mercifully lined with ham and mint.

The province of Cádiz takes the place of honour in Andalucían cuisine and some specialities to look out for are *cañailles* (sea snails), *pastel de pichones* (pigeon paté), *calamares con habas* (squid with beans), *archoba* (a highly seasoned fish dish) or *bocas* (small crab).

Córdoba, too, has a fine culinary tradition, including dishes with a strong Arab and Jewish influence, like *calderetas*, lamb stew with almonds. But Córdoba is really the home of one of the most famous Andalucían dishes, *rabo de toro*, a spicy concoction of bull's tail, onions and tomatoes. Try also the *buchon* (rolled fish filled with ham, dipped in breadcrumbs, then fried).

As one might expect, the Sierras offer dishes based on the game and wild herbs found in the mountains. Here freshwater lakes teem with trout, and on the slopes wild asparagus grows. The town of Jaén is particularly well known for its high-quality oil and vinegar, and delectable salads are a feature of most menus (try the *pipirrana*).

The Costa del Sol's traditional beachside delicacy is sardines, speared on a stick and cooked over a wood fire—best when eaten with a good salad and washed down with chilled white wine. *Boquerones* (fresh fried white bait) feature widely in restaurants and *tapas* bars, along with *pijotas*, small hake that suffer the indignity of being sizzled with tail-in-mouth. All over the region you will find *pinchitos*, a spicier version of its Greek cousin the *souvlaki*, a mini-kebab of lamb or pork marinated in spices. To finish off your meal there are any number of desserts (*postres*) based on almonds and custards, and the Arab influence once again shows through in, for example, the excellent sweetmeats from Granada and the *alfajores* from Huércal, Almería.

The presence of 1.5 million foreign residents, mainly clustered along the southern coast, has had an effect on the Costa del Sol culinary scene, although Spanish restaurants still manage to hold their own. A bewildering choice of Indonesian, Belgian, Swedish, Chinese, French, Italian and numerous other nationalities' cuisines confront the tourist. The standard is in fact quite high in most 'ethnic' restaurants, and prices are reasonable because of the fierce competition. A host of British establishments (mostly pubs) offer the whole shebang: roast beef, Yorkshire pudding and three veg, apple pie and custard that would put your granny to shame, and all for under 700 pts.

Be careful, though. Spain still has plenty of bad restaurants. The worst offenders are often those with the little flags and 10-language menus in the most touristy areas, and in general you'd do better to buy some bread, Manchego cheese and a bottle of Valdepeñas red and have a picnic, than throw away your pesetas there. If you dine where the locals do you'll be assured of a good deal, if not necessarily a good meal. Almost every restaurant offers a *menú del día*, or a *menú turístico*, featuring an appetizer, a main course, dessert, bread and drink at a set price, always a certain percentage lower than if you had ordered the items *à la carte*. These are always posted outside the restaurant, in the window or on the plywood chef at the door; decide what you want before going in if it's a set-price menu, because these bargains are hardly ever listed on the menu the waiter gives you at the table.

If you're travelling on a budget you may want to eat one of your meals a day at a *tapas bar* or **tasca**. *Tapas* means 'lids', and they started out as little saucers of goodies served on top of a drink. They have evolved over the years to form a main part of the world's greatest snack culture. Bars that specialize in them have platter after platter of delectable titbits—shellfish, slices of omelette, mushrooms baked in garlic, vegetables in vinaigrette, stews. All you have to do is pick out what looks best and order a *porción* (hors d'oeuvre), or a *ración* (big helping) if it looks really good. It's hard to generalize about prices, but on the average 400 pts of *tapas* and wine or beer really fill you up. You can always save money in bars by standing up; sit at that charming table on the terrace and prices jump considerably.

27

Another advantage of *tapas* is that they're available at what most Americans or Britons would consider normal dining hours. Spaniards are notoriously late diners; 2 is the earliest they would consider sitting down to their huge 'midday' meal, which can often turn into a marathon affair, then after work at 8 a few *tapas* at the bar hold them over until supper at 10 or 11. After living in Spain for a few months this makes perfect sense, but it's exasperating to the average visitor. On the coasts, restaurants tend to open earlier to accommodate foreigners (some as early as 5) but you may as well do as the Spaniards do.

Sticklers for absurd bureaucracy and measurement, the Spanish government rates restaurants by forks (this has become a bit of a joke—a car repair shop in Granada has rated itself two wrenches). The forks have nothing to do with the quality of the food, though they hint somewhat at the prices. Unless it's explicitly written on the bill (*la cuenta*), service is *not* included in the total, so tip accordingly.

Between restaurants and *tascas* are **comedors** (literally, dining-rooms) often tacked onto the backs of bars, where the food and decor are usually drab but cheap, and **cafeterías**, usually those places that feature photographs of their offerings of *platos combinados* (combination plates) to eliminate any language problem. **Asadors** specialize in roast meat or fish; **marisqueras** serve only fish and shellfish; you'll usually see the sign for 'pescados y mariscos' on the awning. Keep an eye out for **ventas**, usually modest family-run establishments offering excellent *menus del día* for working people. They specialise in typical Andaluz dishes of roast kid or lamb, rabbit, *paella*, game (partridge crops up often) and many pork dishes, *chorizo* sausage and varieties of ham. Try and visit one on a Sunday lunchtime when all the Spanish families go out—with a bit of luck things may get out of hand, and guitars and castanets could appear from nowhere, in which case abandon all plans for the rest of the day. (For menu and restaurant vocabulary see Language section at the end of the book.)

Eating Out in Gibraltar
This doesn't just mean sausage, chips and beans, though there are plenty of establish-ments serving such honest fare. Restaurants have become more competitive and people more selective, to the extent that you can find some excellent varieties of southern Mediterranean dishes in particular, some French classics and a healthy choice of many other nations' cuisines, at prices admittedly higher than in southern Spain, but lower than the average of other European countries. Pub grub can be good, too, but beware the fast-food alternatives unless your pockets are empty and your taste buds dead.

Drinking

No matter how much other costs have risen in Spain, **wine** has remained awesomely inexpensive by northern European or American standards; what's more, it's very good and there's enough variety from the various regions of the country for you to try something different every day. A restaurant's *vino del lugar* or *vino de la casa* is always your least expensive option while dining out; it usually comes out of a barrel or glass jug and may be a surprise either way. Some 20 Spanish wine-regions bottle their products under the strict controls, imposed by the National Institute, of *Denominación de Origen* (these almost always have the little maps of their various regions pasted on the back of the bottle). In many parts of Andalucía you may have difficulty ordering a simple bottle of white wine, as, on requesting *una botella de vino blanco de la casa*, you will often be served something resembling diluted sherry. To make things clear, specify a wine by name or by region—for example *una botella de Rioja blanco*, and the problem should be solved. Spain also produces its own champagne, known as *cava*, which is often just as good as the French, and notably cheaper.

Some Andalucían wines have achieved an international reputation for high quality. Best known is the Jerez, or what we in English call sherry. When a Spaniard invites you to have a *copa* (glass) it will nearly always be filled with this Andalucían sunshine. It comes in a wide range of varieties: *Manzanillas* are very dry, *fino* is dry, light and young (the famous *Tío Pepe*); *Amontillados* are a bit sweeter and rich and originate from the slopes around Montilla in Córdoba province; *olorosos* are very sweet dessert sherries, and can be either brown, cream, or *amoroso*. Nearby Huelva province produces the *Condado Pálido* and *Condado Viejo*, the first similar to the *finos* and the second *secos, semisecos*, whilst the *dulce* is comparable to *olorosos*. The white wines of Córdoba grown in the Villaviciosa region are again making a name for themselves, after all but being wiped out by phylloxera in the last century. In Sevilla, wine is produced in three regions: Lebrija; Los Palacios (white table wines); and Aljarafe, where full-bodied wines are particular favourites. Jaén also has three wine-producing regions—take your bottle along to the local *bodega* when you are here, as many wines are on tap only. In Bailén, the white, rosé and red table wines resemble those of the more famous La Mancha vineyards. Torreperogil, east of Ubeda, produces clarets, but only a limited number are bottled. In the west of the province, Lopera white wines are also sold from the barrel. Málaga and Almería do not produce much wine, although the sweet, aromatic wines of Málaga are famous, especially the *Málaga Virgen*.

Spanish brandy is extremely palatable; the two most popular brands are *103* (very light in colour) and *Soberano*, both drunk extensively by Spanish labourers at 7 am, and by British OAPs from Torremolinos to Estepona on sunny winter afternoons. *Anís* (sweet or dry) is also quite popular. *Sangría* is the famous summertime punch of red wine, brandy, mineral water, orange and lemon with ice, but beware—it's rarely made very well.

Many Spaniards prefer **beer**, which is also good, though not quite the bargain wine is. The most popular brands are *Cruzcampo* and *San Miguel*—most bars sell it cold in bottles or on tap; try *Mahón* Five Star if you see it. Imported whisky and other spirits are pretty inexpensive, though even cheaper are the versions Spain bottles itself, which may come close to your home favourites. Gin, believe it or not, is often drunk with Coca-Cola. Bacardi and Coke is a popular thirst-quencher; with a flourish worthy of a *matador* the barman will zap an ice-filled tumbler in front of you, and heave in a quadruple measure.

Coffee, tea, all the international soft-drink brands and the locally-made *Kas* round out the average café fare. If you want tea with milk, say so when you order, otherwise it will probably arrive with a piece of lemon. Coffee comes with milk (*café con leche*) or without (*café solo*). Spanish coffee is good and strong, and if you want a lot of it order a *doble* in a *vaso*; one of those will keep you awake even through the guided tour of any museum.

Drinking in Gibraltar

You can drink to your heart's delight in Gibraltar, but your liver may be happy to know that costs are about double the Spanish equivalent. Pub opening times follow Britain—

open all day till 11; wines and spirits are cheap in the supermarkets and off-licences, but no bargain in restaurants or pubs.

Fiestas and Annual Events

One of the most spiritually deadening aspects of Francoism was the banning of many local and regional fiestas. These are now celebrated with gusto, and if you can arrange your itinerary to include one or two you'll be guaranteeing an unforgettable holiday. Besides the ones listed below, there are literally thousands of others, and new ones spring up all the time.

Holidays celebrated throughout Spain are Holy Week (*Semana Santa*), the week preceding Easter; *Corpus Christi* in late May; 25 July, the feast day of Spain's patron, Santiago; and 15 August, the Assumption of the Virgin. No matter where you are there are bound to be fireworks or processions on these dates, especially for *Semana Santa* and *Corpus Christi*. Dates for most festivals tend to be fluid, flowing towards the nearest weekend; if the actual date falls on a Thursday or a Tuesday, Spaniards 'bridge' the fiesta with the weekend to create four-day whoopee. Check dates at the tourist office in advance.

Many village patronal fiestas feature *romerías* (pilgrimages) up to a venerated shrine. Getting there is half the fun, with everyone in local costume, riding on horseback or driving covered wagons full of picnic supplies. Music, dancing, food, wine and fireworks are all necessary ingredients of a proper fiesta, while the bigger ones often include bullfights, funfairs, circuses and competitions. *Semana Santa* is a major tourist event, especially in Sevilla, but unless you're prepared to fight the crowds to see the *pasos* (ornate floats depicting scenes from the Passion) carried in an excruciating slow march to lugubrious tuba music, and accompanied by children and men decked out in costumes later copied by the Ku Klux Klan, you may want to skip it; the real revelry takes place after Easter.

Fiestas or *ferias* are incredibly important to Andalucíans, no matter what the cost in money and lost sleep; a celebration of being alive in a society constantly aware of the inevitability of death. There are festivities for every stratum of society—from the elite of Sevilla to the humble fieldworker.

Calendar
January
1–2   **Granada**, commemoration of the city's capture by the Catholic Kings.
5   **Málaga**, Epiphany parade of Los Reyes Magos.
        Gibraltar, Three Kings Cavalcade.
February   *Carnival* usually pops up in mid-February. **Cádiz** has perhaps the best in Spain and certainly the oldest: parades, masquerades, music and fireworks in abundance.
March   *Semana Santa*: the most important celebrations are in **Sevilla**, with over 100 processions, broken by the singing of *saetas* (weird laments); **Málaga** and **Granada** put on major 'dos'.

April

Last week — **Sevilla**'s *April Feria*, originally a horse-fair, now grown into the greatest festival of Andalucía. Costumed parades of the gentry in fine carriages, lots of flamenco, bullfights, and drinking. **Andújar** (Jaén) the *Romería of the Virgin de la Cabeza*: pilgrimage from all over Andalucía and procession to the sanctuary nearby in the Sierra Morena.

End of April
beginning of May — **Jerez** Horse Fair; equestrian events and sherry tasting.

April–June — **Gibraltar** Festival.

May

1–2 — **Navas de San Juan** (north of Ubeda), pilgrimage in honour of *Nuestra Señora de la Estrella*; one of the most important pilgrimages in the province of Jaén. During the night, the popular *mayos* are sung in front of the church.

First week — **Jerez de la Frontera**, much like the April Fair in Sevilla; first Friday, **Jaca** re-enacts the victory over the Moors by local women; in **Granada** , everyone dresses up and decorates the streets with carpets and flowers for the *Fiesta de la Santa Cruz*.

2nd week
(every 3rd year) — **Córdoba**, Concurso Nacional de Arte Flamenco; 100 singers, guitar players and dancers participate.

Pentecost
Seventh Sunday
after Easter — **El Rocío** (Huelva), the biggest *romería* in Spain. Pilgrims converge on this tiny spot in Las Marismas south of Sevilla, in gaily decorated wagons for a week of wild carrying-on. The religious aspect is secondary.

27–31 — **Sanlúcar de Barrameda**, the *Manzanilla* wine fair. Vast quantities of fried fish and shellfish are consumed, helped down by equally copious amounts of *Manzanilla*; dancing, singing and sporting events.

Corpus Christi — Usually falls at the end of May (Thursday after Trinity Sunday), initiating four days of festivities, especially at **Zahara de la Sierra** (Cádiz).

June

15–July 15 — **Granada**, *Festival Internacional de Música y Danza* attracts some big names from around the world; classical music, jazz and ballet; also flamenco competitions in odd-numbered years.

2nd week — **Marbella**, *Feria de San Bernabe*, with big-name events.

23–26 — **Alhaurin de la Torre** (Málaga), fair and festival in honour of the patron St John with entertainment including parade of giant figures and the *torre del cante*, one of the best flamenco gatherings in the region.

31

July

First Sunday	**Córdoba**, International Guitar Festival—classical, flamenco and Latino.
16	**Málaga**, Virgen del Carmen, decorated boats along waterfront with firework display.
Last two weeks	**Lebrija** flamenco festival. **La Línea** summer fair.
End of July	**Almería** festival, including jazz concerts.

August

3	**Huelva** *Colmbinas*; bullfights and other sporting events.
5	**Trevelez** (Granada) has a midnight pilgrimage up Mulhacén, Spain's highest mountain.
First fortnight	**Ronda** Pedro Romero festival; bullfights, equestrian parades, folk groups.
15–16	Assumption of the Virgin and San Roque festivities at **Vejar** (Cádiz) with flamenco.
Last week	**Sanlucar de la Barrameda** (Cádiz), exaltation of the Río Guadalquivir and major flamenco events; **Toro**, Fiesta de San Augustine, with bulls and a 'fountain of wine'.

September

First week	**Jerez** has a *Vendimia* wine festival.
8	The **Virgin's Birthday** with celebrations in many places, especially at **Alájar** (Huelva). Far livelier and more popular than most pilgrimages; carriages and riders dressed in typical Andalucían costumes. Around this date **Ronda** puts on an 18th-century-style bullfight in its historic ring.
Second week in September	**Chipiona** flamenco singing and dancing, running of the bulls, bullfights.
End of September beginning of October	**Ubeda**, fair, stalls, bullfights.

October

15–23	**Jaén**, festival of St Luke, bullfights, cultural and sporting events.
21	**Gibraltar**, Trafalgar Day Ceremony.

Part II

TOPICS

Bullfights

In Spanish newspapers, you will not find accounts of the bullfights on the sports pages; look in the 'arts and culture' section, for that is how Spain has always thought of this singular spectacle. Bullfighting combines elements of ballet with the primal finality of Greek tragedy. To Spaniards it is a ritual sacrifice without a religion, and it divides the nation irreconcilably between those who find it brutal and demeaning, an echo of the old Spain best forgotten, and those who couldn't live without it. Its origins are obscure. Some claim it derives from Roman circus games, others say it started with the Moors; in the Middle Ages the bull faced a mounted knight with a lance.

There are bullrings all over Spain, and as far afield as Arles in France and Guadalajara, Mexico, but modern bullfighting is quintessentially Andalucían. It had its beginnings around the year 1800 in Ronda, when Francisco Romero developed the basic pattern of the modern *corrida*; some of his moves and passes, and those of his celebrated successor, Pedro Romero, are still in use today. The first royal *aficionado* was Fernando VII, the reactionary post-Napoleonic monarch who also brought back the Inquisition. He founded the Royal School of Bullfighting in Sevilla, and promoted the spectacle across the land as a circus for the discontented populace. Since the Civil War, bullfighting has gone through a period of troubles similar to boxing in the US. Scandals of weak bulls, doped-up bulls, and bulls with the points of their horns shaved have been frequent. Attempts at reform have been made, and all the problems seem to have decreased bullfighting's popularity only slightly.

In keeping with its ritualistic aura, the *corrida* is one of the few things in Andalucía that begins strictly on time. The show commences with the colourful entry of the *cuadrillas*

33

(teams of *toreros*) and the *alguaciles*, officials dressed in 17th-century costume, who salute the 'president' of the fight. Usually three teams fight two bulls apiece, the whole taking only about two hours. Each of the six fights, however, is a self-contained drama performed in four acts. First, upon the entry of the bull, the members of the *cuadrilla* tease him a bit, and the *matador*, the team leader, plays him with the cape to test his qualities. Next comes the turn of the *picadores*, on padded horses, whose task is to slightly wound the bull in the neck with a short lance or *pica*, and the *bandilleros*, who agilely plant sharp darts in the bull's back while avoiding the sweep of its horns. The object of these wounds is to weaken the bull physically without diminishing any of its fighting spirit, and to force it to keep its head lower for the third and most artistic stage of the fight, when the lone *matador* conducts his pas-de-deux with the deadly, if doomed, animal. Ideally, this is the transcendent moment, the *matador* leading the bull in deft passes and finally crushing its spirit with a tiny cape called a *muleta*. Now the defeated bull is ready for 'the moment of truth'. The kill must be clean and quick, a sword thrust to the heart. The corpse is carried out to the waiting butchers.

More often than not the job is botched. Most bullfights, in fact, are a disappointment, especially if the *matadors* are beginners, or *novios*, but to the *aficionado* the chance to see one or all of the stages performed to perfection makes it all worthwhile. When a *matador* is good, the band plays and the hats and handkerchiefs fly; an excellent performance earns the reward from the president of one of the bull's ears, or both; or rarely, for an exceptionally brilliant performance, both ears and the tail.

You'll be lucky to see a bullfight at all; there are only about 500 each year in Spain, mostly coinciding with holidays or a town's fiesta—during Sevilla's *feria* there is a bullfight every afternoon at the famous Maestranza ring, while the rings in Málaga and Puerto Santa María near Cádiz are other major venues. Tickets can be astronomically expensive and hard to come by, especially for a well-known *matador*, sometimes scalpers buy out the lot. Get them in advance, if you can, and directly from the office in the *plaza de toros* to avoid the hefty commission charges. Prices vary according to the sun—the most expensive seats are entirely in the shade.

City Slickers

You're on the train for Córdoba, passing the hours through some of the loneliest landscapes in Europe. For a long time, there's been nothing to see but olive trees—gnarled veterans, some of them planted in the time of Ferdinand and Isabella. You may see a donkey pulling a cart. At twilight, you pull in at the central station, and walk four blocks down to the Avenida del Gran Capitán, an utterly Parisian boulevard of chic boutiques and pompous banks, booming with traffic. The loudspeakers from the *Galerias Preciados* department store broadcast the latest singles of Lisa Stansfield and The Pet Shop Boys.

You don't often see Andalucíans going off on picnics in the country. The ground is dry, vegetation usually sparse, and the sun can seem like a death-ray even in winter. Climate has always forced people here to seek their pleasure elsewhere; it is the impetus behind their exquisite gardens, and it has made of them the most resolutely urban people in Europe.

In city centres the air is electric, a cocktail of motion, colour, and fragrances that goes to your head like the best *manzanilla*. It has probably been much the same for over 2000 years; the atmosphere may be hard to recapture, but we can learn a lot by looking at decoration and design.

We know little about city life in Roman times—only that for relatively small populations, towns like Italica had amphitheatres and other amenities comparable to any in the empire. The cities of Moorish Spain were a revelation—libraries, public gardens and street lighting, at a time when feudal Europe was scratching its carrot rows with a short stick. Their design, similar to that of North African and Middle Eastern cities, can be traced (with some difficulty), in Granada, Córdoba and Sevilla today.

It is difficult to say how many of Andalucía's Moorish cities were inherited from Roman Baetica, and how much introduced by the Moors themselves. Enclosure was the key word: a great mosque and its walled courtyard at the centre, near the fortified palace (*alcazar* or *alcazaba*) and its walled gardens. Along with the markets and baths, these were located in the *medina*, and locked up behind its walls each night. The residential quarters that surrounded the *medina* were islands in themselves, a maze of narrow streets where the houses, rich or poor, looked inwards into open patios while turning blank walls to the street. Some of these survive, with their original decoration, as private homes in Granada's Albaicín.

In Roman times, the patio was called a *peristyle*. The gracious habit of building a house around a colonnaded central court was perfected by the Greeks, and became common across the Mediterranean in Roman times. Today, while most of us enjoy the charms of our cramped flats and dull, squarish houses, the Andalucíans have never given up their love of the old-fashioned way. In Córdoba especially, the patios of the old quarters spill over with roses, wisteria and jasmine; each year there is a competition for the prettiest.

Besides the houses, some of the cellular quality of Moorish cities survived the Reconquista. In 16th-century Sevilla, thick with artful bandits, the silversmiths had their own walled quarter (and their own cops to guard it). The Moorish urban aesthetic evolved gracefully into the modern Andalucían; the simple, unforgettable panorama of almost any town—an oasis of brilliant white rectangularity, punctuated sharply by upright cypresses and by the warm sandstone of churches, palaces and towers. One Spanish invention, combining Italian Renaissance planning with native tradition, was the arcaded, rectangular square usually called *Plaza Mayor*. The best are in Madrid and Salamanca, but many Andalucían towns have one, and there is a huge dilapidated specimen in Córdoba. Architecturally unified—the four walls often seem like a building turned inside-out—the *Plaza Mayor* translated the essence of the patio into public space. Such a square made a perfect stage for the colourful life of a Spanish city; not coincidentally, Spanish theatres in the great age of Lope de Vega and Calderón took the same form, with three sides of balconies, the fourth for the stage, on the narrow end, and a Shakespearean 'pit' at ground level.

In the last two centuries, while the rest of Spain continued to create innovations in urban design and everyday pageantry, impoverished Andalucía contributed little—some elegant bullrings, exquisite redesigns of the old Moorish gardens, grand boulevards like the Alameda of Málaga and the *paseos* of Granada, and some eccentric decorations, such as the gigantic, sinister stone birds of prey that loom over most city centres— symbols of an insurance company. Since the 70s and the end of Francoism, one can sense a momentum of slickness gathering steam: a touch of anonymous good design in a shop sign, new pavements and lighting, ambitious new architecture with a splash of colour and surprise. Last Christmas, we noticed the *El Corte Ingles* department store in Málaga entirely covered in computer-controlled electric lights, nearly a vertical acre of permanent fireworks, flashing peacock tails and other patterns in constantly changing brilliant colours; as spectacular and futuristic a decoration as any city has ever had. Watch out for these sharp Andalucíans—and for Spaniards in general. While we fog-bound northerners are nodding off with Aunty at twelve o'clock, they may well be plotting the delights of the future.

Dust in the Wind

The poets of al-Andalus devoted most of their attention to sensuous songs of love, nature, wine, women and boys, but amidst all the lavish beauty there would linger, like a *basso continuo*, a note of refined detachment, of melancholy and futility. Instead of forgetting death in their man-made paradises, the poets made a point of reminding their listeners of how useless it was to become attached to these worldly delights. After all, only God is forever, and why express love to something that would one day turn to dust? Why even attempt to build something perfect and eternal—the main ingredients of the lovely, delicate Alhambra are plaster and wood. The Nasrid kings, were they to return, might be appalled to find it still standing.

The Christians who led the Reconquista had no time for futility. In their architecture and art they built for eternity, plonking a soaring church right in the middle of the Great Mosque and an imperial palace intruding on the Alhambra; literal, lapidarian, emanating the power and total control of the temporal Church and State. Their oppression reduced the sophisticated songs of the Moorish courts to a baser fatalism. The harsh realities of everyday life encouraged people to live for the moment, to grab what happiness they could in an uncertain world. This uncertainty was best expressed by the 17th-century Spanish playwright Calderón de la Barca, especially in his great *La Vida es Sueño* (Life is a Dream), known as the Catholic answer to *Hamlet*.

There wasn't much poetry in Granada between 1492 and the advent of Federico García Lorca, born in 1898 in the Vega just outside of town. Lorca, a fine musician as well as a poet and playwright, found much of his inspiration in what would be called nowadays Granada's 'alternative' traditions, especially those of the gypsies. In 1922, Lorca was a chief organizer of Granada's first *cante jondo* festival, to bring flamenco singing to international attention and prevent it from sliding into a hackneyed Andalucían joke. In 1927, he published the book of poems that made him the most popular poet in Spain, the *Romancero Gitano* (Gypsy Ballads); his plays, like *Noces de sang* (Blood Wedding) and *Yerma*, have the lyrical, disturbing force of the deepest *cante jondo*. But of post-Reconquista Granada he was sharply critical, accusing Ferdinand and Isabella of destroying a much more sophisticated civilization than their own—and as for the modern inhabitants of Granada, they were an imported reactionary bourgeois contingent from the north, not 'real' Andalucíans. Lorca criticized, but he kept coming back, and had dreams of bringing the city's once-great culture back to life.

In Granada, a commemorative park at Víznar marks the spot where on 18 August, 1936, local police or rebel soldiers took Lorca and shot him dead. No one knows who gave the orders, or the reason why; the poet had supported the Republic but was not actively political. When news of his secret execution leaked out, it was an embarrassment to Franco, who managed to hush up the affair until his own death. But most historians agree that the killing was a local vendetta for Lorca's outspoken views of his hometown, a blood sacrifice to the stone god of Ferdinand and Isabella and Charles V who fears all change, closing (one can only hope, once and for all) a full circle of bittersweet futility, frustration, and death.

Flamenco

For many people, flamenco is the soul of Spain—like bullfighting—an essential part of the culture that sets it apart from the rest of the world. Good flamenco, with that ineffable quality of *duende*, has a primitive, ecstatic allure that draws in its listeners until they feel as if their very hearts were pounding in time with its relentless rhythms, their guts seared by its ululating Moorish wails and the sheer drama of the dance. Few modern experiences are more cathartic.

As folklore goes, however, flamenco is a newborn. It began in the 18th century in Andalucía, where its originators, the gypsies, called one another 'flamencos'—a derogatory term dating back to the days when Charles V's Flemish (*Flamenco*) courtiers bled Spain dry. These gypsies, especially in the Guadalquivir delta cities of Sevilla, Cádiz, and Jerez, sang songs of oppression, lament, and bitter romance, a kind of blues that by the 19th century began to catch on among all the other downtrodden inhabitants of Andalucía.

Yet despite flamenco's recent origins, the Andalucían intelligentsia, especially Lorca and Manuel de Falla, found (or invented) much to root it deeply in the south's soil and soul. Its rhythms and Doric mode are as old as Andalucía's ancient Greek settlers; its spirit of improvisation and spontaneity date from the famous Córdoba school of music and poetry, founded in 820 by Abu al-Hassan Ali Ibn Nafi, better known as Ziryab, the 'Blackbird' (see History); the half-tonal notes and lyrics of futility of the *cante jondo*, or deep song, the purest flamenco, seem to go straight back to the Arab troubadours of al-Andalus. But just how faithfully the music of al-Andalus was preserved among the gypsies and others to be reincarnated as flamenco will never be known; the Arabs knew of musical notation, but disdained it in their preference for improvisation.

By the late 19th century, flamenco had gone semi-public, performed in the backrooms of cafés in Sevilla and Málaga. Its very popularity in Spain, and the enthusiasm set off by Bizet's *Carmen* abroad, began seriously to undermine its harsh, true quality. At the same time, flamenco influence spread into the popular and folk repertories to create a happier, less intense genre called the *sevillana* (often songs in praise of you know where). When schoolchildren at a bus stop in Cádiz burst into an impromptu dance and hand-clapping session, or when some old cronies in Málaga's train station bar start singing and reeling, you can bet they're doing a *sevillana*. In Europe, only the Greeks dance and sing their own music as much, for the pure joy of it.

In the 1920s attempts were made to establish some kind of standards for the real thing, especially *cante jondo*, though without lasting results; the 'real, original flamenco' was never meant to be performed as such, and will only be as good as its 'audience'. This should ideally be made up of other musicians and flamenco *aficionados*, whose participation is essential in the spontaneous invariably late-night combustion of raw emotion, alcohol, drugs and music, to create *duende*. With so many intangible factors, your chance of getting in on some genuine soul-stirring flamenco are about as rare as getting in on a genuine soul-stirring bullfight. But perhaps it is this very fleeting, hard-to-pin-down quality that makes both arts so compelling in the midst of a programmed, homogenized world.

The Founding Father

Andalucía For itself, for Spain and for Humanity; so reads the proud device on the regional escutcheon, hurriedly cooked up by the Andalucíans after the regional autonomy laws of the 70s made them masters in their own house once again. Above the motto we see a strong fellow, mythologically underdressed and accompanied by two lions. Though perhaps more familiar to us for his career among the Hellenes, he is also the first Andalucían—HERCULES DOMINATOR FUNDATOR.

The Greeks themselves admit that Hercules found time for two extended journeys to the distant and little-known West. In the eleventh of his Twelve Labours, the Apples of the Hesperides caper, he made it as far as the environs of Tangier, where he dispatched the giant Antaeus. The tenth Labour brought Hercules into Spain, sailing in the golden goblet of Helios and using his lion skin for a sail. In the fabled land of Tartessus, on the 'red island' of Erytheia, he slew the three-headed titan Geryon and stole his cattle. Before heading back to Greece, he founded the city of Gades, or Cádiz, on the island (Cádiz, surrounded by marshes is, in a sense, an island). He also erected his well-known Pillars, Gibraltar and Mount Abyle, across the way in Africa. His return was one of the all-time bad trips; whenever you're crazed and dying on some five-hour 'semi-direct' Andalucían bus ride (say, Granada to Córdoba *via* Rute), think of Hercules, marching Geryon's cows through Spain and over the Pyrennees, then making a wrong turn that took him halfway down the Italian peninsula before he noticed the mistake. After mortal combats with several other giants and monsters, he finally made it to Greece—but then his nemesis Hera sent a stinging blue-tail fly to stampede the cattle. They didn't stop until they reached the Scythian Desert.

To most people, Hercules is little more than mythology's most redoubtable Dog Warden, rounding up not only Cerberus, the Hound of Hell, but most of the other stray monsters that dug up the roses and soiled the footpaths of the Heroic Age. But there is infinitely more than this to the character of the most-travelled, hardest-working hero of them all. In antiquity, wherever Hercules had set foot the people credited him with founding nations and cities, building roads and canals, excavating lakes and draining swamps. And there is the intellectual Hercules, the master of astronomy and lord of the zodiac, the god of prophecy and eloquence who taught both the Latins and the Spaniards their letters. One version has it that the original Pillars of Hercules were not mountains at all, but columns, like those of the Temple of Jerusalem, connected with some alphabetical mysticism.

Ancient mythographers had their hands full, sorting out the endless number of deities and heroes known to the peoples of Europe, Africa and the Middle East, trying to decide whether the same figure was hiding behind different names and rites. Varro recorded no less than 44 Herculeses, and modern scholars have found the essential Herculean form in myths from Celtic Ireland to Mesopotamia. Melkarth, the Phoenician Hercules, would have had his temples in southern Spain long before the first Greek ever saw Gibraltar. Not a bad fellow to have for a founding father—and a reminder that in Andalucía the roots are as strong and as deep as in any corner of Europe.

Getting Them Back

In the 70s Robert Graves recalled overhearing two London secretaries talking about their vacations; 'I went to Majorca this year', says one. Her friend asks, 'Where's that?' and receives the answer: 'I don't know, I flew.' But the boom years of the Spanish package tour are definitely over. The drop in visitors is ringing alarm bells in Spain, and Europe's most intelligent and capable tourism bureaucracy is making a determined effort to put the country back in its former position, by means of a far-sighted and extensive change of image.

The down-market profile of resorts like Torremolinos will take a long time to change in the minds of the foreign public, who understandably but somewhat mistakenly connect it with tattooed lager louts, late-night punch-ups and raucous discos belting out music until dawn. There's a fair degree of snobbery involved in these attitudes; who in Britain, for example, boasts of having just spent a holiday on the Costa del Sol, with destinations such as Turkey, Florida and the Caribbean beckoning at affordable prices? The principal obstacle to attracting and sustaining mass tourism is the quality of holiday and destination on offer. Whilst the independent traveller is happy to pack guide book, camera and sensible shoes and head off on a cultural pilgrimage to Granada's Alhambra, Córdoba's Mezquita, Sevilla's Giralda or the Cádiz Carnival, and along the way experience and indulge in the *real Andalucía*, the majority of visitors are interested in less ethereal pursuits, and the ingredients for their fun are beaches, hotels, food and entertainment at a reasonable price.

Spain, of course, can meet these criteria—too well, some malcontent Hispanophiles would say; those who think that the country has sacrificed its integrity to provide monstrous concrete resort playgrounds, paint them white and pass them off as Andalucían *pueblos*. So what can be done? It's too late to tear down what already exists, but it's time the government pushed the stop-button on the coastal developments, on the Costa del Sol particularly, but no less so on the Costa de la Luz, where full-scale construction would mean, and in some places has already meant, the ruination of an untamed stretch of coast. Control future development, improve the existing infrastructure and abolish Spain's reputation as solely a paradise for sun-seeking tipplers, and maybe more visitors will come for the most genuine of motives—to get a balanced view of a country rich in history, culture and fun.

Hot-blooded Andalucían Women

Andalucía holds roughly a sixth of Spain's people, which means one twelfth of the population consists of the most sultry, sensuous women in Europe. ¡Ah, señores, how they arch their supple torsos in an improvised *sevillana*, clicking their magic castanets! ¡Dios, how provocative they are behind the iron grilles of their windows with their come-hither-burning-black-eyes over flickering fans, serenaded by their handsome guitar-strumming *caballero*, tossing him a red rose of promise and desire!

Ever since the first boatload of dancing girls from Cádiz docked at the slave-markets of ancient Rome, the women of Andalucía have had to put up with this—an extraordinary reputation for grace, beauty, and amorous dispositions. Travellers' accounts and novels elaborate on their exotic charms, spiced by the languor of the Moorish harem odalisque and the supposed promiscuity of the passionate gypsy. After all, when Leperello counts off his master's conquests in Mozart's *Don Giovanni*, which country comes out on top? Spain, of course, with 1003 victims to the arch-libertine's art of persuasion.

Nothing kept this fond male fancy afloat as much as the fact that nubile Andalucían women were tantalizingly inaccessible, thanks to a rigid Latin code of honour second to none. It took the Industrial Revolution, the Sevilla Tobacco Factory, and a French visitor, Prosper Mérimée to bring this creature of the imagination out into the open, in the form of the beautiful gypsy tomato *Carmen* (1845), rendered immortally saucy in Bizet's opera of 1873. Step aside, Don Juan, or be stepped on! This new stereotype was as quick to light up a cheroot as to kick aside her sweetheart for a strutting matador in tight trousers. Not surprisingly, it wasn't long before the Tobacco Factory and its steamy, scantily-clad examples of feminine pulchritude (labouring for a handful of pesetas a day) attracted as many tourists as the Giralda tower.

Alas, where is the kitsch of yesteryear? Modern young Andalucían women are, like modern Andalucían men, among the most normal, mentally well-balanced people in the world. Ask them about the cloistered señoritas of the past and they'll laugh. Ask them about the unbridled Carmen, and they'll laugh. Ask them about the bizarre wind called the *solano* that troubles Cádiz in the springtime, a wind that in the old days drove the entire female population en masse to the beach, where they would fling off their clothes and dive into the sea to seek relief while the local cavalry regiment stood guard. Ask them about it, and they'll just laugh.

Roses of the Secret Garden

Western art and Islamic art are two worlds that will never agree. Even today, the sort of folk who believe in the divinity of Michelangelo or the essential greatness of the Baroque can be found in print, sniffing at the art of the Alhambra as merely 'decorative'. On the other side, you will discover a state of mind that can dismiss our familiar painting and sculpture as frivolous, an impious obsession with the appearances of the moment that ignores the transcendent realities beneath the surface. A powerful idea was in the air, in the 7–8th centuries, perhaps a reaction against the worldliness and incoherence that drowned classical civilization. It was not limited to Islam alone; the 'iconoclastic' controversy in Byzantium, following the attempt of Emperor Leo III to end the paganistic veneration of icons, was basically the same argument.

However this argument started, Islam grew up with an aversion to figurative art. At the same time, Islam was gaining access to the scientific and mathematical heritage of Greece and Rome, and finding it entirely to its liking. A new approach to art gradually took form, based on the sacred geometry of Byzantine architecture, and on a trend of mathematical mysticism that goes back to Pythagoras. Number, proportion, and symmetry were the tools God used to create the world. The same rule could be found in every aspect of creation, and could be reproduced in art, courtesy of the simple methods of Euclidean geometry. This geometry now found its place not only in the structure of a building, but also in its decoration.

Once the habit of thinking this way was established, it profoundly affected life and art in all the Islamic world, including Spain. The land itself became a careful mosaic, with neat rows of olive trees draped over the hills and the very beans and carrots in the gardens laid out in intricate patterns (Andalucían farmers still do it; you can see a remarkable example of such a landscape from the *mirador* in Ubeda). While nature was being made to imitate art, Muslim artists, consciously or not, often imitated the hidden processes of nature—as in the Córdoba mosque, growing like a crystal with the columns and aisles of each new addition. Often, they created novelties by changing scales, reducing and replicating old forms to make new, more complex ones. One example would be the Visigothic horseshoe arch. You can see it in its simplest form at Córdoba or Madinat az-Zahra; later, as in Sevilla's Alcazar, the same arch is made of smaller versions of itself. And in the Alhambra, you'll see arches made of arches made of arches, seeming to grow organically down from the patterns on the walls. A tree or a snowflake finds its form in much the same way. Fans of Chaos theory, take note—the Moors had anticipated fractals and Koch curves 600 years ago.

Three dimensions is the domain of the mundane shell, the worldly illusion. The archetypes, the underlying reality, can be more fittingly expressed in two. With their straight-edge and compass, Islamic artists developed a tradition of elaborate geometrical decoration, in painted tiles, stucco, or wooden grilles and ceilings. The highest levels of subtlety reached by this art were in Isfahan, Persia, in Egypt, and in Granada. The foundation, as in all constructive geometry, is the circle—*man's heart is the centre, heaven the circumference*, as a medieval Christian mystic put it. From this, they wove the exquisite patterns that embellish the Alhambra, exotic blooms interlaced in rhythms of 3, 5, 6, 8 or 12. This is not the shabby, second-hand symbolism of our times. A 12-pointed flower does not *symbolize* the firmament and the 12 signs of the zodiac, for example; it *recalls* this, and many other things as well. For philosophers, these patterns could provide a meditation on the numerical harmony of creation; for the rest of us, they stand by themselves, lovely, measured creations, whispering a sweet invitation to look a bit more closely at the wonders around us. The patterns of the Alhambra haunt Andalucía to this day. In Granada especially, these geometric flowers are endlessly reproduced on *azulejo* tiles in bars and restaurants, and in the *taracea* work boxes and tables sold in the Alcaiceria.

One of the favourite games of the Islamic artists was filling up space elegantly, in the sense a mathematician understands that word. In geometry, only three regular polygons, when repeated, can entirely fill a plane. One is the hexagon—as in a honeycomb; the others are the square—as on a chessboard—and the equilateral triangle. Some not-so-regular polygons (any triangle or parallelogram, for example) can do it too. Try and find some more complex forms; it isn't easy. One modern artist fascinated by these problems was M. C. Escher, whose tricks of two-dimensional space are beloved of computer programmers and the other Pythagoreans of our own age. The first four figures below can fill a plane.

41

The first, with a little imagination and geometrical know-how, could be made into one of Escher's space-filling birds or fish. The third doesn't quite do the job, but properly arranged it creates a secondary pattern of eight-pointed stars (fig. 5) in between. For a puzzle, try and multiply each of the four on paper to fill a plane. Answers can be found on the walls of the Alhambra.

By now, you may suspect that these shapes were not employed without reason. In fact, according to the leading authority on such matters, Keith Critchlow (in his book *Islamic Patterns*), the patterns formed by figs 1 and 3 mirror the symmetrical arrangement of numbers in a magic square. Triangular figs 2 and 4 are based on the *tetractys*, a triangle of numbers closely related to the magic squares that was a favourite study of the Pythagoreans. But a Spanish Muslim did not need to be a mathematician to appreciate the lesson of this kind of geometry. Everyone understood the basic tenet of Islam: that creation is One: harmonious and complete. Imagine some cultured minister of a Granadan king, musing under the arcades of the Court of the Lions, reflecting perhaps on the nature that shaped the roses in the court, and how the same laws are proclaimed by the ceramic blossoms within.

Part III
HISTORY

Visigothic crown

Southern Spain has been inhabited since the remotest antiquity. Neanderthal man lived here (in Gibraltar, *c.* 50 000 BC), and later peoples contributed cave paintings around Ronda. Neolithic cultures, with their dolmens and burial mounds begin to appear around the Iberian coasts about 4000. About 800 BC, the native Iberians are joined by other peoples, notably the Celts from over the Pyrenees, who occupied much of the north and centre of Spain. The great mystery of this era is the fabled kingdom of **Tartessos**, roughly modern Andalucía, the only place where the anarchistic Iberians ever founded a state. Phoenician records mention it, and in the *Book of Kings* it appears as 'Tarshish', its great navy bringing wares of Spain and Africa to trade with King Solomon. With great wealth from the mines of the Rio Tinto and the Sierra Morena, Tartessos reached its height about 800–700, just in time to be digested by more high-powered civilizations from the east.

700–50 BC: Phoenicians, Carthaginians, Romans

The **Phoenicians** 'discovered' Spain perhaps as early as 1100 BC, founding Gades (Cádiz), claimed to be the oldest city in Western Europe. They were after Spain's mineral resources—copper, tin, gold, silver and mercury—and their successful exploitation of Spain made the Phoenicians the economic masters of the Mediterranean. Their rivals, the **Greeks**, arrived about 636, founding a trading post at Mainake near Málaga.

By this time, the Phoenicians of the Levant were in decline, and **Carthage**, their western branch office, was building an empire out of their occupied coasts in Spain and North Africa. About 500 BC, the Carthaginians gobbled up the last remains of Tartessos and stopped the Greek infiltration. The Carthaginians contributed little to Spain, but they maintained the status quo until 264–241 BC, when **Rome** drubbed them in the First Punic War. In the rematch, the Second Punic War that began in 218, the Romans under Scipio Africanus conquered Spain while Hannibal was chasing rainbows in Italy (with a largely Spanish army).

Unlike their predecessors, the Romans were never content to hold just a part of Spain. Relentlessly, they slogged over the peninsula, subjugating one Celtic or Iberian tribe after another, a job that was not completed until about 50 AD. Rome had to send its best—Cato, Pompey, Julius Caesar and Augustus were all commanders in the Spanish conquest. Caesar, in fact, was governor in Andalucía, the most prosperous part of the peninsula, and the one that adapted most easily to Roman rule and culture.

AD 50–409: Roman *Bætica*

At first, the Romans called the region simply 'Further Spain', but eventually it settled in as *Bætica*, from the Bætis, the ancient name for the Guadalquivir. For the next four centuries, it would be a prosperous, contented place, by grace of its mineral and agricultural wealth the richest Roman province west of Tunisia. Besides wine, oil and metals, another export was dancing girls—Bætica's girls were reputed to be the hottest in the empire. And for the choicer Roman banquets, there was *garum*, a highly prized condiment made of fish guts. Modern gourmets have been trying to guess the recipe for centuries.

New cities grew up to join Cádiz, Italica and Málaga. Of these the most important were **Hispalis** (Sevilla) and **Corduba** (Córdoba). Among the cosmopolitan population were Iberians, Celts, Phoenicians, Italians, and a sizeable minority of Jews. Rome settled them here in great numbers in the Diaspora as far from home as they could possibly put them; they were to play an important and constructive role in Spanish life for the next 1500 years. The province also had a talent for keeping in the mainstream of imperial politics and culture. Vespasian had been governor here, and Bætica gave birth to three of Rome's best emperors: Trajan, Hadrian and Theodosius. To Latin literature, it contributed Lucan, both Senecas, Martial and Quintilian.

409–711: Roman Twilight and the Visigoths

By the 4th century, the crushing burden of maintaining the defence budget and the government bureaucracy sent Spain's economy into a permanent regression. Cities declined, and in the countryside the great landowners gradually squeezed the majority of the population into serfdom or outright slavery. Thus when the bloody, anarchic **Vandals** arrived in 409, they found bands of rural guerrillas, or *bagaudae*, to help them in smashing up the remnants of the Roman system. The Vandals moved on to Africa in 428, leaving nothing behind but, maybe, the name Andalucía—perhaps originally *Vandalusia*.

The next uninvited guests were the **Visigoths**, a ne'er-do-well Teutonic folk who had been pushed westwards by the Huns. After sacking Rome in 410, they found their way into Spain four years later. By 478 they had conquered most of it, including Andalucía, and they established an independent kingdom stretching from the Atlantic to the Rhone. The Visigoths were illiterate, selfish and bloody-minded, but persistent enough to endure, despite endless dynastic and religious quarrels; like most Germans, they were Arian heretics. There weren't many of them, only a warrior elite that never formed more than a small fraction of the population. For support they depended on the landowners, who were making the slow but logical transition from Roman *senatores* to feudal lords.

Despite all the troubles, Andalucía at least seems to have been doing well—probably better than anywhere else in Western Europe—and there was even a modest revival of learning in the 7th century, the age of St Isidore, famous scholar of Sevilla. King Leovigild (573–86) was an able leader; his son Reccared converted to orthodox Christianity in 589; both brought their state to the height of its power as much by internal reform as military victories. Allowing the grasping Church a share of power, however, proved fatal to the Visigoths. Their depredations against the populace, and their persecutions of Jews and heretics made the Visigothic state as many enemies within as it ever had across its borders.

711–756: the Muslim Conquest

The great wave of Muslim Arab expansion that began in Muhammad's lifetime was bound to wash up on Spain's shores sooner or later. A small Arab force arrived in Spain in 710, led by **Tarif**, who gave his name to today's Tarifa on the straits. The following year brought a larger army—still only about 7000 men—under **Tariq ibn-Ziyad** who quickly defeated the Visigoths near Barbate, a battle in which King Roderick was killed. Within five years, the Arabs had conquered most of the peninsula.

The ease of the conquest is not difficult to explain. The majority of the population was delighted to welcome the Arabs and their Berber allies. The overtaxed peasants and persecuted Jews supported them from the first. Religious tolerance was guaranteed under the new rule; since the largest share of taxes fell on non-believers, the Arabs were happy to refrain from seeking converts. The conquest, however, was never completed. A small Christian enclave in the northwest survived, the Kingdom of Asturias that became the nucleus of modern Spain. Muslim control of most of Spain was solid, but hampered by dissension almost from the start between the Arabs and the neglected Berbers, and between the various tribes of the Arabs themselves.

756–1031: the Emirate of al-Andalus

Far away in Damascus, the political struggles of the Caliphate were being resolved by a general massacre of the princes of the Ummayyad dynasty, the successors of Muhammad, as the Abbasids replaced them on the throne. One Ummayyad escaped—**Abd ar-Rahman**; he fled to Córdoba, and gained the support of Ummayyad loyalists there. After a battle in May 756, he proclaimed himself Emir, the first leader of an independent **Emirate of al-Andalus.**

Under this new government, Muslim Spain grew strong and prosperous. Political unity was maintained only with great difficulty, but trade, urban life and culture flourished. Though their domains stretched as far as the Pyrenees, the Ummayyad emirs referred to it all as *al-Andalus*. Andalucía was its heartland and Córdoba, Sevilla, and Málaga its greatest cities, unmatched by any others in western Europe. Abd ar-Rahman began the Great Mosque in Córdoba, a brilliant and unexpected start to the culture of the new state.

After Abd ar-Rahman, the succession passed without difficulty through Hisham I (788–96), Al-Hakam I (796–822), and Abd ar-Rahman II (822–52). One of Abd ar-Rahman's innovations, the creation of a professional army and palace secretariat, helped considerably in maintaining stability. The latter, called the *Saqaliba*, a civil service of imported slaves, was made up largely of Slavs and black Africans. The new dynasty seems also to have worked sincerely to establish justice and balance among the various contentious ethnic groups. One weakness, shared with most early Islamic states, was the personal, non-institutional nature of rule. Individuals and groups had only the Emir to address their grievances to, while governors in distant towns had so much authority, they often began to think of themselves as independent potentates—a cause of frequent rebellions in the reign of Muhammad I (852–86).

In the tenth century, al-Andalus enjoyed its golden age. **Abd ar-Rahman III** (912–961) and **Al-Hakam II** (961–76) collected tribute from the Christian kingdoms of the north, and from North African states as far as Algiers. In 929, Abd ar-Rahman III assumed the title of Caliph, declaring al-Andalus entirely independent of any higher political or religious authority. When the boy Caliph Hisham II came to the throne in 976, effective power was seized by his chamberlain Ibn Abi-'Amir, better known as **Al-Mansur** ('the victorious'), who recaptured León, Pamplona and Barcelona from the Christians, and even raided the great Christian shrine of Compostela, in Galicia, stealing its bells to hang up as trophies in the Great Mosque of Córdoba.

al-Andalus, at the height of its fortunes, was one of the world's great civilizations. Its wealth and stability sustained an impressive artistic production—obvious today, even from the few monuments that survived the Reconquista. Also, art and life were growing closer. About 822, the famous Ziryab had arrived in Córdoba from Baghdad. A great musician and poet, Ziryab also revolutionized the manners of the Arabs, introducing eastern fashions, poetic courtesies, and the proper way to arrange the courses of a meal. It wasn't long before the elite of al-Andalus became more interested in the latest graft of Shiraz roses than in riding across La Mancha to bash swords with the malodorous Asturians.

Keeping such a diverse, sophisticated population in balance was a more concrete accomplishment: Latinized Baeticans and residual Celtiberians, Yemenites, Jews, Arabs, Syrians, Slavs, Berbers, Black—all the while accomodating three religions and ensuring mutual tolerance. At the same time, they made it pay. Their cities thrived, far in advance of any of their neighbours, Muslim or Christian. Córdoba, with al-Hakam's great library, became a centre of learning; Málaga was renowned for its singers, and Sevilla for the making of musical instruments. The countryside was more prosperous than it has been before or since. The Arabs introduced cotton, rice, dates, sugar, oranges and much else. Irrigation, begun under the Romans, was perfected, and even parched Almería became a garden.

At this time, when backward Christian Europe was just beginning to blossom, al-Andalus and Byzantium were its exemplars and schoolmasters. Religious partisanship and western pride have always obscured the relationship; how much we really owe al-Andalus in scholarship—especially the transmission of Greek and Arab science—in art and architecture, in technology, and in poetry and the other delights of civilization, has never been completely explored. Contacts were more common than is generally assumed. Christian students were not unknown in Toledo or Córdoba—like the French monk who became Pope Sylvester II in 997.

Throughout the 10th century, the military superiority of al-Andalus was great enough to have finally erased the Christian kingdoms had the Caliphs cared to do so; it may have been a simple lack of aggressiveness and determination that held them back. The Muslim-Christian wars of this period cannot be understood as a prelude to the Crusades, or to the bigotry of Ferdinand and Isabella. Religious fanaticism, in fact, was lacking on both sides. Frontier chiefs could switch sides more than once without switching religions. The famous El Cid spent more time working for Muslim rulers than Christians; all the kings of Leon had some Moorish blood, and the mother of Abd ar-Rahman III was a Basque.

After the death of al-Mansur in 1002, the political situation began to change dramatically. His son, Abd al-Malik, inherited his position and held the state together despite increasing tensions until his death in 1008; all the while Hisham II remained a pampered prisoner in the palace-city of Madinat-az-Zahra, outside Córdoba. The lack of political legitimacy in this ministerial rule contributed to the troubles that began in 1008, along with the increasing distance between government and people that Madinat az-Zahra (begun by Abd ar-Rahman III in 936) symbolized. Historians also suggest that the great wealth of al-Andalus had made the nation a bit jaded and selfish, that the rich and powerful were scarcely inclined to compromise or sacrifice for the good of the whole.

Whatever the reason, the Caliphate disintegrated with startling suddenness after 1008. Nine Caliphs ruled between that year and 1031, most of them puppets of the Berbers, the **Saqaliba** or other factions. Civil wars and city riots became endemic; Madinat az-Zahra itself was destroyed, and Córdoba sacked, by Berber troops in 1013. By 1031, when the Caliphate was formally abolished, an exhausted al-Andalus had split into some 30 squabbling states.

1031–1492: the Reconquista

The years after 1031 are known as the age of the **taifas**, or 'Party Kings', so-called because most of them owed their position to one of the political factions. Few of these self-made rulers slept easily, in an era of constant intrigues and revolts, shifting alliances and pointless wars. The only relatively strong state was that of Seville, founded by former governor Muhammad ibn-Abbad and continued by his sons, who managed to annex Córdoba and several other towns.

The total inability of these rulers to work together made the 11th century a party for the Christians. Alfonso VI, King of Castile and León, collected tribute from most of the *taifas*, including even Seville. In 1085, with the help of the legendary warrior El Cid, he captured Toledo. The loss of this key fortress-city alarmed the *taifas* enough for them to request assistance from the **Almoravids** of North Africa, fanatical Berbers who had recently established an empire stretching from Morocco to Senegal. The Almoravid leader Yusuf crossed the straits and defeated Alfonso in 1086. Yusuf liked al-Andalus so much he decided to keep it, and by 1110, the Almoravids had gobbled up the last of the surviving *taifas*. Under their rule, al-Andalus became more of a consciously Islamic state than it had ever been before, uncomfortable for the Christian Mozarabs and even for the cultured Arab aristocrats, with their gardens and their poetry.

Popular rebellions put an end to Almoravid rule in 1145, and two years later their power in Africa was defeated and replaced by that of the **Almohads**, a nearly identical military-religious state. By 1172, they had control of most of southern Spain. Somewhat more tolerant and civilized than the Almoravids, the Almohads' rule coincided with a cultural reawakening in al-Andalus, a period that saw the building of La Giralda in Seville. Literature and art flourished, and in Córdoba lived two of the greatest philosophers of the Middle Ages: Ibn Rushd (Averroës) and Moses Maimonides. The Almohads nevertheless shared many of the Almoravids' limitations. Essentially a military state, with no deep support from any part of the population, they could win great victories over the Christians (as at Alarcos, in 1195) but were never able to take advantage of them.

At the same time, the Christian Spaniards were growing stronger and gaining a new sense of unity and national consciousness. The end for the Almohads, and for al-Andalus, came with the **Battle of Navas de Tolosa** in 1212, when an army from all Christian Spain under Alfonso VII destroyed the Almohad power forever. Alfonso's son, **Fernando III**, captured Córdoba (1236) and Sevilla (1248), and was made a saint for his trouble. **Alfonso X** 'the Wise', noted for his poetry and the brilliance of his court, completed the conquest of western Andalucía in the 1270s and 1280s.

In the conquest of Seville, important assistance had been rendered by one of Ferdinand's new vassals, **Muhammad ibn-Yusuf ibn-Nasr**, an Arab adventurer who had conquered Granada in 1235. The **Nasrid Kingdom of Karnattah** (Granada) survived partly from its cooperation with Castile, and partly from its mountainous, easily defensible terrain. For the next 250 years it was the only remaining Muslim territory on the peninsula. As a refuge for Muslims from the rest of Spain, Granada became al-Andalus in miniature, a sophisticated and generally peaceful state, stretching from Gibraltar to Almería. It produced the last brilliant age of Moorish culture in the 14th century, expressed in its poetry and in the art of the Alhambra.

In the rest of Andalucía, the Reconquista meant a profound cultural dislocation, as the majority of the Muslim population chose to flee the rough northerners and their priests. The Muslims who stayed behind (the Mudejars, meaning those 'permitted to remain') did not fare badly at first. Their economy remained intact, and many Spaniards remained fascinated by the extravagant culture they had inherited. In the 1360s, King Pedro of Castile was signing his correspondence 'Pedro ben Xancho' in a flowing Arabic script, and spending most of his time in Seville's Alcazar, built by artists from Granada. Throughout the period, though, this culture and the society that created it were becoming increasingly diluted, as Muslims either left or converted, while the Castilians imported large numbers of Christian settlers from the north. Religious intolerance, fostered by the Church, was a growing problem.

The final disaster, for Andalucía and for Spain, came with the marriage of **King Ferdinand of Aragon** and **Queen Isabella of Castile**, *Los Reyes Católicos*, creating a united Spain. The glory of the occasion has tended to obscure the historical realities. If Ferdinand and Isabella did not invent genocide, they did their hypocritical best to sanctify it, forcing a maximalist solution to a cultural diversity they found intolerable. In 1481, they began the final war with Granada. The capital fell in 1492, the same year Columbus sailed from Andalucía to the New World. Also in that year, Ferdinand and Isabella expelled the Jews from Spain; already, the Inquisition they created was in full swing, terrorizing converted Jews and Muslims and effectively putting an end to all differences of opinion, religious or political.

1492– : Spanish Andalucía

Under the conditions of Granada's surrender in 1492, the Mudejárs were to be allowed to continue their religion and customs unmolested. Under the influence of the Church, however, Spain soon reneged on its promises and attempted forced conversion, a policy cleverly designed to justify itself by causing a revolt. The First Revolt of the Alpujarras (1500), the string of villages near the city in the Sierra Nevada, resulted in the expulsion of all Muslims who failed to convert—the majority of the population had already fled—as well as decrees prohibiting Moorish dress and customs such as public bathhouses.

Beyond that, the Spanish purposely impoverished the Granada territories, ruining their agriculture and bankrupting the important silk industry with confiscatory taxes and a ban on exports. The Inquisition enriched the Church's coffers, attaching the entire property of any converted Muslims who could be found guilty of backsliding in the faith. A second revolt in the Alpujarras occurred in 1568, after which Philip II ordered the prohibition of the Arabic language and the dispersal of the remaining Muslim population throughout the towns and cities of Castile. Intolerance had become the a way of life; in the same year, the Inquisition began incinerating suspected Protestants in Sevilla.

In the 16th century, the new nation's boundless wealth, energy and talent were squandered by two rulers even more vile than *Los Reyes Católicos*. Charles I, a Habsburg who gained the throne by marriage when Ferdinand and Isabella's first two heirs died, emptied the treasury to purchase himself election as Holy Roman Emperor. Outside Spain he is better known as **Charles V** (for the Imperial title), a ghoulish, sanctimonious tyrant who had half of Europe in his pocket and dearly wanted the rest. His megalo-maniac ambitions bled Spain dry, a policy continued by his son **Philip II**, under whom Spain went bankrupt twice.

Throughout the century, Andalucía's ports were the base for the exploration and exploitation of the new world. Trade and settlement were planned from Sevilla, and gold and silver poured into the city each year from the Indies treasure fleet. Of this, what did not immediately go to finance the wars of Charles and Philip was gobbled up by the nobility, the Genoese bankers—or by inflation, the 16th-century 'price revolution' caused by the riches of America. The historical ironies are profound; amidst all this opulence, Andalucía was rapidly declining from one of the richest and most cultured provinces of Europe to one of the poorest and most backward. Ferdinand and Isabella had begun the process, distributing the vast confiscated lands of the Moors to their friends, or to the Church and military orders; from its birth the new Andalucía was a land of huge estates, exploited by absentee landlords and worked by sharecroppers—the remnants of the original population as well as the hopeful colonists from the north, reduced in a generation or two to virtual serfdom.

By the 17th century, the destruction of Andalucía was complete. The Church's terror had done its work, eliminating any possibility of intellectual freedom and reducing the population to the lowest depths of superstition and subservience. Their trade and manufactures ruined, the cities stagnated; agriculture suffered as well, as the complex irrigation systems of the Moors fell into disrepair and were gradually abandoned. The only opportunity for the average man lay with emigration, and Andalucía contributed more than its share to the American colonies. The shipments of American bullion peaked about 1610–20, and after that the decline was precipitous.

For almost the next two centuries, Andalucía has no history at all. The perversions of Spain's rulers had exhausted the nation. Scorned for its backwardness, Spain was no longer even taken seriously as a military power. The War of the Spanish Succession, in which the English seized Gibraltar (1704), replaced the Habsburgs with the **Bourbons**, though their rule brought little improvement. The one bright spot in the century was the reign of **Charles III** (1759–88), a reformer who expelled the Jesuits, attempted to revive trade and resettled the most desolate parts of Andalucía. New towns were founded; the *Nuevos Poblaciones* such as La Carolina and Olavide.

Despite three centuries of decay, Andalucíans responded with surprising energy to the French occupation during the Napoleonic Wars. The French gave them good reason to, stealing as much gold and art as they could carry, and blowing up castles and historical buildings just for sport. As elsewhere in Spain, irregulars and loyal army detachments assisted the British under Wellington. In 1808, a force made up mostly of Andalucians defeated the French at the Battle of Bailen. In 1812, a group of Spanish liberals met in Cádiz to declare a Constitution, and under this the Spanish fitfully conducted what they call their **War of Independence**.

With victory, however, came not reforms and a constitution, but reaction and the return of the Bourbons. The confusing century that followed would see the loss of the American colonies, along with coups, counter-coups, civil wars on behalf of pretenders to the throne (the two Carlist Wars of the 1830s and 70s), a short-lived republic and several *de facto* dictatorships. Andalucía, disappointed and impoverished as ever, contributed many liberal leaders. The desperate peasantry, meanwhile, had become one of the most radicalized rural populations in Europe.

At first, this manifested itself as simple outlawry, especially in the Sierra Morena. In 1870, an Italian agitator and associate of Bakunin named Fanelli brought **Anarchism** to Andalucía. In a land where government had never been anything more than institutionalized oppression, the idea was a hit. Anarchist-inspired guerrilla warfare and terrorism increased steadily, reaching its climax in the years 1882–86, directed by a secret society called the Mano Negra. Violence continued for decades, met by fierce repression by the hated but effective national police, the Guardia Civil.

The coming of the democratic Second Republic in 1931 brought little improvement. Peasant rebellions intensified, especially under the radical right-wing government of 1934–36, when attempted land seizures led to incidents like the massacre at Casas Viejas in 1934. With the army uprising that began the **Civil War** in July 1936, the army succeeded in gaining control of most key cities: as in Sevilla, where a flamboyant officer named Queipo de Llano (later famous as the Nationalists' radio propaganda voice) singlehandedly bluffed and bullied the city into submission, and in arch-reactionary Granada, where the authorities and local fascists massacred thousands of workers and republican loyalists.

Most of the region fell to the Nationalists the following month; thereafter Andalucía saw little fighting, though its people shared fully in Nationalist reprisals and oppression. After the war, in the dark days of the 40s, Andalucía like the rest of Spain knew widespread destitution and, at times, conditions close to famine. Emigration, which had been significant ever since the discovery of America, now became a mass exodus, creating the huge Andalucían colonies in Madrid and Barcelona, and smaller ones in nearly every city of northern Europe.

Economic conditions improved in the 50s, with American loans to help get the economy back on its feet, and the birth of the Costa del Sol, on the empty coast west of Málaga. A third factor, often overlooked, was the quietly brilliant economic planning of Franco's economists, setting the stage for Spain's industrial take-off of the 60s and 70s. In Andalucía, their major contributions were industrial programmes around Sevilla and Cádiz, and a score of dams, providing cheap electricity and ending the endemic, terrible floods.

When King Juan Carlos ushered in the return of democracy, Andalucíans were more than ready. Felipe Gonzalez, the Socialist charmer from Sevilla, has been running Spain since 1982, and other Andalucíans are well represented in every sector of government and society. They took good advantage of the revolutionary regional autonomy laws of the late-70s, building one of the most active regional governments, and giving Andalucía some control over its destiny for the first time since the Reconquista. Five centuries of misery and misrule cannot be redeemed in a day. The average income is less than half of that in Catalunya or the Basque country; the unemployment rate is brutal. None of this will be readily apparent, unless you go through the more dismal suburbs of Sevilla or Málaga, or in the mountain villages of Almería province where the new prosperity is still a rumour. In the flashy, vibrant cities and the tidy whitewashed villages, Andalucíans hold fast to their ebullient, extrovert culture, living as if they were at the top of the world. Things have never been better, and the future looks bright.

Part IV

ANDALUCIA

Sevilla

Qui non ha vista Sevilla, non ha vista marravilla
(Who hasn't seen Sevilla, has seen no wondrous thing)

Hijo de Sevilla, uno bueno por marra villa
(You'll be lucky if you find a good Sevillano)

—Andalucían sayings

Apart from the Alhambra in Granada, the place where the lushness and sensuality of al-Andalus survives best is Andalucía's capital. Sevilla may be Spain's fourth-largest city, but it is a place where you can pick oranges from the trees, and see open countryside from the centre of town. Come in spring if you can, when the gardens are drowned in birdsong and the air becomes intoxicating with the scent of jasmine and a hundred other blooms. If you come in summer, you may melt; the lower valley of the Guadalquivir is one of the hottest places in Europe.

The pageant of Sevilla unfolds in the shadow of **La Giralda**, the Moorish tower that means so much to Sevilla ('the mother of artists, the mould for bullfighters' according to a *Sevillano* poet). It is still the loftiest tower in Spain, and its size and the ostentatious play of its arches and arabesques make it the perfect symbol for this city, full of the romance of the south and the perfume of excess.

At times Sevilla has been a capital, and it remains Spain's eternal city; neither past reverses nor modern industry have been able to shake it from its dreams. That its past glories should return and place it alongside Venice and Florence as one of the jewels in the crown of Europe, a true metropolis with full international recognition and status, is the first dream of every *Sevillano*. They have launched into an extensive programme of building and renovation, manifest in the preparation for the World Fair. The new opera house alone will catapult Sevilla into the cultural limelight, to outdo anything in Madrid or Barcelona. Six new bridges are being built and one of them, nick-named the *Golden Gate*, will soar higher than La Giralda itself, joining the city to the island of Cartuja, focal point of Expo '92.

Most aspects of this city are thriving. The number of licensed businesses rose tenfold between 1984 and 1989, and the number of private cars has increased by over 100,000 in the same period. The tourist trade has risen by 10%, whereas the national figure is a mere 0.3%. Property prices have escalated and rents sky-rocketed, but rising living costs have done little to curb the Sevillanos' zest for life— the bars and restaurants are fuller than ever.

Sevilla is a city very much in love with itself. When a Sevillano sings in the street or in a café, which charmingly enough he often does, the subject of the song is invariably the city itself, and posters advertise concerts with the theme '*Sevilla, porqué te quiero?*' Even the big celebration during Holy Week, although enjoyable to the foreigner (anyone from outside the city), with revelry in every café and on every street corner, is essentially a private one; the Sevillanos celebrate in their own *casetas* with friends, all the time strongly aware that they are being observed by the general public, who can peek but may not enter, at least not without an *enchufe* ('the right connection').

Sevilla is like a beautiful, flirtatious woman; she'll tempt you to her doorstep and allow you a peck on the cheek—whether you get over the threshold depends entirely on your charm.

From Hispalis to Isbiliya to Sevilla

One of Sevilla's distinctions is its long historical continuity. Few cities in Western Europe can claim to have never suffered a dark age, but Sevilla did well after the fall of Rome—and even after the coming of the Castilians. Roman Hispalis was founded on an Iberian settlement, and soon became one of the leading cities of the province of Baetica. So was Italica, the now ruined city just to the northwest; it is difficult to say which was the more important. During the Roman twilight, Sevilla seems to have been a thriving town. Its first famous citizen, St Isidore, is one of the Doctors of the Church and the most learned man of the age, famous for his great *Encyclopedia* and his *Seven Books Against the Pagans*, an attempt to prove that the coming of Christianity was not the cause of Rome's fall. Sevilla was an important town under the Visigoths, and after the Moorish conquest it was second only to Córdoba as a political power and a centre of learning; for a while after the demise of the Western Caliphate, in 1023, it became an independent kingdom, paying tribute to the kings of Castile. Sevilla suffered under the Almoravids after 1091, but enjoyed a revival under their successors the Almohads.

AV. CRUZ ROJA

C. JOSÉ LAGUILLO
C. GONZALO BILBAO
C. JÚPITER
AMADOR DE RÍOS
C. LUIS MONTOTO

MARÍA AUXILIADORA

RONDA DE CAPUCHINOS

C. DEL SOL

C. NAVARROS

SOCORRO

C. SANTIAGO
GARCÍA PÉREZ
S. ESTEBAN
CÉSPEDES
25
Pl. Pilatos

S. JUAN RIBERA
DIEGO DE CÁDIZ
30

Pl. Ponce de Léon

29

Pl. San Leandro
CONDE IBARRA
S. LUIS
24

C. S. LUIS

C. BUSTA TAVERA
C. GERONA
ALHÓNDIGA
CABEZA DEL REY
MÁRMOLES
ABAD

DON FADRIQUE

C. RELATOR

C. JUAN PALMA

Pl. Cristo de Burgos
ARGOTE

C. DE LA FERIA

C. REGINA
Pl. Encarnación
CUESTA ROSARIO
23
22
CONTEROS

C. PERAL

26

Pl. El Salvador
C. COLÓN

CALATRAVA

La Campana
OROPESA
C. SIERPES
TETUÁN
17
AV. DE CONSTI

28

C. JESÚS DEL GRAN PODER
VELÁZQUEZ
C. Nueva
6

27

C. STA CLARA
CARDINALE SPINOLA
Pl. de la Concordia
C. MENDEZ NÚÑEZ

C. LUMBERAS
C. JUAN RABADÁN
C. S. JUAN ÁVILA
ALFONSO XII
S. ELOY
S. ROQUE
CANALEJAS
20
ZARAGOZA
GARCÍA
GARCÍA

C. S. VICENTE
21
CÉSAR
REYES CATÓLICOS

C. TORNEO
C. BAÑOS
BAILEN

MARQUÉS DE PARADAS
C. ARJONA

2
C. LA LEGIÓN

km   0   ½
miles 0   ¼

to Huelva

to Málaga, Córdoba

C. VALPARAÍSO

AV. BORBOLLA

to Cádiz

Pl. de España

ISABELLA CATÓLICA

Parque María Luisa

PASEO DE LAS DELICIAS

AV. CARLOS V

AV. CÁDIZ

C. MENÉNDEZ PELAYO

S. SEBASTIÁN

DEMETRIO DE LOS RÍOS

GAGO

Barrio
Santa
Cruz

Jardines del
Alcázar

University

Alcázar

S. FERNANDO

S. GREGORIO

AV. LA,
RÁBIDA

R. Guadalquivir

C. S. SEBASTIAN

SANTANDER

ALMIRANTE

LOBOS

DOS DE MAYO

TEMPRADO

ARFE

ICIÓN

to Fairgrounds

Pl. de Cuba

C. ASUNCIÓN

C. COLÓN

C. BETIS

C. PAGES DE CORRO

AV. REPÚBLICA

ARGENTINA

N

TRIANA

SEVILLA

Key

1. Tourist Information
2. Estación de Santa Justa, 2 km
3. Estación de Cádiz
4. Main Bus Station
5. Post Office
6. Telephones
7. Airport Bust Stop
8. Torre del Oro
9. Archive of the Indies
10. Museum of Modern Art
11. Casa de Contratación
12. La Giralda
13. Catalina de Ribera
14. Museum of Popular Art
15. Archaeological Museum
16. Guatemala Pavilion
17. Ayuntamiento
18. Hospital de la Caridad
19. La Maestranza Bullring
20. Iglesia La Magdalena
21. Museum of Fine Art
22. Iglesia El Salvador
23. Old University
24. Iglesia San Ildefonso
25. Casa de Pilatos
26. Alameda de Hércules
27. Convent of Sta Clara
28. S. Clemente Monastery
29. La Macarena
30. Walls

The disaster came for Moslem Isbiliya in 1248, 18 years after the union of Castile and León. Ferdinand III's conquest of the city is not a well-documented event, but it seems that more than half the population found exile in Granada or Africa preferable to Castilian rule; their property was divided among settlers from the north. Despite the dislocation, the city survived, and found a new prosperity as Castile's window on the Mediterranean and South Atlantic trade routes (the Río Guadalquivir is navigable as far as Sevilla). Everywhere in the city you will see its emblem, the word *NODO* (knot) with a double knot between the O and D. It recalls the civil wars of the 1270s, when Sevilla was one of the few cities in Spain to remain loyal to Alfonso the Wise. '*No m'a dejado*' ('She has not forsaken me'), Alfonso is recorded as saying; *madeja* is another word for knot, and placed between the syllables NO and DO it makes a clever rebus besides a tribute to Sevilla's loyalty to medieval Castile's greatest king.

From 1503 to 1680, Sevilla enjoyed a legal monopoly of trade with the Americas. The giddy prosperity this brought, in the years when the silver fleet ran full, contributed much to the festive, incautious atmosphere that is often revealed in Sevilla's character. Sevilla never found a way to hold on to much of the American wealth, and what little it managed to grab was soon dissipated in showy excess.

It was in this period, of course, that Sevilla was perfecting its charm. Poets and composers have always favoured it as a setting. Bizet's Carmen rolled her cigars in the Royal Tobacco Factory, and for her male counterpart Sevilla contributed Don Juan Tenorio, who evolved through Spanish theatre in plays by Tirso de Molino and Zorròlla to become Mozart's *Don Giovanni*; the same composer also used the city as a setting for *The Marriage of Figaro*. Modern Sevilla has been loth to leave all this behind, and for the World's Fair in 1992, they hope to show off not only the Sevilla of orange blossoms and guitars, but the Sevilla of the future.

GETTING AROUND   (tel prefix 954)
By air: Sevilla has regular flights from Madrid, Málaga, and Barcelona, less regularly from Lisbon, the Canary Islands and Valencia. The airport is 12 km (7.5 miles) east of the city, and the airport bus leaves from the Bar Iberia on C. Almirante Lobos, near the southern end of Av. de la Constitución (tel 52 59 80).
By train: Currently under construction is the **Estación de Santa Justa**, to the northeast of town on José Laguillo and Avenida Kansas City. Planned to open for 1992, this station will handle all train traffic in and out of the city. In the meantime, all trains arrive and depart from the **Estación de San Bernardo** (also known as **Estación de Cádiz**), tel 441 4360. The central RENFE office is at C. Zaragoza 29, tel 441 4111. There are train connections—to Madrid, a daily *talgo* to Valencia and Barcelona, and to Córdoba, Jerez and Cádiz, among the other frequent regular services to these cities; for trains to Málaga, Ronda and Algeciras, you should watch out for possible train changes at Bobadilla Junction, the black hole of Andalucían railways where all lines cross.
By bus: Almost all lines for Madrid, the Levante, Andalucía and Portugal, leave from the Estación de Autobuses, Prado de San Sebastián. Buses for Jerez and Cádiz run about every 1½ hours, and there are frequent connections to most other points in Andalucía (five daily to Granada, four to Málaga, three to Córdoba and Ubeda, two to the Costa del Sol, Aracena, Almería, La Línea, Tarifa and Algeciras, also three each to Madrid, Valencia and Barcelona. For destinations within the province (eg Carmona, Ecija), buses

depart from outside this station, across the Avenida de Carlos V. Buses for Matalascañas, Huelva, Badajoz and Ayamonte leave from C. Segura 18, while those for Santiponce and the ruins leave from Marqués de Parada every hour or so during the day.

TOURIST INFORMATION
The permanent tourist office is an especially helpful one, at Avenida de la Constitución 21 near the Cathedral (tel 22 14 04). The municipal information centre is near the María Luisa Park next to the American consulate in Avenida María Luisa (tel 23 44 65).

La Giralda
A good place to start your tour of Sevilla is at one of Andalucía's most famous monuments. You can catch the 319 ft tower of **La Giralda** peeking over the rooftops from almost anywhere in Sevilla; it will be your best friend when you get lost in the city's labyrinthine streets. This great minaret, with its *ajimeces* and brickwork arabesques, was also built under the Almohads, just 50 years before the Christian conquest. The surprisingly harmonious spire stuck on top is a Christian addition. Whatever sort of turret originally stood on top was surmounted by four golden balls (or apples, according to one chronicler) stacked up at the very top, designed to catch the sun and be just visible to a traveller one day's ride from the city; all came down in a 13th-century earthquake. On the top of their spire, the Christians added a huge, revolving statue of Faith as a weathervane (many writers have noted the curious fancy of having a supposedly constant Faith turning with the four winds). La Giralda—the weathervane—has given its name to the tower as a whole.

The climb to the top is surprisingly easy; instead of stairs, there are shallow ramps— wide enough for Fernando III to have ridden his horse up for the view after the conquest in 1248 (open daily 10.30–1, 4.30–6.30 summer; 10.30–1, 3.30–5.30 winter).

The Biggest Gothic Building in the Whole World
For a while after the conquest, the Castilians who repopulated Sevilla were content to use the great Almohad mosque, built at the same time as La Giralda. At the turn of the 1400s, in a fit of pious excess, it was decided to build a new Cathedral so grand that 'future ages shall call us mad for attempting it'. If they were mad, at least they were good organizers—they got it up in slightly over a century. The architects are unknown, though there has been speculation that the original master was either French or German.

The exterior, with its great rose window and double buttresses, is as fine as any of the Gothic cathedrals of northern Spain—if we could only see it. Especially on the west front, facing Sevilla's main street, the Avenida de la Constitución, the buildings close in; walking around its vast bulk past the fence of Roman columns joined by thick chains is like passing under a steep and ragged cliff. It's long overdue for a cleaning, and the grime contributes to the effect. Some of the best original sculptural work is on the two portals flanking the main door on the façade: the **Puerta del Bautismo** (left), and the **Puerta del Nacimento** (right).

The groundplan of this monster, roughly 400 by 600 ft, probably covers the same area as did the mosque. On the northern side, the **Patio de los Naranjas** preserves the outline of the mosque courtyard, now planted with orange trees. The Muslim fountain (built around a basin from the previous Visigothic cathedral) survives, along with some of the walls and arches; in the left-hand corner, the Moorish 'Gate of the Lizard' has hanging from it a stuffed crocodile, said to have been a present from an Egyptian emir asking for the hand of a Spanish infanta. Along the eastern wall is the entrance of the **Biblioteca Columbina**, an archive of the explorer's life and correspondence.

The cavernous interior overpowers the faithful with its size more than its grace or beauty. The main altarpiece is the World's Biggest Retablo, almost 120 ft high and entirely covered with carved figures and golden Gothic ornament; it took 82 years to make, and takes about a minute to look at. The cathedral is dark and cold inside, and without the usual nave and transept; its enormous space is ill-defined and disorienting. Just behind the Capilla Mayor and the main altar, the **Capilla Real** contains the tombs of St Ferdinand (Fernando III), conqueror of Sevilla, and of Alfonso the Wise; Pedro the Cruel and his mistress María de Padilla are relegated to the crypt underneath. The art of the various chapels around the cathedral is lost in the gloom, but there are paintings by Murillo in the Capilla de San Antonio (in the north aisle), and an altarpiece by Zurbarán in the Capilla de San Pedro (to the left of the Capilla Real).

In the southern aisle, four stern pall-bearers on a high pedestal support the **Tomb of Christopher Columbus**. They represent the kingdoms of Castile, León, Navarre and Aragón. Columbus has been something of a refugee since his death. In the 16th century his remains were moved for unknown reasons from Valladolid to the island of Santo Domingo, and after Dominican independence from there to the Havana Cathedral. In 1899, after Cuba became independent, he was brought to Sevilla, and this idiosyncratic monument put up to honour him. In the Dominican Republic, they'll tell you Columbus is still buried in Santo Domingo, and of course most Spaniards are convinced Columbus was born in Spain; it is appropriate that the life of this most elusive character should have mysteries at both ends.

THE SACRISTY
Most of the Cathedral's collections are housed in a few chambers near the turn-stiles at the main entrance. In the **Sala Capitular**, Sevilla's bishop can sit on his throne and pontificate under the unusual acoustics of an elliptical Baroque ceiling, with an *Immaculate Conception* by Murillo. The adjacent **Sacristy** contains paintings by Zurbarán, Murillo, Van Dyck and others, most in dire need of restoration. Spare a moment for the reliquaries. Juan de Arfe, maker of the world's biggest silver monstrances, is represented here with one that seems almost a small palace, complete with marble columns. Spain's most famous, and possibly most bizarre reliquary, is the **Alfonsine Tables**, filled with over 200 tiny bits of tooth and bone. They were said to have belonged to Alfonso the Wise and were made to provide extra-powerful juju for him to carry into battle.

The Archive of the Indies
As in most medieval cathedrals, Sevilla's porches, the Patio of the Orange Trees, and often even the naves and chapels were public ground, used to transact all sorts of business. A 16th-century bishop put an end to this practice, but prevailed upon Philip II to construct an exchange, or **Lonja**, for the merchants next to the Cathedral. Philip sent his favourite architect, Juan de Herrera, then still busy with El Escorial, to design it. The severe, elegant façades are typically Herreran, and the stone balls and pyramids on top are practically the architect's signature. By the 1780s, little commerce was still going on

in Sevilla, and what was left of the American trade passed through Cádiz, so Charles III converted the lonely old building to hold the **Archive of the Indies**, the repository of all the reports, maps, drawings and documents the crown collected during the age of exploration. The collection, the richest in the world, has not even yet been entirely sifted through by scholars; but they are always worth a look (open daily except Saturday and Sunday 10–1).

The Alcazar

It's easy to be fooled into thinking this is a Moorish palace; some of its rooms and courtyards seem to come straight from the Alhambra. Most of them, however, were built—by Moorish workmen, to be sure—for King Pedro the Cruel of Castile in the 1360s. The Alcazar and its king represent a fascinating dead-end of Spanish history and culture, the possibility that al-Andalus might have assimilated its conquerors instead of being destroyed by them.

Pedro was an interesting character. In Froissart's *Chronicle*, we have him described as 'full of marveylous opinyons ... rude and rebell agaynst the commandements of holy churche'. Certainly he didn't mind having his Moorish artists, lent by the Kings of Granada, adorn his palace with sayings from the *Koran* in Kufic calligraphy. Pedro preferred Sevilla, still half-Moorish and more than half-decadent, to Old Castile, and he filled his court here with Moorish poets and dancers, and Moorish bodyguards—the only ones he trusted. Unfortunately he was not the man for the job of cultural synthesis. The evidence, in as far as it is reliable, suggests he richly deserved his honorific 'the Cruel'; his brother Don Fadrique is only one of many he is said to have assassinated in this palace. One of Her Majesty's biggest crown jewels was a gift from Pedro to the Black Prince—he murdered an ambassador from Granada to get it off his turban.

Long before Pedro, the Alcazar was the palace of the Moorish governors. Begun under Abd ar-Rahman II in the 840s, it assumed its present form gradually over the next four centuries. Important additions were made under the Almohads; the Alcazar was their capital in al-Andalus. Almost all the decorative work you see now was done under Pedro, some by the Granadans and the rest by Muslim artists from Toledo; altogether it is the outstanding production of Mudejár art in Spain.

The Alcazar is entered through a little gate on the Plaza del Triunfo, on the south side of the Cathedral (open every day 9–12.45, 3–5.30; Saturday and Sunday 9–1.30). The first courtyard, the **Patio de la Monteria**, has beautiful arabesques, with lions amid castles for Castile and León mixed in; this was the public court of the palace, where visitors were received, corresponding to the Mexuar at the Alhambra. At the far end of the Patio is the lovely **façade** of the interior palace, decorated with inscriptions in Gothic and Arabic scripts.

Much of the best Mudejár work can be seen in the adjacent halls and courts; their seemingly haphazard arrangement was in fact a principle of the art, to increase the surprise and delight in passing from one to the next. The **Patio de Yeso** (plaster) is largely a survival of the Almoravid palace of the 1170s, itself built on the site of a Roman *praetorium*. The **Patio de las Doncellas** (entered through the gate of Pedro's façade) is the largest of them, a little more ornate than the rooms of the Alhambra—built at the same time and possibly by some of the same craftsmen. It leads to the **Salon de los Embajadores**, a small, domed chamber that is the finest in the Alcazar despite jarring additions from the time of Charles V. In Moorish times this was the throne room. Another small court, the **Patio de la Muñecas** ('of the dolls') where King Pedro's bodyguards cut down Don Fadrique, takes its name from two tiny faces on medallions at the base of one of the horseshoe arches—a little joke on the part of the Muslim stone-carvers. The columns here come from the ruins of Medinat az-Zahra.

Spanish kings after Pedro couldn't leave the Alcazar alone. Ferdinand and Isabella spoiled a large corner of it for their **Casa de Contratación**, a planning centre for the colonization of the Indies. There's little to see in it: a big conference table, Isabella's bedroom, a model of the *Santa María* in wood and a model of the royal family (Isabella's) in silver. Charles V added a **palace** of his own, as he did in the Alhambra. This one isn't much, either, but it contains a spectacular set of **Flemish tapestries** showing finely detailed scenes of Charles' campaigns in Tunisia.

Within its walls, the Alcazar has extensive and lovely **gardens**, with reflecting pools and palm trees, avenues of clipped hedges, and lemons and oranges everywhere. The park is deceptively large, but you can't get lost unless you find the little **labyrinth** near the pavilion built for Charles V in the lower gardens. Outside the walls, there are more gardens, a formal promenade called the **Plaza Catalina de Ribera**, with two monuments to Columbus, and the **Jardines de Murillo**, small though beautifully landscaped, bordering the northern wall of the Alcazar.

West of the Cathedral

Avenida de la Constitución, passing the façade of the cathedral, is Sevilla's main street. Between it and the Guadalquivir are mostly quiet neighbourhoods, without the distinction of the Barrio Santa Cruz but still with a charm of their own. On Calle Temprado, behind a colourful Baroque façade (1647), is the **Hospital de la Caridad**.

Founded in the 16th century, the Hospital's original benefactor was a certain Miguel de Mañara, a reformed rake who may have been the prototype for Tirso de Molina's Don Juan. Though it still serves its intended purpose as a charity-home for the aged, visitors come to see the art in the hospital chapel. The best is gone, unfortunately—in the lobby they'll show you photographs of the Murillos Napoleon stole. Among what remains are three works of art ghoulish even by Spanish standards. Juan de Valdés Leal (1622–90) was a competent enough painter, but warmed to the task only with such subjects as you see here: a bishop in full regalia decomposing in his coffin, and Death snuffing out your candle while bestriding paintings, church paraphernalia, and books. Even better than these is the anonymous, polychrome bloody Jesus, surrounded by smiling Baroque *putti*, who carry, instead of harps and bouquets, whips and scourges.

On the river is another citadel of Sevillan *duende*, **La Maestranza bullring** (1760). Not as big as Madrid's, it is still a lovely building, and perhaps the most prestigious of all *Plazas de toros*. It also carries the third-busiest schedule, after Madrid and Barcelona, and you may be fortunate enough to see a *corrida* while in town. The bullring's name comes from the big **Maestranza arsenal** across the street.

Continuing north, as you near the San Eloy district, full of raucous bars and hotels, you'll pass the 1704 **La Magdalena**, on Calle San Pablo, with an eccentric Baroque façade decorated with sundials; among the art inside are two paintings of the *life of St Dominic* by Zurbarán, and gilded reliefs by Leonardo de Figueroa.

Museo de Bellas Artes
This excellent collection is housed in the 1612 **Convento de la Merced**, on Calle San Roque (open daily except Monday, 10–2 and 4–7; Saturday and Sunday mornings only). There are some fine medieval works—sweetly naive-looking virgins, and an especially expressive triptych by the 'Master of Burgos' from the 13th century. The Italian sculptor Torregiani (the fellow who broke Michelangelo's nose, and who died in a Sevilla prison) has left an uncanny barbaric wooden **St Jerome**. This saint, Jeronimo in Spanish, is a favourite in Sevilla, always pictured with a rock and a rugged cross instead of his usual lion; as the Doctor of the Church, he helped most to define the concepts of heresy and self-mortification.

The museum has a roomful of Murillos (the painter was Sevillan and is buried in the Barrio Santa Cruz), including an *Immaculate Conception* and many other artful missal-pictures. Much more interesting are the works of Zurbarán, who could express spirituality without the simpering of Murillo or the hysteria of the others. His series of **female saints** is especially good, and the *Miracle of Saint Hugo* is perhaps his most acclaimed work. Occasionally even Zurbarán slips up; you may enjoy the *Eternal Father* with great fat toes and a triangle on his head, a *St Gregory* who looks like the scheming church executive he really was, and the wonderful *Apotheosis of St Thomas Aquinas*, where the great Scholastic philosopher rises to his feet as if to say 'I've got it!'. Don't miss El Greco's portrait of his son Jorge. There are also more Valdés Leal—heads on plates, and such—and works by Jan Brueghel, Ribera, Caravaggio and Mattia Preti.

Calle Sierpes

Sevilla's business and shopping area has been, since Moorish times, the patch of narrow streets north of La Giralda. **Calle Sierpes** ('serpent street') is its heart, a sinuous pedestrian lane lined with every sort of old shop. Just to the north, **El Salvador** is a fine Baroque church by Leonardo de Figueroa, picturesquely mouldering; the base of its tower was the minaret of an important mosque that once stood here; the plaza in front is a popular hangout of Sevilla's youth, as well as their backpacking cousins from northern Europe.

On the **Plaza Nueva**, Sevilla's modern centre, you can see the grimy 1564 **Ayuntamiento**, with a fine, elaborate plateresque façade. From here, Avenida de la Constitución changes its name to Calle Tetuán. Sevilla has found 100 ways to use its *azulejos*, but the best has to be in the **billboard** on this street for 1932 Studebaker cars; so pretty that no one's had the heart to take it down.

Barrio Santa Cruz

If Spain envies Sevilla, Sevilla envies this neighbourhood, a tiny, exceptionally lovely quarter of narrow streets and whitewashed houses. It is the true homeland of everything *Sevillana*, with flower-bedecked patios and iron-bound windows through which the occasional nostalgic young man still gets up the nerve to embarrass his sweetheart with a serenade.

Before 1492, this was the Jewish quarter of Sevilla; today it's the most aristocratic corner of town. In the old days there was a wall around the barrio; today you may enter through the Jardines de Murillo, the Calle Mateos Gago behind the cathedral apse, or from the **Patio de las Banderas**, a pretty Plaza Mayor-style square next to the Alcazar. On the eastern edge of the Barrio, **Santa María la Blanca** (on the street of the same name) was a pre-Reconquista church; some ancient details remain, but the whole was rebuilt in the 1660s, with spectacular rococo ornamentation inside and paintings by Murillo.

The University

Sevilla has a building even larger than its cathedral—twice as large, in fact, and probably better known to the outside world. Since the 1950s it has housed parts of the city's **University** and it does have the presence of a college building, but it began its life in the 1750s as the state Tobacco Factory. In the 19th century, it employed as many as 12,000 women to roll cigars—as historians note, the biggest female urban proletariat in the world. One of its members, of course, was Bizet's Carmen. These sturdy women, with 'carnations in their hair and daggers in their garters', hung their capes on the altars of the factory chapels each morning, rocked their babies in cradles while they rolled cigars, and took no nonsense from anybody.

The Tower of Gold

The Moorish **Torre del Oro** stands on the banks of the Guadalquivir. In the days of the explorers, ships were still small enough to make this the maritime centre of the city; with a little imagination you can picture the scene when the annual silver fleet came in: the great, low-riding galleons tossing ropes to stevedores on the quay, the crowds and scrambling children, the King's officials and their battalions of guards, more than a few Indians, probably, and the agents of the Flemish and Italian bankers in the background, smiling bemusedly while mentally plotting the most expeditious means of finessing the booty out of Spain. For over a century the fleet's arrival was the event of the year, the turning-point of an annual feast-or-famine cycle when all debts would be made good, and long-deferred indulgences could finally be had.

The Torre del Oro, built by the Almohads in 1220, was the southernmost point of the city's fortifications, constructed on a now demolished extension of the walls to guard the river; from it a chain would be stretched across the Guadalquivir in times of trouble. It took its name from the gold and *azulejo* tiles that covered its 12-sided exterior in the days of the Moors. The interior now houses a small **Maritime Museum** (open daily except Monday, 10–2, Sunday till 1). On the Guadalquivir, however, there probably won't be a ship in sight. The water you see, in fact, isn't the Guadalquivir at all; the river has been canalized around the city to the new ports to the south, leaving the old bed a backwater.

María Luisa Park

For all its old-fashioned grace Sevilla has been one of the most forward-looking and progressive cities of Spain in this century. In the 1920s, while they were redirecting the Guadalquivir and building the new port and factories that are the foundation of the city's growth today, the Sevillanos decided to put on an exposition. In a tremendous burst of energy, they turned the entire southern end of the city into an expanse of gardens and grand boulevards. The centre of it is **María Luisa Park**, a paradisical half-mile of palms and orange trees, elms and Mediterranean pines, covered with flower beds and dotted with hidden bowers, ponds and pavilions. Now that the trees and shrubs have reached their maturity, the genius of the landscapers can be appreciated—this is one of the loveliest parks in Europe.

Two of the largest pavilions on the **Plaza de America** have been turned into museums; the **Archaeological Museum** (open daily except Sunday and Monday, 10–2) has one of the best collections of pre-Roman jewellery and icons, reproductions of the fine goldwork of the 'Treasure of Carambelo', and some tantalizing artefacts from mysterious Tartessos. The Romans are represented, as in every other Mediterranean archaeology museum, with copies of Greek sculpture and oversized statues of emperors—also a mosaic of the *Triumph of Bacchus*, another of Hercules, architectural fragments, some fine glass, and finds of all sorts from Italica and other nearby towns.

Across the plaza, the **Museum of Popular Art and Customs** (open daily except Monday, 10–2) is Andalucía's attic, with everything from ploughs and saucepans to *azulejo* tiles, flamenco dresses (polka dots weren't always the style), musical instruments, religious bric-à-brac and exhibits for the city's two famous celebrations, Holy Week and the April Fair.

The Plaza de España

In the 1920s at least, excess was still a way of life in Sevilla, and to call attention to the Exposición Iberoamericana they put up a building even bigger than the Tobacco Factory.

With its grand Baroque towers (stolen gracefully from Santiago de Compostela), fancy bridges, staircases and immense colonnade, it is World's Fair architecture at its grandest and most outrageous. Much of the fanciful neo-Spanish architecture of 1930s Florida and California may well have been inspired by this building. Sevillanos gravitate naturally to it at weekends, to row canoes in the Plaza's canals and nibble curious pastries. One of the things Sevilla is famous for is its painted *azulejo* tiles; they adorn nearly every building in town, but here on the colonnade a few million of them are devoted to maps and historical scenes from every province in Spain.

Casa de Pilatos

On the eastern fringes of the old town, the Barrio de Santa Cruz fades gently into other peaceful pretty areas—less ritzy, though their old streets wear more palaces. One of these, built by the Dukes of Medinaceli (1480–1571) is the **Casa de Pilatos** on Plaza Pilatos. The dukes like to tell people that it is replica of 'Pontius Pilate's house' in Jerusalem (Pilate, without whom Holy Week would not be possible, is a popular figure; there's a common belief that he was a Spaniard). It is a pleasant jumble of Mudéjar and Renaissance work, with a lovely patio and lots of *azulejos* everywhere. The entrance, a mock-Roman triumphal arch done in Carrara marble by sculptors from Genoa, leads through a small court into the **patio principal**, with 13th-century Granadan decoration, beautiful coloured tiles, and rows of Roman statues and portrait busts—an introduction to the dukes' excellent collections of antique sculpture in the surrounding rooms, including a Roman copy of a Greek herm (boundary marker, with the head of the god Hermes), imperial portraits, and a bust of Hadrian's boyfriend, Antinous (open daily 9–6.30; 400 pts).

Behind the Casa de Pilatos, **San Esteban**, rebuilt from a former mosque, has an altarpiece by Zurbarán; around the corner on Calle Montoto are remains of an **Almoravid acqueduct**. **San Ildefonso**, on Calle Aguilas, has a pretty yellow and white 18th-century façade. Another post-1492 palace with Mudejár decoration, several streets north on Calle Busta Tavera, is the huge **Palácio de las Dueñas**.

Macarena and Triana

The north end of Sevilla contains few monuments; most of it is solid, working-class neighbourhoods clustered around Baroque parish churches. The **Alameda de Hércules**, a once fashionable promenade adorned with copies of ancient statues, is in the middle of one of the shabbier parts. **Santa Clara** and **San Clemente** are two interesting monasteries in this area; Santa Clara includes a Gothic tower built by Don Fadrique, Pedro the Cruel's brother; its pretty chapel has one of Sevilla's best *artesonado* ceilings. North of Calle San Luis, a stretch of the city's **Moorish walls** survive, near the **Basilica of La Macarena**, which gives the quarter its name. The Basilica is the home of the best-worshipped of Sevilla's idols, a delicate Virgin with glass tears on her cheeks who always steals the show in the Holy Week parades. Like a film star she makes her admirers gasp and swarm around her, crying 'O la hermosa! O la guapa!' The small adjacent **museum**, is divided between La Macarena's trinkets and costumes of famous bullfighters.

South from here, along Calle San Luis, you'll pass another Baroque extravaganza, Leonardo de Figueroa's **San Luis**, built for the Jesuits (1699–1731), with twisted columns and tons of encrusted ornament. **San Marcos**, down the street, has one of Sevilla's last surviving Mudejár towers.

Across the Guadalquivir from the bullring is the neighbourhood of **Triana**, an ancient suburb that takes its name from the Emperor Trajan. It has a reputation as the 'cradle of flamenco' and its workmen make all Sevilla's *azulejo* tiles. Queipo de Llano's troops wrecked a lot of it at the start of the Civil War, but there are still picturesque, white streets overlooking the Guadalquivir, and quite a few bars and clubs.

Italica

Eight km (5 miles) north of the city, the only significant Roman ruins in Andalucía are at **Italica**, a city founded in the 3rd century BC by Scipio Africanus as a home for his veterans. Italica thrived in the Imperial age. The Guadalquivir had a reputation for constantly changing its course in the old days, and this may explain the presence of two important cities so close together. Three great emperors, Trajan, Hadrian and Theodosius, were born here. The biggest ruins are an **amphitheatre**, with seating for 40,000, some remains of temples, and a street of foundations of villas. Surviving mosaics portray Hercules and Bacchus, a Cretan Labyrinth, and battle of Pygmies and cranes. (Open Tuesday–Saturday 9.30–6.00, Sunday 9.00–3.00.)

The village of Santiponce, near the ruins, has a fine Gothic-Mudejár monastery built for the Cistercians in 1301: **San Isidoro del Campo**, with another gruesome Saint Jerome, carved in the 1600s by Juan Montañes, on the altarpiece.

64

Expo '92

Despite the sour grapes attitude of their fellow Andalucíans that the Sevilla World Fair will not be ready in time, the bulldozers, trucks and cement mixers are going hell for leather at the moment to have Expo '92 fully finished well before the deadline. Over 80 countries will be participating and up to 20 million visitors are expected, nearly half of those from outside Spain. The theme of the Expo organisers' pavilions is 'Route of Discoveries', as 1992 marks the 500th anniversary of the discovery of the New World; the Expo site incorporates Cartuja Island, where Columbus is known to have stayed while he mulled over his ambitions and geographical theories. Apart from the national pavilions, 20 international bodies will present their greatest contributions to human progress, the sciences, technology and art.

The thematic pavilions are: **The 15th-century Pavilion**, the exterior of which represents the roundness of the earth, will explain what the world was like at that time; **The Pavilion of Discovery** houses a set of exhibitions on the great discoveries which have been made from the 16th century on; **The Navigation Pavilion** is devoted to geographical discoveries and scientific expeditions; **The Pavilion of the Present and Future** demonstrates the latest advances in fields as varied as energy, communications, robotics, artificial intelligence, genetic engineering and astronomy.

But the present frantic construction doesn't stop at pavilions. There are landscaped gardens, tree-lined avenues and shady parks on the drawing board, to allow you to escape the fierce summer heat of Sevilla. There will also be a vast programme of music, drama, dance and sport.

Other Diversions

Take a **river cruise** along the Guadalquivir. Two companies do it daily (at 3.45 and 4.30), both from around the Torre del Oro. See a **bullfight** in the famous Maestranza if you can (but don't just turn up! Get tickets as far ahead as you can; prices at the ring office will be cheaper than at the little stands on C. Sierpes). If you've been longing to experience **flamenco**, Sevilla is probably the place to do it. The touristy flamenco factories will hit you for 1000 pts and up per drink. Bars in Triana and other areas do it better for less, but try to find an enthusiast (it shouldn't be hard) to steer you straight. They do play other kinds of music in Sevilla, and a little publication called *El Giraldillo*, available around town, has listings.

WHERE TO STAY   (tel prefix 954)
Not many of Sevilla's hotels are distinctive in any way, but there are plenty of rooms all over the centre (during Holy Week and the April Fair you should book even for inexpensive *hostales*, preferably a year ahead).

Alfonso XIII***** (C. San Fernando 2, tel 422 28 50); built for the Exposición Iberoamericana in 1929, this luxury hotel is named after the unfortunate monarch then reigning. Probably *the* prestige hotel of southern Spain, in a huge building in landscaped grounds next to the University. It's been recently remodelled, and all the brass is polished up nicely; Sevilla society still meets around its lobby fountain and bars (17,000–30,000 pts for a palatial double). **Hotel Colón******* (C. Canalejas 1, tel 422 29 00); this has recently been totally refurbished for the 1992 Expo and in former times was a haunt of bullfighters and their hangers on. It is a grand and extremely comfortable place to stay (17,000–28,500 pts for a double). **Hotel Simon*** (Garcia de Vinuesa 14, tel 422 66 60); just off the Av. de la Constitución by the Cathedral, is in a restored 18th-century mansion, and is also quite popular (4,000–6,500 pts for a double; high season is March and April). **Hostal Atenas**** (C. Caballerizas 1, tel 421 80 47); quiet and very nice, in a good location between the Pl. Pilatos and Cathedral. Take a cab, it's hard to find. Doubles 3500–5500 pts with bath. By the Macarena walls, the **Macarena Sol****** is another classy establishment; the lobby has a beautiful *azulejo* tiled fountain, service is excellent and while not exactly central, it's well placed for the Expo. The roof-top terrace has views over the city, and a swimming pool. Rates are very reasonable for this category: 16,000 pts (San Juan de Rivera 2, tel 437 57 00). Near the Prado de San Sebastián, the **Meliá Sevilla****** is a very pleasant modern hotel within easy walking distance of the city centre, and has some lovely suites (23,000 pts; 15,500 pts for double rooms; Doctor Pedro Castro 1, tel 442 26 11).

For inexpensive *hostales*, the Barrio Santa Cruz is surprisingly the best place to look. Even in July and August, you'll be able to find a place on the quiet side-streets off Mateos Gago. The **Monreal*** is closest to the Cathedral, a lively place with almost too much character and a good cheap restaurant when they feel like opening it (C. Rodrigo Caro 8, tel 421 41 66; doubles 5500–9000 pts). **Pensión Toledo***, Santa Teresa 15, tel 421 53 35, is respectable and good value (doubles 3500 pts).

The biggest selection of all, however, is along **C. San Eloy** just east of the now defunct Córdoba station; it's theatrically urban any hour of the day.

EATING OUT (tel prefix 954)
Restaurants here are a little more expensive than in most of Spain, but even around the Cathedral and the Barrio Santa Cruz, there are few places that can simply be dismissed as tourist traps. Remember that in the evening the Sevillanos, even more than most Andalucíans, enjoy bar-hopping for *tapas*, rather than sitting down to one meal; two Sevillanos in a bar is a party, three is a fiesta.

A few places have attractions beyond the cuisine: **La Albahaca** in Plaza Santa Cruz has tables outside and three dining rooms creating a romantic and relaxing atmosphere. Specialities include scorpion fish with fennel and peanuts; mushrooms with green asparagus; partridge with endives. Prices start at around 4000 pts per head (tel 422 07 14). Splendidly situated on the corner of the Jardines Alcazar, opposite the university, is one of Sevilla's best-loved restaurants, the **Egaña–Oriza**. It serves the best of Andaluz and Basque cuisine. Among its tempting delights are: spider crab mousse, and escalope of goose in pear sauce (4500 pts minimum with wine; San Fernando 41, tel 422 72 11; closed Sun and August). North of La Giralda, you can dine well on French and Italian specialities at **San Marco** (Cuna 6, tel 421 24 40), in a large, old, elegantly decorated Sevilliana house: try the ravioli stuffed with sea bass, crayfish salad in *Marie-Rose* sauce, tournedos of duck foie gras; 4000–5000 pts. By the cathedral, in the narrow Argote de Molino (at no. 26) is **Mesón Don Raimundo**, a restaurant in what was once a convent. No enforced abstinence here, though. You can pig out on the large selection of fish, shellfish, and game dishes (3000–4000 pts; tel 422 33 55; closed Sun evening). On the same street is the lively *tapas* bar **Bodega La Andana**, where hordes of Sevilla's *caballeros* and *señoritas* spill out onto the pavement, particularly at weekends, to mis-spend their youth. Around the corner you can eat decently at the bar-restaurant **Gonzalo**, with the Giralda looming overhead. There's a reasonably priced and varied-menu, but the walls could do with a lick of paint (corner of Alemanes and Argote de Molina; around 1200 pts). In the same vicinity, **Los Duendes** (Conteros 45, tel 422 35 95) has a *menú del día* for 750 pts.

Along the Triana side of the Guadalquivir, you can dine with a view of the Torre del Oro and La Giralda at the restaurant **Río Grande** (C. Betis s/n, tel 427 39 56). The kitchen here specializes in regional cuisine (3500 pts), and on a Sunday afternoon if there's a good *corrida*, you can join in the roars of *olé* that erupt from the bullring on the opposite bank. Along from here is **Ox's**, with Basque novelties—cod-stuffed peppers, fish and steaks (at least 3000 pts; C. Betis 61, tel 427 9585; closed Sun and August). **Kiosko de las Flores** serves light fish-lunches of *boquerones*, among other things. The place is an informal café-bar, right by the Puente de Isabel II, and part of it looks over the water. Prices are a little high—a glorified fishy snack with a drink costs 1300 pts. Americans love **El Mesón** at C. Dos de Mayo 26, tel 421 30 75, full of nostalgic photographs of bullfighters partying with visiting US journalists and writers (1800–2500 pts).

A little difficult to find, but well worth the search, is the best *tapas* bar in Sevilla, and the most charming in all of Andalucía. North of the cathedral, between the church of San Pedro and the convent Espíritu Santu, at Gerona 42 is **El Rinconillo**; the place dates back to 1670 and is decorated in moody brown *azulejo*; here lively Sevilliana *cognoscenti* gather to dabble at the tasty nibbles, but their real purpose is to model their designer clothes and spend the evening in loud animated high-brow chatter.

Sevilla's cheapest restaurants lurk around C. San Eloy. Some almost give meals away, and they're worth the price. It's better to stick with the *tapas* and *mariscos* bars here and in the little streets of C. Tetuan and C. Sierpes.

SHOPPING
All the paraphernalia associated with Spanish fantasy, like *mantillas*, *castanets*, wrought iron, gypsy dresses and Andalucían dandy suites, *azulejo* tiles and embroidery, is available here. Most of it's made here, and if you're interested in tours or just shopping, ask the Tourist Information office what's currently available. There are two branches of *El Corte Inglés*, where the well-heeled Sevillanos shop, and even a branch of *C&A* on C. Sierpes. *Vertice* is a bookshop with a small selection of English-language literature and local guide-books and history books, on M. Gago near the cathedral.

Travelling from Sevilla

GETTING AROUND
There is no train service for the towns around Sevilla, but plenty of buses—especially for Carmona and Ecija, from where you can easily find a connecting bus for Córdoba.

South from Sevilla

If you're on your way to Jerez or Cádiz, stops at a few towns on the way will make an interesting alternative to the big four-lane highway. **Alcalá de Guadaira** is jocularly known in Sevilla as Alcalá de los Panadores ('of the bakers'), as it used to supply the city with its daily bread. Its **castle** is the best-preserved Almohad fortress in Andalucía. Just outside Utrera, the tiny village of **Palmar de Troya** received a visit in 1968 from the Virgin Mary (to little girls, as usual) that has led to the founding of a new church, the 'Orden de la Santa Faz'. They have their own Pope in Palmar and include among their saints Franco, José Antonio and Ramon Llull. In **Lebrija**, the church of **Santa María de la Oliva** is really a 12th-century Almohad mosque, with a typical Middle Eastern roof of small domes and a tower that is a miniature version of La Giralda, built by a Basque architect in the 19th century.

Take care before you start any rambles in the countryside; this area south of Sevilla contains some of the best-known ranches where fighting bulls are bred, and the bulls are always allowed to run free.

From Sevilla to Córdoba

There are two ways to go, both of approximately equal length. The train, and most of the buses, unfortunately take the duller route through the flat lands along the Guadalquivir. The only landmark here is the Spanish–Moorish **castle of Almodovar del Río** , perched romantically on a height planted with olive trees, overlooking the river. The southern route (the NIV) also follows the Guadalquivir valley, though the scenery is a little more varied, and the road passes through two fine towns: Carmona and Ecija.

TOURIST INFORMATION
Carmona: Plaza de las Descalzas (tel 954 14 22 00) near the church of Santa María.
Ecija: in the *Ayuntamiento*, Plaza de España (tel 954 833062).

Carmona
The first town along the NIV, Carmona, seems a miniature Sevilla. It is probably much older. Remains of a Neolithic settlement have been found around town; the Phoenician colony that replaced it grew into a city and prospered throughout Roman and Moorish times. Pedro the Cruel favoured it and rebuilt most of its extensive **Alcazar**. Sitting proudly on top of the town, with views over the valley, this fortress is now a national *parador*.

Carmona is well worth a day's exploration. Its walls, mostly Moorish fortifications built over Roman foundations, are still standing, including a grand gateway on the road from Sevilla, the **Alcazar de la Puerta de Sevilla** (open to the public Fri and Sat 11–1, Sun 11–2). Continue through the arch and up to the palm-decked Plaza de San Fernando, where the under-16s and over-60s gather; the Ayuntamiento here has a Roman mosaic of Medusa in its courtyard. Next, take Calle Martín Lopez up to the lofty 15th-century church of **Santa María**, built on the site of an old mosque. The old quarters of town have an ensemble of fine palaces and Mudejár and Renaissance churches. On one of these, **San Pedro** (1466), you'll see another imitation of La Giralda, *La Giraldilla*—though not as fussily ornate as her big sister, she has a cleaner exterior. Carmona's prime attraction is just west of the town, as you enter from Sevilla: the **Roman necropolis**, a series of rock-cut tombs. Some, like the 'Tomb of Servilia', are elaborate creations with subterranean chambers and vestibules, pillars, domed ceilings and carved reliefs (open daily except Monday, 10–2 and 4–6, Sun 10–2). Near the entrance to the site are remains of the Roman amphitheatre, forlorn and unexcavated.

Twenty eight km south of Carmona on the C339, **Marchena** still retains many of its wall defences, dating from Roman times with later Moorish and Christian additions. Of its gates, the arch of **La Rosa** is best, and in the **Torre de Oro** there is a new archeological museum. The Gothic church of **San Juan Bautista** has an altar retablo by Alejo Fernández and a sculpture by Pedro Roldán. There's also a small museum with a collection of paintings by Zurbarán. Nearby **El Arahal** is a bleached white town worth visiting for its Baroque monuments, notably the church of **La Victoria** of Mudéjar origin.

Ecija

Ecija makes much of one of its nicknames, the 'city of towers' and tries to play down the other—the 'frying-pan of Andalucía', which isn't exactly fair. Any Andalucían town can overheat you thoroughly on a typical summer's day, and if Ecija is a degree hotter and a little less breezier than most, only a born Andaluz could tell the difference. Ask one, and you'll soon learn that the Andaluces are the only people yet discovered who talk about the weather more than the English.

Don't be put off by the clinical outskirts of the town, nor by the ill-concealed gasometers; all is forgiven when you reach the **Plaza de España**, one of the loveliest in Andalucía, charmingly framed by tall palms and centred on an exquisite fountain. There's a church façade on the 18th-century **Santa María** that wouldn't look out of place in a Sergio Leone movie. The atmosphere here is laid-back, and once you've finished rubber-necking the steeples, choose your favourite corner of the plaza and do what the locals do—sit and watch. Most of the **towers** are sumptuously ornate late-Baroque, rebuilt after the great earthquake of 1755, the one that flattened Lisbon. Santa María has one, along with **San Juan Bautista**, gaily decorated in coloured tiles, and **San Gil**. This last is the highest of the towers, and within are paintings by Alejo Fernández and Villegas Marmolejo.

Ecija also has a set of Renaissance and Baroque palaces second only to Ubeda's in Andalucía; most of these showy façades can be seen on or near the **Calle de los Caballeros**. Worth visiting is the **Mudejár Palace**, dating from the 14th century, where you can find some interesting archeological remains, part Mudéjar, part Baroque, some Roman mosaics, reliefs, coins and glass. Two small museums are to open in 1991—one in the **Peñaflor Palace** on Calle de Castellar, with exhibits of 18th-century art and sculpture, contemporary art and local traditional costumes; the palace itself (1728), with its grandiose façade and lovely patio, is one of the outstanding works of Andalucían Baroque. The other museum, the **Santa Barbara Museum of Sacred Art** will have a more religious theme, and will also include furniture, silverware and handicrafts from the 16th to 19th centuries.

In the evening the town buzzes; after the big city crush of Sevilla, you might find that this is the perfect place to spend a couple of days—busy enough to be interesting, but not too frantic.

WHERE TO STAY   (tel prefix 954)

In Carmona, the **Parador Nacional Alcazar del Rey Don Pedro****, tel 414 10 10, occupying a section of Cruel Pete's castle, has commanding views, a garden, pool and luxurious furnishings for 9500–11,500 pts for a double. Or sleep just as well at any of the town's attractive little pensions and *hostales*. Two good ones are: **Casa Carmelo*** (C. San Pedro 15, tel 414 05 72) and the **Pensión Comercio*** (C. Torre del Oro, tel 414 00 18), both for around 3000 pts.

Marchena has two *hostales*, the **Ponce*** (Plaza de Alvarado 2, tel 84 31 80) and **La Rubia*** (C. San Sebastian s/n), both with rooms for 2500–3500 pts.

Ecija's hotels are mostly motels on the outskirts, serving traffic on the Madrid–Cádiz highway. **Ciudad del Sol**** is the best in town, with friendly service and air-conditioned rooms (C. Cervantes 42, tel 83 03 00; 5000 pts for a double). If that's full try the **Astigi**** on the same road (tel 83 01 62; 5500 pts). A minute's walk from the main plaza, in a little back street behind the fabulously named Gasolina Bar, will take you to the delightful little **Fonda Santa Cruz**. The simple rooms open out to the tiled courtyard, and were probably stables once (no phone, 2500 pts).

EATING OUT

In Carmona, the restaurant **San Fernando** in Plaza San Fernando has the best reputation in town and the highest prices (4000 pts); you'll find all the local dishes here. Fish features largely on the menu at the **Parador**, but prices are more reasonable, and at **El Ancla** (Bonifacio 4, tel 414 15 18), where a full fish meal with wine will set you back a moderate 2500 pts. **Mesón de la Reja** is on the main street as you enter from Sevilla. With cool *azulejo* interior, it's a good place to try *cola de toro* and down a beer, while keeping an eye on the bus departures opposite (about 800 pts). (Incidentally, if you need bus information, don't ask the drivers— the only person who knows for sure is the man behind the bar at the bus stop.)

In Marchena you can find the local specialities in the two restaurants on Travesia de San Ignacio: **Los Muleros**, tel 84 31 99 and **El Fogón**, both for around 1500 pts.

In Ecija the best place in town is the **Bodegón del Gallego** (Calle A. Aparicío 3, tel 83 00 08), which concentrates on Andaluz dishes (2500 pts). Also in the heart of town, the **Pasareli** looks like any modern cafeteria, but there's a surprisingly efficient little restaurant tucked away in the corner, where you can eat well from a large selection of meat and fish for under 2000 pts (Pasaje Virgen del Rocío, tel 83 20 24).

CÓRDOBA

There are a few spots around the Mediterranean where the presence of past glories becomes almost tangible, a mixture of mythic antiquity, lost power and dissipated energy that broods over a place like a ghost. In Istanbul you can find it, in Rome, or among the monuments of Egypt, and also here on the banks of the Guadalquivir at Córdoba's southern gate. Looking around, you can see reminders of three defunct empires: a Roman bridge, a triumphal arch built for Philip II and Córdoba's great Mosque, over 1000 years old. The first reminds us of the city's beginnings, the second of its decline; the last one scarcely seems credible, as it speaks of an age when Córdoba was the brilliant metropolis of all Europe, city of half a million souls, a place faraway story-tellers would use to enthral audiences in the rude halls of the Saxons and Franks.

Detail of a window in the Great Mosque at Córdoba

The little plaza by the bridge concentrates melancholy like a magnet; there isn't much left for the rest of the town. Unlike Rome or Istanbul, Córdoba seems largely free of the burden of the past. Its recent growth has allowed it a chance to renovate its sparkling old quarters and monuments. With the new prosperity has come a contentment the city probably hasn't known since the Reconquista.

Everyone who visits Andalucía comes for the Great Mosque, but you should spare some time to explore the city itself. Old Córdoba is one of the largest medieval quarters of any European city, and certainly the biggest in Spain. More than Sevilla, it retains its Moorish character, in a maze of whitewashed alleys opening into the loveliest patios in all Andalucía.

History

Roman *Corduba*, built on the site of an Iberian town, was almost from the start the leading city of interior Spain, capital of the province of Hispania Ulterior, and later of the reorganized province of Baetica. Córdoba had a reputation as the garden spot of Hispania; it gave Roman letters Lucan and both Senecas among others, testimony to its prominence as a city of learning.

Córdoba became Christianized at an early date. Ironically, the True Faith got its come-uppance here in 572, when the Arian Visigoths under Leovigild captured the city from Byzantine rule. When the Arabs arrived, they found it an important town still, and it became the capital of al-Andalus when Abd ar-Rahman established the Ummayad Emirate in 756. For 300 years, Córdoba enjoyed the position of unqualified leader of al-Andalus. It is hard to take the chroniclers at face value—3000 mosques and 80,000 shops, a library of 400,000 volumes, in a city stretching for 16 km (10 miles) along the banks of the Guadalquivir. We can settle for half that, for accuracy's sake, and still be

to Medinat az-Zahra

Pl. de Toros

AV. DE A

AV. DE CÁDIZ

to Seville

AV. MEDINA AZAHARA

HERNAN RUIZ

AV. CERVANTES

CAPITÁN

DE TEJ

ARFE

RONDA

AV. DE GRAN

CONCEPCIÓN

GONDOMAR

J. M. HERRERO

ALBÉNIZ

AV. ANTONIO
MAURA

GRAN VÍA DEL PARQUE

DÁMASO

CORTÉS

AV. REPÚBLICA ARGENTINA

Jardines de la Victoria

PASEO DE LA VICTORIA

FERNÁN NÚÑEZ

S. FELIPE

Pl. de las
Tendillas

AL

CL.
MA

AV. GRAL BORROSO

ALMANZOR

PASTOR

BUEN

DEA NES

BARROSO

JESÚS Y MARÍA

C. REY HEREDIA

S. VITOR

VILLAR

C. S. FERN

Pl. Campo
Santo

La Mezquita

C. GONZALEZ

LUCA

Arab Walls

Alcazar

RONDA ISASA

R. Guadalquivir

Roman Bridge

N

[3]
[6]
[4]
[18]
[5]
[14]
[13]
[12]
[15]
[2]
[1]
[16]
[7]
[17]
[8]
[10]
[11]
[9]

0   km   ½
0   miles   ½

MÉRICA

12 DE OCTUBRE

ARES

19

Pl. de Colón

20

AV. OBISPO PÉREZ MUÑOZ

to Linares

1

MARROQUÍES

MISERICORDIA

C. LARA

RONDA DEL MARRUBIAL

Arab Walls

21

CONDE DE PRIEGO

22

LÓPEZ CRIADO

C. ZARCO

23

Pl. S. Agustín

C. MONTERO

C. FRAILES

FONSO XIII

UDIO CELO

C. ALFAROS

S. PABLO

C. PARRAS

26

C. MARÍA AUXILIADORA

27

STA MARÍA DE GRACIA

C. ESCAÑUELA

Pl. de la Corredora

C. GUTIÉRREZ DE RÍOS

MUNICES

C. ARMAS

25

Pl. S. Pedro

ALFONSO XII

CAMPO MADRE DE DIOS

24

NO

C. LINEROS

C. AGUSTÍN MORENO

RONDA DE LOS MÁRTIRES

CÓRDOBA

Key
1. Tourist Office
2. Municipal Tourist Office
3. Train Station
4. Post Office
5. Telephones
6. Main Bus Station
7. Puerta del Puente
8. Torre La Calahorra
9. C. de las Flores
10. Sta Victoria
11. Archaeological Museum
12. Casa del Indiano
13. Municipal Museum
14. Almodovar Gate
15. Synagogue
16. Archbishop's Palace
17. Mills
18. S. Nicolás
19. Convento de La Merced
20. Malmuerta Tower
21. Cristo de los Faroles
22. Sta Marina
23. Marqués de Viana Palace
24. Museum of Fine Arts
25. S. Pedro
26. S. Lorenzo
27. S. Andrés

impressed. Beyond doubt, Córdoba was a city without equal in the West as a centre of learning; it would be enough to mention two 12th-century contemporaries, Averroës, the Muslim scientist and Aristotelian philosopher who contributed so much to the rebirth of classical learning in Europe, and Moses Maimonides, the Jewish philosopher (and later personal physician to Saladin in Palestine) whose reconciliation of faith and reason were assumed into Christianity by Thomas Aquinas.

Medieval Córdoba was a great trading centre, and its luxury goods were coveted throughout Western Europe; the old word *cordwainer* is a memory of Córdoba's skill in leather goods. At its height, picture Córdoba as a city of bustling international markets, great palaces, schools, baths and mosques, with 28 suburbs and the first street lighting in Europe. Its population, largely Spanish, Moorish and Arab, included students and merchants from all over Europe, Africa and Asia, and an army and palace secretariat made up largely of Slavs and Blacks. In it Muslims, Christians, and Jews lived in harmony, at least until the coming of the fanatical Almoravids and Almohades. We can sense a certain amount of decadence; street riots in Córdoba were an immediate cause of the breaking-up of the Caliphate in 1031, but here, as in Sevilla, the coming of the Reconquista was an unparalleled catastrophe. When Ferdinand III captured the city in 1236, much of the population chose flight over putting themselves at the mercy of the priests. Three centuries of Castilian rule sufficed to rob Córdoba of all its glories and turn it into a shrunken and depressed backwater. Only in the last 100 years has it begun to recover; today Córdoba is an industrial city, though you wouldn't guess it from its immaculately restored centre. It is the third city of Andalucía, and the first and only big town since Franco's death to have elected a communist mayor and council.

GETTING AROUND

By train: Córdoba is on the major Madrid–Sevilla rail line, so there are always plenty of trains in both directions, besides two daily *talgos* to Madrid, and Málaga, one *talgo* daily to Cádiz, Valencia and Barcelona, and regular trains to Huelva, Algeciras and Alicante. Trains for Granada, Málaga and Algeciras pass through Bobadilla Junction, and may require a change. Córdoba's station is on the Avenida de America, 1.6 km (1 mile) north of the Mezquita (tel (957) 47 93 02).

By bus: Buses for Granada, Cádiz and Málaga and most nearby towns leave from the Alsina Graells terminal on Avenida Medina Azahara 29 (tel (957) 23 64 74); for Madrid (three daily), Sevilla (three daily), Valencia (three daily) and Barcelona (one a day), the Ureña firm has its office at Avenida de Cervantes 22 (tel (957) 47 23 52). Other firms do go to Sevilla—but the train's a better bet for that city and for Málaga. The Córdoba bus network is complicated and it's always best to check with tourist information as to times and departure points. Any bus for Lora del Rio or Palma del Rio (Alsina Graells) will drop you off at Medinat Az-Zahra, but you'll have to walk about 2 km (1.3 miles) to the site.

TOURIST INFORMATION   (tel prefix 957)

The Provincial Office is on C. Torrijos 10 (tel 47 12 35). The Municipal office is in the Juderia on Pl. Judah Levi (tel 47 20 00). It's definitely worth a stop at either to get a detailed map, for Córdoba has the biggest and most labyrinthine old quarter in Spain. To arrange personal guides to the mosque and other sights, telephone 48 69 97 or 41 06 29.

La Mezquita

This is the local name for Abd ar-Rahman's Great Mosque. **Mezquita** means 'mosque' and even though the building has officially been a cathedral for 750 years, no one could ever mistake its origins. Abd ar-Rahman, founder of a new state, felt it necessary to construct a great religious monument for his capital. As part of his plan, he also wished to make it a centre of pilgrimage to increase the sense of divorce from eastern Islam; Mecca was at the time held by his Abbasid enemies. Islam was never entirely immune to the exaltation of holy relics, and there is a story that Abd ar-Rahman had an arm of Mohammed to legitimize his mosque as a pilgrimage site. The site, at the centre of the city, had originally held a Roman temple of Janus, and later a Visigothic church.

Only about one-third of the mosque belongs to the original. Successive enlargements were made by Abd ar-Rahman II, Al-Hakam, and Al-Mansur. Expansion was easy; the plan of the mosque is a simple rectangle divided into aisles by rows of columns, and its size was increased to serve a growing population simply by adding more aisles. The result was the second-largest of all mosques, exceeded only by the one in Mecca. After 1236, it was converted to use as a cathedral without any major changes. In the 1520s, however, the city's clerics succeeded in convincing the Royal Council, over the opposition of the Córdoba city government, to allow the construction of a choir and high altar, enclosed structures as is typical in Spanish cathedrals. Charles V, who had also opposed the project, strongly reproached them for the desecration when he saw the finished work—though he himself had done even worse to the Alhambra and Sevilla's Alcazar.

Most people come away from a visit to the Mezquita somewhat confused. The endless rows of columns and red-and-white striped arches make a picture familiar to most of us, but actually to see them in this gloomy old hall may not increase one's understanding of the work. They make a pretty pattern, but what does it mean? It's worth going into some detail, for learning to see the Mezquita the way its builders did is the best key we have to understanding the refined world of al-Andalus.

Before entering, take a few minutes to circumnavigate this massive and somewhat forbidding pile of bricks. Spaced around its 2,250 feet of wall are the original entrances and windows, excellent examples of Moorish art. Those on the western side are the best, from the time of al-Mansur: interlaced Visigothic horseshoe arches, floral decorations in the Roman tradition, and Islamic calligraphy and patterns, a lesson in the varied sources of this art.

The only entrance to the mosque today is the **Puerta del Perdón**, a fine Mudejár gateway added in 1377, opening to the **Patio de los Naranjos**, the original mosque courtyard, planted with orange trees, where the old Moorish fountain can still be seen. Built into the wall of the courtyard, over the gate, the original minaret—a legendary tower said to be the model for all the others in al-Andalus—has been replaced by an ill-proportioned 16th-century bell tower. From the courtyard, the mosque is entered through a little door, the **Puerta de las Palmas**, where they'll sell you a ticket and tell you to take off your hat. Inside, it's as chill and old as Sevilla Cathedral.

Now here is the first surprise. The building is gloomy only because the Spanish clerics wanted it that way. Originally there was no wall separating the mosque from the courtyard, and that side of the mosque was entirely open. In the courtyard, trees were planted to continue the rows of columns, translating inside to outside in a remarkable tour-de-force that has never been equalled in architecture. To add to the effect, the entrances along the other three walls would have been open to the surrounding busy markets and streets. It isn't just a trick of architecture, but a way of relating a holy building to the life of the city around it. In the Middle East, there are many medieval mosques built on the same plan as this one; the pattern originated with the first Arabian mosques, and later in the Ummayyad Mosque of Damascus, one of the first great shrines of Islam. In Turkey they call them 'forest' mosques, and the townspeople use them like indoor parks, places to sit and reflect or talk over everyday affairs. In medieval Christian cathedrals, whose doors were always open, it was much the same. The sacred and the secular become blurred, or rather the latter is elevated to a higher plane. In Córdoba, this principle is perfected.

In the aesthetics of this mosque, too, there is more than meets the eye. Many European writers have seen it as devoid of spirituality, a plain prayer-hall with pretty arches. To the Christian mind it is difficult to comprehend. Christian churches are modelled after the Roman basilica, a government hall, a seat of authority with a long central aisle designed to humble the suppliant as he approaches the Praetor's throne—or altar. Mosques are designed with great care to free the mind from such behaviour patterns. In this one, the guiding principle is a rarefied abstraction—the same kind of abstraction that governs Islamic geometric decoration. The repetition of columns is like a meditation in stone, a mirror of Creation where unity and harmony radiate from innumerable centres.

Another contrast with Christian churches can be found in an obscure matter—the distribution of weight. The Gothic masters of the Middle Ages learned to pile stone upwards from great piers and buttresses to amazing heights, to build an edifice that seems to aspire upwards to heaven. Córdoba's architects amplified the height of their mosque only modestly by a daring invention—adding a second tier of arches on top of the first. They had to, constrained as they were by the short columns they were recycling from Roman buildings, but the result was to make an 'upside-down' building, where weight increases the higher it goes, a play of balance and equilibrium that adds much to the mosque's effect.

There are about 580 of these columns, mostly from Roman ruins and Visigothic churches the Muslims pulled down; originally, legend credits there being an even thousand. Some came from as far as Constantinople, a present from the emperors. The same variety can be seen in the capitals—Roman, Visigothic, Moorish and a few mysteries. The surviving jewel of the mosque is its **mihrab**, added in the 10th century under al-Hakam II, an octagonal chamber set into the wall and covered by a beautiful dome of interlocking arches. A Byzantine emperor, Nicephoras Phocas, sent artists to help with its mosaic decoration, and a few tons of enamel chips and coloured glass cubes for them to work with. That these two states should have had such warm relations isn't that surprising; any enemy of the Pope and the Western Christian states in those days was a friend of Constantinople. Though the mihrab is no longer at the centre of the Mezquita, it was at the time of al-Hakam II ar-Rahman; the aisle extending from it was the axis of the original mosque.

Looking back from the mihrab, you will see what once was the exterior wall, built in Abd ar-Rahman II's extension, from the year 848. Its gates, protected indoors, are as good as those on the west façade, and better preserved. Near the mihrab is the **Capilla**

de Villaviciosa, a Christian addition of 1377 with fancy convoluted Mudejár arches that almost succeed in upstaging the Moorish work. Behind it is a small chapel usually closed off. Fortunately, you can see most of the **Capilla Real** above the barriers; its exuberant stucco and *azulejo* decoration are among the greatest works of Mudejár art. Built in the 14th century as a funeral chapel for Ferdinand IV and Alfonso XI of Castile, it is contemporary with the Alhambra and shows some influence from the styles developing in Granada.

Far more serious intrusions are the 16th-century **Coro** and **Capilla Mayor** (high altar). Not unlovely in themselves, they would not offend anywhere else but here. Fortunately the Mezquita is so large that from many parts of it you won't even notice them. Begun in 1523, the plateresque Coro (choir) was substantially altered in the 18th century, with additional stucco decoration, as well as a set of Baroque choir stalls by Pedro Duque Cornejo. Between the Choir and Capilla mayor is the tomb of Leopold of Austria, Bishop of Córdoba at the time the works were completed (and interestingly, Charles V's uncle). For the rest of the Christian contribution, dozens of locked, mouldering chapels line the outer walls of the mosque. Never comfortable as a Christian building, today the Cathedral seems to be hardly used at all, and regular Sunday masses are generally relegated to a small corner of the building.

Around the Mezquita

The masses of souvenir stands, cafés and tourists that surround the Mezquita on its busiest days do their best to recreate the atmosphere of the Moorish *souks* that once thrived here, but walk a block in any direction and you'll enter the essential Córdoba— whitewashed lanes with glimpses into dreamily beautiful patios, each one a floral extravaganza. One of the best is a famous little alley called **Calle de los Flores** ('street of the flowers') just a block north of the Mezquita.

Below the Mezquita, along the Guadalquivir, the plaza called **Puerta del Puente** (mentioned above) marks the site of Córdoba's southern gate with a decorative **arch** put up in 1571, celebrating the reign of Philip II. The very curious Churrigueresque monument next to it is called the **Triunfo** (1651) with a statue of San Rafael (the angel Raphael). Wild Baroque confections such as this are common in Naples and South Italy (under Spanish rule at the time); there they are called *guglie*. Behind the plaza, standing across from the Mezquita, is the Archbishop's Palace, built on the site of the original Alcazar, the palace of Abd ar-Rahman.

The **Roman Bridge** over the Guadalquivir probably isn't Roman at all any more; it has been patched and repaired so often practically nothing remains of the Roman work. Another statue of Raphael can be seen in the middle—probably replacing an old Roman image of Jupiter or Mercury. The stern-looking **Calahorra Tower** (1369, over Moorish foundations) once guarded the southern approaches of the bridge; now it contains a small **museum** of Córdoba's history, with old views and plans of the city, and the armour of Gonzalo Fernández de Córdoba, the 'Gran Capitan' who won much of Italy for Ferdinand and Isabella. It also has an historical multivision extravaganza which is expensive and for the dedicated tourist.

Just to the west, along the river, Córdoba's **Alcazar de Los Reyes Cristianos** was rebuilt in the 14th century and used for 300 years by the officers of the Inquisition.

There's little to see, but a good view of the Mezquita and the town from the belvedere atop the walls. The **gardens** are peaceful and lovely, an Andalucían amenity much like those in Sevilla's Alcazar. On the river's edge you'll see an ancient **waterwheel**. At least some of the Moors' talent for putting water to good use was retained for a while after the Reconquista. This is the mill that disturbed Isabella's dreams when she stayed at the Alcazar; it was rebuilt only in the early 1900s. If you continue walking along the Guadalquivir, after about a kilometre you'll come to Cruz Conde Park and the new **Córdoba Zoo**, where you can see a rare black lion who probably doesn't enjoy being called 'Chico' (open daily 10 am to sunset).

The Juderia

As in Sevilla, Córdoba's ancient Jewish quarter has recently become a fashionable area, a nest of tiny streets between the Mezquita and Avenida Dr Fleming. Part of the Moorish walls can be seen along this street, and the northern entrance of the Juderia is the old **Almodovar gate**. The streets are tricky, and it will take some effort to find Calle Maimonides and the 14th-century **Synagogue**, of which little remains but a wall of Alhambra-style arabesques and Hebrew inscriptions. On Calle Ruano Torres, the 15th-century **Casa del Indiano** is a palace with an eccentric façade.

The name of the **Municipal Museum** is somewhat misleading—it's mostly about bullfights. Manolete and El Cordobés are the city's two recent contributions to Spanish culture; here you can see a replica of Manolete's sarcophagus, the furniture from his home (!) and the hide of Islero, the bull that did him in, along with more bullfight memorabilia than you ever thought existed. The turn-of-the-century Art-Nouveau posters are beautiful, and among the old prints you can pay homage to the memory of the famous taurine malcontent Moñudo, who ignored the *toreros* and went up into the stands after the audience (on Plaza Maimonides, open daily 9–1.30, 4–7).

White Neighbourhoods

From the mosque you can walk eastwards through well over a mile of twisting white alleys, a place where the best map in the world wouldn't keep you from getting lost and staying lost. Though it all looks much the same, it's never monotonous: every little square, fountain or church stands out boldly, and forces you to look at it in a different way than you would a modern city—another lesson in the Moorish aesthetic. These streets have probably changed little since 1236, but their best buildings are a series of **Gothic churches** built soon after the Reconquista. Though small and plain, most are exquisite in a quiet way. Few have any of the usual Gothic sculptural work on their façades, to avoid offending a people accustomed to Islam's prohibition of images. The lack of decoration somehow adds to their charm. There are a score of these around Córdoba, and nothing like them elsewhere in the south of Spain. **San Lorenzo**, on Calle María Auxiliadora, is perhaps the best, with a rose window designed in a common Moorish motif of interlocking circles. Some 15th-century frescoes survive around the altar and on the apse.

San Pablo, on the street of the same name, is early-Gothic (1241, 5 years after the Christian conquest) but contains a fine Mudejár dome and ceiling. **San Andres**, on

Calle Varela, two streets east of San Pablo, **Santa Marina** on Calle Morales, and the **Cristo de los Faroles** on Calle Alfaros are some of the others. Have a look inside any you find open; most have some Moorish or Mudejár work in their interiors, and many of their towers (like San Lorenzo's) were originally minarets. **San Pedro** off Calle Alfonso XII, was the Christian cathedral under Moorish rule, though largely rebuilt in the 1500s.

The neighbourhoods have other surprises, if you have the persistence to find them. **Santa Victoria** is a huge austere Baroque church on Calle Jesus y María, modelled after the Roman Pantheon. Nearby on Plaza Baez, a fine 16th-century palace houses the **National Archaeological Museum**, the largest in Andalucía (open daily 10–2 and 4–8, Sunday 10–2) with Roman mosaics, a two-faced idol of Janus that probably came from the temple under the Mezquita, and an unusual icon of the Persian *torero*-god Mithras; also some Moorish-looking early Christian art, and early funeral steles with odd hieroglyphs. The large collection of Moorish art includes some of the best work from the age of the Caliphate, including finds from Medinat-az-Zahra.

East of Calle San Fernando, the wide street that bisects the old quarter, the houses are not as pristinely whitewashed as those around the Mezquita. Many parts are a bit run down, which does not detract from their charm. In the approximate centre of the city is the **Plaza de la Corredera**, an enclosed 'Plaza Mayor', like the famous ones in Madrid and Salamanca; this ambitious project, surrounded by uniform blank façades (an echo of the *estilo desornamentado*, was never completed. Now neglected and a bit eerie, the city is trying to rehabilitate it a little at a time.

Continuing south, the **Museo de Belles Artes** is on the lovely **Plaza del Potro** (mentioned by Cervantes, along with the little *posada* that still survives on it); its collections include works of Valdez Leal, Ribera, Murillo and Zurbarán, two royal portraits by Goya, and works by Córdoban artists of the 15th and 16th centuries. Beware the 'museum' across the plaza, dedicated exclusively to the works of a local named Julio Romero de Torres, the Spanish Bouguereau. Much prized by the Córdobans, this turn-of-the-century artist's *œuvre* consists almost entirely of naked ladies. Eastwards from here, the crooked whitewashed alleys continue for almost a mile, as far as the surviving stretch of **Moorish Walls** along Ronda del Marrubial.

Plaza de las Tendillas

The centre of Roman Córdoba, by chance, has become the centre of the modern city. Córdoba is probably the slickest and most up-to-date city in Andalucía (Sevilla would argue), and it shows in this busy district of crowded pavements, modern shops, cafés and wayward youth. The contrast with the old neighbourhoods is startling, but just a block off the plaza on Calle Gondomar, the beautiful 15th-century **San Nicolás Church** will remind you you're still in Córdoba. And in the other direction, well-preserved remains of a collapsed **Roman Temple** , one of the most complete Roman monuments in Spain, have been discovered on the Calle Nueva near the Ayuntamiento. The city has been at work re-assembling the walls and columns; already the front pediment is largely complete.

Next to the **Plaza de Colón**, a park a few blocks north of the Plaza de las Tendillas, the **Torre de Malmuerta** ('Bad Death') takes its name from a commander of this part of the old fortifications who murdered his wife in a fit of passion; it became the subject of a

79

well-known play by Lope de Vega, *Los Comendadores de Córdoba*. Across the plaza is a real surprise, the rococo **Convento de Merced** (1745), an enormous building that has recently been restored to house the provincial government and often hosts cultural exhibitions on various subjects. Don't miss it: the façade has been redone in its original painted *esgrafiado*, almost decadently colourful in pink and green, and the courtyards and grand staircases inside are incredible—more a palace than a monastery.

Medinat az-Zahra

Five miles northwest of the centre of Córdoba, the Caliph Abd ar-Rahman III began to build a palace in the year 936. The undertaking soon got out of hand, and with the almost infinite resources of the Caliphate to play with, he and his successors turned Medinat az-Zahra ('city of the Flower', named for one of Abd ar-Rahman's wives) into a city in itself, with a market, mosques, schools and gardens, a place where the last Caliphs could live in isolation from the world, safe from the turbulent street politics of their capital. Hisham II was kept a virtual prisoner here by his able vizir al-Mansur.

The scale of it is pure Arabian Nights. One chronicler records an ambassador, being taken from Córdoba to the palace, finding his path carpeted the entire 8 km (5 mile) route and lined from end to end with maidens to hold parasols and refreshments for him. Stories were told of the palace's African menageries, its interior pillars and domes of crystal, and curtains of falling water for walls; another fountain was filled with flowing mercury. Such carrying-on must have aroused a good deal of resentment; in the disturbances that put an end to the Caliphate, Medinat az-Zahra was sacked and razed by Berber troops in 1013.

After serving as a quarry for 900 years it's surprising anything is left at all; even under Muslim rule, columns from the palace were being carted away as far as Marrakesh. But in 1944 the royal apartments were discovered, with enough fragments to permit a restoration of a few arches with floral decorations. One hall has a roof on, and more work is under way, but as yet the rest is only foundations.

WHERE TO STAY (tel prefix 957)
Near the Mezquita, of course. Even during big tourist assaults the advantages outweigh the liabilities.

The **Meliá Córdoba****** is a big modern hotel right in the middle of the Jardines de la Victoria, on the edge of the Judería. It has every conceivable luxury the chain is known for, including a pool and TV—but a double room will set you back 14,000 pts—rather overpriced, considering the service (tel 29 80 66). The **Adarve****** has rooms which look out onto the floodlit walls of of the Mezquita, literally just a few metres from your balcony. The breakfasts are somewhat meagre, though, and service could do with a polish; there's an underground carpark, something to consider in this part of town (Mag. González Francés 15, tel 48 11 02; 16,000 pts). Also next to the mosque is the **Maimonides*****, again with underground parking, but prices are not much lower (Torrijos 4, tel 47 15 00; 13,000 pts). Five minutes north of the train station is the **Las Adelfas******, a modern hotel set in spacious gardens with a pool and beautiful views over Córdoba, elegant rooms and excellent service, and a bargain at present for its rates in this category—10,000 pts (Paseo de la Arruzafa s/n, tel 27 74 20).

In the Judería, 200 metres or so from the Mesquita is the attractive, affordable and immaculate **Albucasis****, with a charming flower-filled courtyard; it's one of the prettiest hotels in Córdoba (C. Buen Pastor II, tel 47 86 25; 7700–8500 pts). **Marisa****, C. Cardinal Herrero 6 (tel 47 31 42) is a simple but well-run establishment opposite the Patio de las Naranjas. The location is the only real amenity, but it will do for the price (4800–6000 pts for a double with bath).

Hostal Seneca*, C. Conde y Luque 5, tel 47 32 34, just north of the Mezquita, is the real find among the inexpensive *hostales*, with a beautiful patio full of flowers, nice rooms and sympathetic management. Not surprisingly, it's hard to get a room (3000–3600 pts a double without bath).

Plenty of other inexpensive *fondas* can be found in the area east of the Mezquita, especially on and around C. Rey Heredia. The **Fonda Agustina** on nearby C. Zapatería Vieja (tel 47 08 72) is clean and central (2200 pts for a double).

If this area is full, or if you have a car and do not care to brave the old town's narrow streets and lack of parking, there are a few hotels in the new town and on the periphery worth mentioning. The **Parador Nacional La Arruzafa******, on the outskirts of town (Avda. de la Arruzafa, tel 27 59 00) isn't in an historic building, but offers a pool, tennis courts and air-conditioned rooms and a view (doubles 11,000–14,000 pts). Off the Plaza de Tendillas, the **Boston***, C. Malaga 2 (tel 47 41 76) has modern clean rooms that are air-conditioned at night and popular with a young American crowd (3000–3600 pts). **Hostal Las Tendillas****, C. Jesús y María 1 (tel 22 30 29), has simple and unpretentious doubles for 2000 pts.

EATING OUT

Sitting in the heart of the old Jewish quarter, **El Churrasco** is Córdoba's best-loved restaurant (C. Romero 16, tel 29 08 19), located in an old town house. Before eating in one of the lovely rooms or on the elegant patio, see if you can first have a glass of *montilla* and some *tapas* in the bodega just up the street from the restaurant. It's not officially open to the public, but if you get there when it's not busy, the owner may open it up for you, especially if you are in a party. Painstakingly restored by the owner, the house and courtyard(complete with well) are decorated with local handicrafts and antiques, and the wine cellar is vast. Upstairs is a salon where the top gourmets of the city meet once a month, including the rogue El Cordobés. The restaurant itself specializes in grilled meats but try also the excellent *dorada*, covered in salt and oven-baked, sole with garlic from the oven, salmon and swordfish steaks. In winter braziers are put under tables making it possible to dine on the patio all year round, and there's a personal parking service. Relatively speaking, it's not expensive— count on 3000–4000 pts (closed Thur, Aug and Christmas).

Rival to El Churrasco is one of the best-known restaurants in Andalucía, **El Caballo Rojo** (Cardenal Herrero 28, tel 47 53 75). Its menu is based on traditional Andaluz cooking and old Arab recipes—*samorejo* with cured ham, artichokes in Montilla wine, Mozarabic angler fish, lamb with honey, *cola de toro* (3500 pts). Adjoining is the pleasant little **El Burlaero**, where you can eat out in the courtyard or in the room upstairs. Specialities include *rabo de toro*, *Paloma Torcaz*, *perdis*, *jabali* (full meal for less than 2000 pts; C. La Hoguera 5, tel 47 27 19). In the Campo Santo de los Mártires (No. 1) the **Almudaina** is in an attractive old house dating from the 16th century, and is a cool and sophisticated spot to eat. Its menu varies from day to day, depending on market availability, and special attention is paid to local produce. Look out for: *ensalada de pimientos, alcachofas a la Cordobés, verduras a la crema de espinacas* and *lomo relleno a la Pedrocheña* (*menú del día* 2000 pts, à la carte 3500 pts and up; tel 47 43 42; closed Sun evening). More quality surroundings and fare are at **Oscar's** (Plaza de Chirinos 6, tel 47 75 17), where the emphasis is on fish—*ensalada de salmón marinado, lubina al vino oloroso de Montilla, lomos de merluza con langostinos en salsa de ajo* (3500–4500 pts; closed Sun and Aug).

Just around the corner from the Mezquita, **El Tablón** is a restaurant with character, offering one of the best bargains in the city, with a choice of *menús del día* or *platos combinados* starting at under 600 pts, glass of wine included (Cardenal Gonzalez 75, tel 47 60 61).

On the corner of C. Deanes and Buen Pastor is the take-it-or leave-it **Bodegan Rafaé**, with true bodega atmosphere and food. Sausages drape from barrels, religious figurines hang next to fake bulls' heads, the radio and TV are on simultaneously; *cola de toro* with a glass of wine at one of the vinyl-topped tables will cost you an exorbitant 550 pts. Some other inexpensive choices are around Plaza de las Tendillas. For the young, or young at heart, a lively spot is **El Campeon**, near Plaza de las Tendillas in one of those narrow streets (Munda 8). Here students gather amid the dotty decor to order enormous glass tankards of beer and sangria, and enjoy the loud music and snack food in one of the half-dozen tiny rooms with wooden benches (tel 47 02 07).

Don't forget that Córdoba is the heart of a wine-growing region; there are a few bodegas in town that appreciate visitors: **Bodega Campos**, on C. Colonel Cascajo; and **Bodega Doña Antonia**, Avda. Virgen Milagrosa 5, really a small restaurant serving its own wines.

SHOPPING

Córdoba is famous for its silverwork—try the shops in José Cruz Grande, where you'll get better quality than in the old quarter round the mosque. Handmade crafts are made on the premises at *Meryan*, Calle de los Flores 2 (tel 47 59 02), where they specialize in exquisitely embossed wood and leather furniture. For antiques, there's one shop with a very good selection of Spanish art and furniture in Plaza San Nicolás, and they'll arrange packing and shipment. High-quality ladies' and gents' suede and leather goods are sold at *Sera*, on the corner of Rondo de los Teares and Cruz Conde.

North of Córdoba

The N432 out of Córdoba leads north to the Sierra Morena, the string of hills which curtain the western part of Andalucía from Extremadura, Castilla and La Mancha. This area is the **Valley of Los Pedroches**, fertile grazing lands for the pig, sheep and goats and an important hunting area for deer and wild boar. Thousands of these animals are stalked and shot in the numerous annual hunts, or *monterías*. It's also healthy hiking territory, but keep yourself visible at all times—you don't want to be mistaken for someone's supper. This area is also widely known for its supreme quality *Jamón Iberico* (locally cured ham) and other pork products.

82

GETTING AROUND
Although buses do run from Córdoba up into the Sierra and villages of Los Pedroches, they are infrequent and very time-consuming. To explore the best parts, you really need a car.

A road winds 80 km up to **Bélmez**, with its Moorish castle perilously perched on a rock, from which there are panoramic views over the surrounding arid countryside. **Peñar-roya-Pueblonuevo**, is a dull industrial town that has fallen into decline, but is useful here as a reference point. Over the next two years the province of Córdoba is planning to straighten out the bends and flatten the annoying bumps, allowing easier access to the surrounding villages. Sixteen km west on the N432 the village of **Fuente Obejuna** is best remembered for the 1476 uprising of its villagers, who dragged their tyrannical lord from his palace and treated him to a spectacularly brutal and bloody end. The event is the subject of the drama *Fuenteovejuna* by Lope de Vega.

Forty four km east of Peñarroya (take the C421, then C420) is the village of **Pozoblanco**, famous for the last *corrida* of the renowned bullfighter Francisco Rivera, better known as Paquirri. Gored, he died in the ambulance on the way to Córdoba; presumably, bouncing around on those roads didn't help. Paquirri's widow, the singer Pantoja, soared to even greater heights of popularity on his death, the Spanish public obsessed as ever by the drama of life and the proximity of death. **Pedroche**, 10 km away, is a sleepy little village with a fine 16th-century Gothic church, with a proud, lofty spire. This place too has had its fair share of drama—in 1936 communist forces shot nearly one hundred of the menfolk. Beyond the villages of **Villanueva de Córdoba** and **Cardeña** to the east is the **Natural Park of Cardeña**; rolling hills forested in oak, more stag-hunting grounds and ideal rambling terrain.

WHERE TO STAY AND EAT   (tel prefix 957)
North of Córdoba there's nothing in the way of deluxe accommodation, but the area has a small selection of one- and two- star hotels. Two and a half km out of Pozoblanco (Ctra Vva de la Serena-Andújar, Km 129), in a listed historic building is the quiet **San Francisco****, with tennis courts and rooms with bath for 6000 pts (tel 10 14 35). Villanueva de Córdoba has **Demetrius***, a place that offers no frills for its 2500 pts rooms (Ctra de Cardeña s/n, tel 12 02 94). Similarly, in Cardeña the **Paco*** has simple, cheap and clean rooms for 2500 pts (Plaza Independencia 6, tel 17 41 09). Though there's no reason to stay in Peñarroya-Pueblonuevo, you may like to use it as a base for your day trip. The **Sevilla*** is the most comfortable place to stay, rooms with bath go for 3800 pts (Miguel Vigara 15, tel 56 01 00), while **El Sol*** has basic rooms for 2600 pts (El Sol 24, tel 56 80 50).

This area is famed throughout Andalucía for its Iberian ham and suckling pig, the excellent *salchichon* from Pozoblanco, and the strong, spicy cheese made from ewes' milk. There are no oustanding restaurants around; drop in on a family *venta* and see what the day's special is, or head for the *tapas* bars in the villages. Better still grab some goodies from a supermarket and have a picnic out on the slopes.

From Córdoba to Ubeda

In this section of the Guadalquivir valley the river rises into the heights of the Sierra Morena; endless rolling hills covered with neat rows of olive trees and small farms make a memorable Andalucían landscape. The three large towns along the way, **Andújar**, **Bailén** and **Linares**, are much alike, amiable industrial towns still painted a gleaming white.

This area is Andalucía's front door, from where the roads and railways from Madrid branch off for Sevilla and Granada. Many important battles were fought nearby, including Navas de Tolosa near La Carolina, in 1212, that opened the way for the conquest of al-Andalus; and Bailén, in 1808, where a Spanish-English force gave Napoleon's boys a sound thrashing and built up Spanish morale for what they call their War of Independence.

The NIV snakes along the Guadalquivir valley, and 42 km east of Córdoba it brings you to the delightfully placed town of **Montoro**, sitting on a bend in the river. The facetious-looking tower that rises above the whitewashed houses belongs to the Gothic-Mudejár church of **San Bartolomé**, in the main square, Plaza de España; here also is the 16th-century **Ducal Palace**, with a *plateresque* façade. The beautiful 15th-century bridge that connects Montoro to its suburb, Retamar, is known as the Puente de Las Doñadas, a tribute to the women of the village who sacrificed their jewellery to help finance its construction. Seek out the kitsch **Casa de las Conchas**, a house and courtyard done out in sea shells.

Approaching **Andújar**, a further 35 km down the NIV, you'll find the countryside dominated by huge, blue sunflower-oil refineries like fallen space stations. Sunflowers, like olives, are a big crop in the region and much in evidence in late summer. Nothing remains of Andújar's Moorish castle, but there are a couple of surprises in this town which might tempt you to linger a while. The church of **Santa María**, in the plaza of the same name, has in one chapel the *Immaculate Conception* by Pacheco, Velázquez's teacher, and in another chapel the magnificent *Christ in the Garden of Olives*, the work of El Greco.

A possible diversion, 30 km north of Andújar on the J501, is the **Santuario de la Virgen de la Cabeza**. Although very little is left of the 13th-century sanctuary, and the present one is disappointing, it's worth packing a picnic and enjoying the drive; when you get there you'll be rewarded with panoramic views of the whole area. One of southern Spain's biggest fiestas is the annual *romería* here to the sanctuary on the last Sunday in April, when a quarter of a million pilgrims trek up on foot, horseback, carts and donkeys. The day before there's a competition for the best-decorated carriage.

Twenty-seven kilometres further east on the NIV is the modern, unprepossessing town of **Bailén**. The tomb of the Spanish general Castaños, who so cleverly whipped the French troops and sent Napoleon back to the drawing board, is in the Gothic parish church of the **Encarnación**, which also has a sculpture by Alonso Cano. But don't dally here—the real treat is to be found 11 km to the north on the NIV at **Baños de la Encina**, where the 10th-century Moorish castle is one of the best preserved in all Andalucía, and evokes the glory of a by-gone age. Dominating the town, the castle has 14 sturdy towers, scarcely touched by time, and from the walls you get a sweeping vista of the olive groves and distant peaks beyond Ubeda.

Twenty kilometres north of here on the NIV is **La Carolina**, a model of 18th-century grid planning. The village owes its existence to forward-thinking Charles III, who imported a few thousand German artesans in the late-1700s and set them to work excavating the lead and copper mines, tilling the fields and herding sheep. A side-effect of this colonization was supposed to be the decline of banditry in the then wild and unpopulated hills. But within two generations almost all the Germans had died off or fled. The town and surrounding area are best known now as a big game-hunting reserve, particularly for partridge.

From Bailén the N322 heads eastward to the mining town of **Linares**, birthplace of the guitarist Andrés Segovia, who later moved on; others weren't so lucky—in 1947 the great bullfighter Manolete had an off day and met his end at the horns of a bull in the ring here. If things had gone well for him, he might have gone to view the finds from the Roman settlement of nearby *Cástulo*, housed in the town's **archaeology museum**, but unfortunately the last thing he probably saw was the ornate Baroque portal of the hospital **San Juan de Dios**. From Linares it's a 27 km run to Ubeda; a little more than halfway you'll pass an elegant castle at **Canena**.

WHERE TO STAY AND EAT (tel prefix 953)
On the main Madrid–Cádiz road (at Km 358) is the **Montoro****, with doubles at 3500 pts (tel 16 07 92). Andújar has a bigger selection, but less reason to stay. The best here is **Don Pedro***** (Gabriel Zamora 5, tel 50 12 74) in the centre of town, with pleasant rooms for 4500 pts, and a tavern-style restaurant which specialises in game dishes; meal with wine about 2000 pts. There's a modern **Parador***** just outside Bailén, with pleasant gardens, air-conditioning and pool—rates are a reasonable 7500 pts (Ctra. Nacional IV, Km 296, tel 67 01 00). It also houses a restaurant and average *tapas* bar. In Linares the **Anibal***** is the jumbo in town (6500–7500 pts for double with bath; Cid Campeador 11, tel 65 04 00); and for dining **Mesón Castellano** is the place to go (2500 pts; Puente 5, tel 69 00 09; closed Sun, July and Aug). In La Carolina the hotel **Perdiz****** has a pretty good restaurant and as its name ('partridge') implies, has seasonal game dishes (2500 pts). Rates for the hotel, which has a pool, are 8000 pts a double (Ctra NIV, Km 269, tel 66 03 00).

Baeza

> *Campo de Baeza, soñaré contigo cuando no te vea...*
> Fields of Baeza, I will dream of you when I can no longer see you...
> —Antonio Machado, 19th/20th century

Sometimes history offers its recompense. The 13th-century Reconquista was especially brutal here; nearly the entire population fled, many of them moving to Granada, where they settled the Albaicín. The 16th century, however, when the wool trade was booming in this corner of Andalucía, was good to Baeza, leaving it a distinguished little town of neatly clipped trees and tan stone buildings, with a beautiful ensemble of monuments in styles from Romanesque to Renaissance. It seems a happy place, serene and quiet as the olive groves that surround it.

GETTING AROUND
Come to Baeza by train at your own risk. The nearest station, officially named Linares-Baeza, is far off in the open countryside, 20 km away. A bus to Baeza usually meets the train, but if you turn up at night or on a Sunday you may be stranded. Baeza's bus station,

in a residential area without many street signs, is incredibly difficult to find—keep asking. Baeza is a stop on the Ubeda–Córdoba bus route.

TOURIST INFORMATION
Plaza del Pópulo, tel (953) 74 04 44.

First among the 16th-century monuments are the **Cathedral** , on Plaza Santa María, a work of Andrés de Vandelvira. This replaced a 13th-century Gothic church (surviving chancel and portal), which in turn took the place of a mosque; a colonnade from this can be seen in the cloister. For the best show in town, drop a coin in the box marked *custodia* in one of the side chapels; this will reveal, with a noisy dose of mechanical *duende*, a rich and ornate 18th-century silver tabernacle. The fountain in front of the cathedral, the **Fuente de Santa María**, with a little triumphal arch at its centre (1564), is Baeza's landmark and symbol. Behind it is the Isabelline Gothic **Casas Consistoriales**, formerly the town hall.

Heading north on the Cuesta de San Felipe, you pass the 15th-century **Palacio de Jabalquinto**, with an eccentric façade covered with coats-of-arms and pyramidal stone studs (a Spanish fancy of that age; you can see others like it in Guadalajara and Salamanca). The prettiest corner of the town is a small square, the **Plaza del Pópulo**, enclosed by decorative pointed arches, containing a fountain with four half-effaced lions; the fountain was patched together with the help of pieces taken from the Roman remains at Cástulo, and the centrepiece, the fearless lady on the pedestal, is traditionally considered to be Imilce, the wife of Hannibal. In Plaza Cardenal Benavides, the façade of the *ayuntamiento* (town hall) is a classic example of Andalucían plateresque, and one of the last (1599).

UBEDA

Even with Baeza for an introduction, the presence of this nearly perfect little city comes as a surprise. If the 16th century did well by Baeza, it was a golden age here, leaving Ubeda a 'town built for gentlemen' as the Spanish used to say, endowed with one of the finest collections of Renaissance architecture in all of Spain. Two men can take much of the credit: Andrés de Vandelvira, an Andalucían architect who created most of Ubeda's best buildings, and Francisco de los Cobos, Imperial Secretary to Charles V, who paid for them. Cobos is a forgotten hero of Spanish history. While Charles was off campaigning in Germany, Cobos had the job of running Castile. By the most delicate management, he kept the kingdom afloat while meeting Charles' ever more exorbitant demands for money and men. He could postpone the inevitable disaster, but not prevent it. Like most public officials in the Spanish Age of Rapacity, though, he also managed to salt away a few hundred thousand ducats for himself, and he spent most of them embellishing his hometown. Like Baeza, Ubeda is a peaceful and happy place; it wears its Renaissance heritage gracefully, and is always glad to have visitors. Tourism is still something of a novelty here.

GETTING AROUND
Ubeda has a new bus station on C. San José, at the western end of town, and various lines connect the city directly to Madrid, Valencia and Barcelona, at least once daily, and more

frequently to Baeza, Córdoba, Sevilla, Jaén and Granada. Cazorla and other villages in the region can easily be reached from Ubeda.

TOURIST INFORMATION
Plaza de los Caídos, s/n, tel (953) 75 08 97.

Ubeda today leaves no doubt how its local politics are going. In the **Plaza de Andalucía**, joining the old and new districts, there is an old metal statue of a fascist Civil War general named Sero, glaring down from his pedestal. The townspeople have put so many bullets into it, it looks like a Swiss cheese. They've left it here as a joke, and have merrily renamed another square from Plaza de Generalísimo to Plaza 1 Mayo. The **Torre de Reloj**, in the Plaza de Andalucía, is a 14th-century defensive tower now adorned with a clock. The plaque near the base, under a painting of the Virgin, records a visit of Charles V.

From here, Calle Real takes you into the heart of the old town. Nearly every corner has at least one lovely palace or church on it. Two of the best can be seen on this street: the early 17th-century **Palacio de Condé Guadiana**, with an ornate tower and distinctive windows cut out of the corners of the building, a common conceit in Ubeda's palaces. Two blocks down, the **Palacio Vela de los Cobos** is in the same style, with a loggia on the top storey.

The home of Francisco de los Cobos' nephew, another Royal Counsellor, was the **Palacio de las Cadenas**, now serving as Ubeda's Ayuntamiento, on a quiet plaza at the end of Calle Real. The side facing the plaza is simple and dignified (the tourist office is here) but the main façade, facing the **Plaza Vázquez de Molina**, is a stately Renaissance creation, the work of Vandelvira.

Plaza Vázquez de Molina

This is the only place in Andalucía where you can look around and not regret the passing of the Moors, for it is the only truly beautiful thing in all this great region that was not built either by the Moors or under their influence. The Renaissance buildings around the Palacio de las Cadenas make a wonderful ensemble, and the austere landscaping, old cobbles, and a plain six-sided fountain create the same effect of contemplative serendipity as any chamber of the Alhambra. Among the buildings are the church of **Santa María de los Reales Alcazares**, a Renaissance façade on an older building with a fine Gothic cloister around the back; the Parador (see below; *Where to Stay*); two sedate palaces, both from the 16th century; and Vandelvira's **Sacra Capilla del Salvador** begun in 1540, the finest of Ubeda's churches, where Cobos is buried.

All the sculpture on the façades of Ubeda is first-class work, and the west front of the Salvador is especially good. This is a monument of the time when Spain was in the mainstream of Renaissance ideas, and humanist classicism was still respectable. Note the mythological subjects on the west front and elsewhere in the church, and be sure to look under the arch of the main door. Instead of Biblical scenes, it has beautifully carved panels of the ancient gods representing the five planets; Phoebus and Diana with the sun and moon; and Heracles, Aeolus, Vulcan and Neptune to represent the four elements. The interior, with its great dome, is worth a look despite a thorough sacking in 1936 (the sacristan lives on the first door on the left of Calle Francisco Cobos, on the north side of the church). Behind El Salvador, the **Hospital de los Honrados** has a delightful open patio—but only because the other half of the building was never completed. South of the plaza, the end of town is only a few blocks away, encompassed by a street called the **Redonda de Miradores**, a quiet spot favoured by small children and goats, with remnants of Ubeda's wall and exceptional views over the Sierra de Cazorla to the east.

Around Ubeda

Calle Montiel, north of El Salvador, has a few more fine palaces; at the foot of the street, on Plaza 1 de Mayo is the 13th-century **San Pablo Church**, much renovated in the 16th; inside is an elegant chapel of 1536, the Capello del Camarero Vago. **San Nicolas de Bari**, further north, was originally a synagogue, and confiscated in 1492, which has left it with one Gothic door and the other by Vandelvira, who oversaw the reconstruction.

On the outskirts of town, near the bus station on Calle Nueva is Vandelvira's most remarkable building, the **Hospital de Santiago**. This huge edifice, currently under thorough restoration after long years of neglect, has been called the 'Escorial of Andalucía'. Both have the same plan, a grid of quadrangles with a church inside. Oddly, both were begun at about the same time, though this one seems to have been started a year earlier, in 1568. Both are supreme examples of the *estilo desornamentado*. The façade here is not as plain as Herrera's; its quirky decoration and clean, angular lines are unique, more like a product of the 20th century than the 16th.

East of Ubeda

If you go this way, you'll be entering a zone few visitors ever reach. The **Sierra de Cazorla**, a jumble of ragged peaks, pine forests, and olive-covered lowlands, offers some memorable mountain scenery, especially around **Cazorla**, a lovely, undiscovered white village of narrow alleys hung at alarming angles down the hillsides.

Cazorla's landmarks are a ruined Renaissance church (again, by Vandelvira) half-open to the sky, and its castle; but there's an even better castle, possibly built by the Templars, just east of town. **La Iruela** is a romantic ruin even by Spanish standards, with a Homage tower on a dizzying height behind. Beyond La Iruela is the pass into the Sierra, the wild territory of hiking, hunting and fishing. The mountain ranges of Cazorla and Seguria make up one of the 10 national parks in Spain. Gun-toting hunters stalk wild boar, deer, mountain goat, buck and *muflón*, and rainbow trout do their best to outwit the patient but determined anglers. Not all visitors are in for the kill, however, and those interested in flora and fauna find the area one of the richest in Europe, with a variety of birdlife that's hard to match.

WHERE TO STAY (tel prefix 953)
In Baeza there are no hotels with pretensions; the **Juanito*** (Avda Arca del Agua s/n, tel 74 00 40) has rooms with bath for 4000–4800 pts and the **Comercio****, C. San Pablo 21 (tel 74 01 00), is a reasonably comfortable lodging where Machado stayed and penned a few poems (2700 pts).

The **Parador Condestable Dávalos*****, an old palace with a glassed-in courtyard, is one of the loveliest and most popular of the chain. All the beamed ceilings and fireplaces have been preserved and the restaurant is the best in town, featuring local specialities from 2100–2500 pts a full dinner. Ask to see the ancient wine cellar (Pl. Vazquez de Molina, tel 75 03 45; 10,000–12,500 pts for a big double room). The rest of Ubeda's hotels are all good bargains; you'll find a large selection on C. Ramón y Cajal, just east of the bus station. At the **Sevilla****, Ramón y Cajal 9, tel 75 06 12, you can get a clean and pleasant double with bath for 2000–2800 pts; the **San Miguel*** is another cheapie, 2200 pts for a double without bath (Avda. Libertad s/n, tel 75 20 49); while at the **Consuelo****, Ramón y Cajal 12, tel 75 08 40, the rooms are a bit fancier for 3800 pts.

Cazorla has a surprising number of hotels, both in town and up in the mountains on the road to the dam and reservoir at El Tranco, 20 km (12.5 miles) north in a beautiful mountain setting. One of these is the **Mirasierra ***, with a restaurant (tel 72 15 44; doubles with bath 2400–2800 pts). The **Parador El Adelantado*****, is a small mountain chalet—only 20 rooms—in another pretty setting in the mountains outside Cazorla, a base for hunting, fishing and walking in the Sierra (tel 72 10 75; doubles 7500–9500 pts). **Don Diego*** is a comfortable little hotel with doubles for 3500–4400 pts (C. Hilario Marcos 163, tel 72 05 45).

EATING OUT
In Baeza the restaurant of the **Hotel Juanito**, Pso. Arca del Agua, is a good one; try the *pastel de perdiz* (partridge in a pastry crust), pheasant with mushrooms, artichokes, *merluza a la Baeza*; dinners average 2000–3000 pts.

Apart from the Parador, there aren't any really good restaurants in Ubeda. The best is **Cusco** (Parque Vandelvira 8, tel 75 34 13) which has local dishes and standard Andaluz fish and meat menus. A smattering of unremarkable places are around C. Ramón y Cajal. **El Olivo** has average fare at average prices (1500 pts; Avda Ramón y Cajal 2, tel 75 20 92). Culinary specialities of Ubeda are the convent cakes, *tocinos de cielo* and Jaén black pudding.

JAÉN

In the middle of the vast tracts of olive groves on which it depends is Jaén, the most provincial of all the Andalucían capitals. Jaén lacks the Renaissance charms of Ubeda or Baeza, but it is a decent, modern town, not as unattractive as many books claim; easily explored on foot in one day, along pleasant pedestrian walkways.

GETTING AROUND
Jaén has direct rail links only with Córdoba (three trains daily) and Madrid (about six). Buses are the best bet for Ubeda or Granada. The bus station is on the Avda de Madrid, near the tourist office. The RENFE station is on the Pso. de la Estación, the main street, at the northern edge of town, by the Plaza de la Concordia.

TOURIST INFORMATION
Arquitecto Berges 1, tel (953) 22 27 37.

Parts of the town well worth a visit include the old Arab quarter, whose weaving, narrow, paved lanes are at the foot of the hill which is crowned by the 13th-century Moorish castle of **Santa Catalina**, built by ibn-Nasr; Jaén was the kingdom of Granada's first capital. Towering above the town, it's an ideal place to take in the views of the wild countryside and the mountains beyond.

The city's pride is its monumental **Cathedral** on Plaza Santa María, begun in 1548 by Andrés de Vandelvira. Vandelvira's work inside has suffered many changes, and the façade isn't his at all; not begun until 1667, Eufrásio López de Rojas' design was the first genuine attempt at Baroque in Andalucía, decorated with extravagant statuary by Pedro Roldán. Adjacent to the cathedral is the **Iglesia del Sagrario**, with a neoclassical interior designed by Ventura Rodriguez. On Calle Martínez Molina, west of the cathedral, an old hospital has been restored to hold a small **museum** of crafts and naive art; the real attraction is the well-preserved ruins of Moorish baths, discovered underneath. Jaén's modern quarters can be a bit dreary, and peculiar at the same time. The centre, Plaza de las Batallas, has an extremely silly winged statue atop a pedestal, commemorating past victories over the Moors. Nearby, on the broad Plaza de la Estación, there is a good archaeological collection in the **Museo Provincial**, with some exceptional Iberian sculptures (open daily except Monday, 10–2 and 4–7, adm).

If you're on the way to Granada, a possible detour is **Alcalá de Real**, with an unusual town square and another picturesque castle, the **Castle of la Mota** on top of a hill. The **Castle of Solera**, in that tiny village just east of Huelina, is an even finer sight; the castle seems to grow out of its narrow crag. Like Cazorla, the views are breathtaking but it will be some trouble to get up to them on foot.

WHERE TO STAY   (tel prefix 953)

The **Parador Castillo de Santa Catalina****** is in the castle overlooking Jaén, tel 26 44 11 (10,000–12,000 pts for a double), and is where General de Gaulle spent time on his memoirs. If you are suffering from writers' block, you might do better at the **Condestable Iranzo*****, near the tourist office on Paseo de la Estación 32. It doesn't have the view, but more luxuries at a better price (7500–9000 pts a double, for an air-conditioned room with TV; tel 22 28 00). Another conveniently placed major hotel is the **Xauen***** further down the Paseo near Plaza Constitución (Plaza Deán Mazas 3, tel 26 40 11; 5500–7000 pts). A couple of acceptable budget hotels are **La Española***, (Bernardo López 9, tel 25 84 34) and **Carlos V*** (Avda de Madrid 4, tel 22 20 91); both have doubles for 2000–2500 pts.

EATING OUT

For dining, the acknowledged best place in the city is **Restaurant Nelson** (Paseo de la Estación 33, tel 22 92 01) decorated very much in the style of an English pub, but that's as far as it goes—you won't find bangers and mash here, but some excellent Spanish and international dishes (2000–3000 pts; closed Sun). For local specialities at their best, try **Casa Vicente** (Arco del Consuelo 1, tel 26 28 16), where a wide-ranging menu concentrates on meat and fish (2000–3000 pts; closed Sun). Very much in the Andalucían tradition is the restaurant **Nuyra** on the Calle Nueva, where grilled meats are particularly good (1500 pts). Look out for the local specialities: Jaén black pudding, a concoction of pork, beef, garlic, paprika, nutmeg and sherry, *cabrito asado* (roast baby kid with garlic), *chorizo* and the famous salad *pipirrana*.

The Andalucían Coasts

Everyone has heard of the Costa del Sol, but there is a good deal more to Andalucía's coasts than just that narrow strip of salty Babylon—about 640 km (400 miles) of it, from the empty spaces of Huelva to the empty spaces of Almería.

Andalucía's Atlantic coast, from Portugal to the Straits of Gibraltar, is not at all scenic, but it has plenty of long golden beaches that haven't yet become too crowded. The image-makers of the Spanish Tourism Ministry have bestowed upon it the name **Costa de la Luz**. The piquant, sea-washed town of **Cádiz** is its major attraction. After Cádiz the mountains close in, until **Algeciras**, a port town with the promise of a side-trip to Morocco, or to a tiny remnant of Spain's colonial empire in Africa, **Ceuta**. Next we stop for fish and chips in **Gibraltar**; there the endless *urbanizaciónes* of the **Costa del Sol** begin, reaching their greatest intensity around **Marbella** and **Torremolinos**. **Málaga** comes next, a busy city not without charm, and after it the only section of the coast with any pretensions to scenery, around **Nerja**. After **Motril**, and the road to Granada, there's more solitude on the **Costa de Almería**, which is in parts pretty, in others nearly a desert.

Altogether, these coasts have only one real purpose—planting yourself on a beach and dozing off. There are the inevitable peripheral attractions (mini-golf, seafood dinners, funfairs, English beer on tap, etc.), but little else. Pack a potent sunscreen and have a good time.

Costa de la Luz
West of Huelva

Coming from the east by bus to **Ayamonte** you'll be deposited next to the pretty square behind the harbour filled with small boats, which you can eye from the comfort of one of the *azulejo* benches. If you're on your way to Portugal, walk through the square and follow the signs for about 500 metres, where a flat-bottomed boat will be waiting to take you and 40 cars across the narrow stretch of the Guadiana river to the Portuguese town of Villa Real de Santo Antonio. The back streets of Ayamonte are not without character and there are plenty of little cafés where you can sit and muse, or bring your diary up to date. Just across the water, the beaches of the resort **Isla Cristina** are more popular with Spaniards than foreigners.

From Ayamonte the N431 heads east to Huelva, passing en route the sleepy town of **Lepe**; the butt of Andalucían jokes, in the same way as the Irish, Polacks and Newfies are elsewhere. Rather sportingly, every May the Leperos hold a festival of humour—and even if they mind the abuse, they're laughing all the way to the bank, for the ever-abundant strawberry, orange and asparagus crops in this area have made the town very wealthy. (Those silver lakes you see along the road are actually sun-tinted plastic sheets protecting the strawberries.)

This stretch of road between Huelva and Ayamonte has no real attraction for the tourist—orange groves interspersed with derelict buildings, scrapyards and mudflats. South of Lepe on the coast are two spots worth a visit—**La Antilla**, with its fine white sandy beach, and **El Rompido**, a pleasant little place that is now being developed for tourism. A little further south, the peninsula of **Punta Umbria** is one of the main tourist resorts of the area; its long sandy beaches offer all types of water sports.

WHERE TO STAY   (tel prefix 955)
In Ayamonte, check to see if the **Parador Costa de la Luz***** has opened after refurbishment. It isn't on the beach, but has fine views over the sea, occupies the site of a long-gone Moorish castle, and a has a big swimming pool (tel 32 07 00; doubles 7500–8000 pts). Ayamonte has a number of inexpensive places, like the **Hostal La Ribera*** (tel 32 02 89, doubles 2500–3000 pts) at Pso. de la Ribera 1, or the **Europa***, Avenida de la Playa 45 (tel 32 01 91; 2600–3400 pts). At Isla Cristina, on the beach you have a choice between **Los Geranios**** (Ctra Isla Cristina-Playa, tel 33 18 00; doubles 4000–4800 pts) and the **El Paraiso**** (Camino de la Playa, tel 33 18 73; doubles 3600–5500 pts). At Punta Umbria the choice is wider: **La Playa**** is the cheapest hotel on the beach (Avda. Océano 95, tel 31 01 12, doubles 3500–4200 pts). All these little resorts have cheaper hotels within reasonable distances of the beaches. In the busy season, phone ahead.

EATING OUT
There's a line of fine little restaurants behind the plaza, on the Paseo de la Ribera, all offering the day's special for around 800 pts; a seafood meal will cost 1500–2000 pts. For shellfish and *paella*, try the **Casino España**. At the restaurant **Barbieri**, you can peep through the palm trees at Portugal. Just around the corner is the **Nuria**, with a busy little bar and a bright, clean little restaurant.

At Isla Cristina, the local favourite is the restaurant **Acosta**, at Plaza Caudillo 13 (tel 33 14 20), for fresh fish and traditional Andalucían stews (1500 pts; closed Mon in winter).

In Punta Umbria you'll raise a few eyebrows if you don't order fish. Long popular is **La Esperanza**, (Plaza Pérez Pastor 7, tel 31 10 45), with satisfying well-cooked dishes at reasonable prices—dogfish with tomato 1500 pts. Another established restaurant is the **El Ayamontino** (Av Andalucía 13, tel 31 03 16), serving tasty fish soup, oven-cooked bream and sirloin steaks (2000 pts).

Huelva

A Huelva una vez y nunca vuelvas.
One trip to Huelva and you don't go back.

This Andaluz saying does seem a little unkind, but the provincial capital *is* full of factories and freshly laid cement; from the outskirts it looks like some dilapidated Balkan town. Hit the centre however and, small as it is, it boasts an incongruously large number of fur shops and amusement arcades. (History will probably prove that Las Vegas was actually founded by a Huelvan.) Another surprise is to be found on its streets, a species now extinct in northern Europe that can occasionally be spotted after nightfall—the crêpe-soled teddy boy.

GETTING AROUND
The train station is on the Avenida de Italia, a 5-minute walk from the centre of Huelva; daily *talgo* to Sevilla and Madrid (change at Linares for Granada and Almería), apart from the regular services to Sevilla, from where there are connections to Cádiz, Jerez, Códoba, other points in Andalucía and Barcelona; also regular trains to Ayamonte, on the Portuguese border. The *Damas* bus company has its station at Avenida de Portugal 9, with services to Sevilla, Granada, Cádiz and Algeciras, and other destinations within the province: Ayamonte, Isla Cristina, Punta Umbria, Mazagón and Matalascañas on the coast, less frequently to Nerva and the mountain villages to the north. The nearest airport is in Sevilla.

TOURIST INFORMATION
Avenida Alemania 1, tel (955) 25 74 03.

The town's tourist brochure, in a unique and disarmingly modest display of candour, states that Huelva 'has no particular historic interest'. The town was severely damaged by the earthquake of 1755, explaining the near-absence of anything older than that; exceptions include the 16th-century Baroque church of **San Pedro**, built on the site of an old mosque, and the **Museo Provincial**, Alameda Sundheim 13 (open daily except Mon, 10–2, 4–7). The town's theatre is an Art-Deco aberration that resembles an Italian ice-cream parlour, but the real curiosity of Huelva is the **Barrio Reina Victoria**, a neighbourhood constructed by, and for, the employees of the English Rio Tinto mining company in the 19th century. The houses, now in a state of disrepair, sport gable ends and chimney pots in true English suburban style. Just out of town, where the Odiel and Tinto rivers meet, is the 118-ft high hooded statue of Christopher Columbus, sculpted by Gertrude Whitney and presented to Spain by the USA in 1929.

Huelvans (also known as *choqueros*, because of their love for *chocos*—cuttlefish) are an isolated bunch, flanked and maybe intimidated by the presence of haughty Sevilla on one side and the expanse of Portugal on the other. They are nonetheless friendly and welcoming, and hoping to put aside centuries of stagnation are optimistic and fervent in their desire to play a more important role in the future of the new Spain and Europe.

North of Huelva

TOURIST INFORMATION
Aracena: Plaza Pozo de las Nieves s/n, tel (955) 11 03 55.

If you have a car you can comfortably explore the little-visited mountain villages in the **Sierra de Aracena**, less than a 2-hour drive from the capital. The N435 takes you to the heart of this area, passing through beautiful forests of holm oaks and cork trees, as the countryside gets more mountainous and the views more scenic. **Aracena** has the big attraction, the **Gruta de las Maravillas**, a spectacular cave of stalagmites and stalactites, underwater lakes and cavernous natural chambers. On the hill above the cave stand the ruins of a **Moorish castle**, once occupied by the Knights Templar, and the church of **Nuestra Señora de los Dolores**, a fine medieval church with a Mudejár tower. Twelve km away to the west on the bumpy H521 is the extremely pretty village of **Alájar**, worth a visit for its natural caves, the *Sillita del Rey* and *Salón de los Machos*; and also the **Hermitage of Nuestra Señora de los Angeles**, with a 13th-century Gothic carving, and wonderful views. From this point you can look down on the mining lands of **Rio Tinto**, excavated as early as Phoenician and Roman times, and bought by a British company in the late 19th century.

Perhaps the best of these villages is the white village of **Almonaster la Real**, in an attractive rural setting, with the remains of a 1000-year-old **mosque**. Nearby **Cortegana** has the 16th-century church of **Divino Salvador**, with three handsome wrought-iron pulpits, and the inevitable ruins of a medieval castle. In **Aroche**, further west, the white houses bask in the sun under the remains of an Almoravid fortress, containing a bullring. There's a small municipal **archaeological museum** and the tiny, unbelievable **Museo del Rosario**—yes, a rosary bead museum. On your way back to Huelva from here, you can stop in **Jabugo** to try the best known and best tasting cured ham in Spain, and don't dare say otherwise. Heading back to Huelva on the N435, **Valverde del Camino** is notable only for its furniture and shoe industries.

WHERE TO STAY (tel prefix 955)
To be honest, there's little to detain you in Huelva for longer than one night, but there's a reasonable selection. The **Luz Huelva****** is out on the Alameda Sundheim near the Columbus monument, with pool, tennis courts and air-conditioned rooms (11,000 pts; tel 25 00 11). The **Tartessos***** is comfortable and in the centre (Martín Alonso Pinzón 13, tel 24 56 11; 7000–8000 pts). **San Miguel**** (Santa María 6, tel 24 52 03) has decent rooms for 3500 pts, and at the bottom of the scale **Paris*** (Rico 6, tel 24 88 16) and **Ruiz*** (Vázquez López 26, tel 24 72 39) both have rooms for 2000–3000, but don't expect any home comforts. In the middle of the Sierra Morena on the road to Portugal, 6 km (3.6 miles) from Aracena, is a grand guesthouse run by a charming English family; lunch is served beside the spring-fed pool. Ring in advance. **Buen Vino**, Los Marines, Huelva, tel 12 40 34. Otherwise, accommodation north of Huelva is limited to simple *hostales*. Aracena has the most comfortable rooms at the modern **Sierra de Aracena****

(Gran Via 21, tel 11 07 75; 4000–4500 pts doubles with bath) and **Sierpes**** (Mesones 19, tel 11 01 47; 3200 pts with bath). In Almonaster la Real **La Cruz*** has doubles for 3500 pts (Los Llanos 8, tel 13 04 35). Jabugo has only **La Aurora*** (Barco 9, tel 12 11 46; 2800 pts).

EATING OUT

Huelva packs some surprises in the culinary department; its markets keep the restaurants well supplied with gleaming fresh seafood and Huelvans like to eat out. For perfectly prepared seafood at affordable prices, head out to **Las Candelas**, Ctra. Punta Umbria at the Aljaraque crossing (tel 31 83 01; closed Sun, 1500 pts). Traditionally the best place in town is **Los Gordos**, Carmen 14, where they concentrate on simple dishes such as shellfish soup and grilled red mullet, but there's also a good selection of meats (tel 24 62 66; closed Sat eve and Sun, 2000 pts). A friendly restaurant that locals claim never disappoints, the **Doñana**, is under the Tartessos Hotel; although better known for its seafood platters, it has an excellent range of meat, notably *Chateaubriand* (Av. Martín Pinzón 13, tel 24 27 73; 2000 pts, closed Sun.) In the busy pedestrian heart of the town **El Timon**, Arq. Peréz Carasa 18, is as a good little Spanish restaurant should be, typical both in its decor and menu. A full dinner with starter, mixed fried fish and wine costs 1600 pts (tel 24 66 28), but the real find in Huelva is the plain, family-run bar **Los Gallegos** on the same street, where delicious *tapas* cost a measly 100–150 pts, *raciones* from 300 pts; *pinchitos, gambas ajillo, merluza frita* or *a la plancha, pulpo a la gallega, calamares*—they're all scrumptious.

Again, in the villages to the north there are no real outstanding restaurants, with the exception of Aracena. At the entrance to the caves, **Casas** is a small rustic place that serves mostly Sierra pork and game dishes (2000 pts; Plaza de San Pedro, tel 11 00 44).

South of Huelva

TOURIST INFORMATION

Mazagón: Edif. Mancomunidad Moguer–Palos, tel (955) 37 60 44.

Matalascañas: Urb. Playa de Matalascañas, tel (955) 43 00 86.
Twenty seven kilometres east of Huelva on the N431 you may visit the once-important town of **Niebla**, now forgotten behind its decayed Romano-Moorish walls. There's a Roman bridge and some interesting old churches and Moorish buildings. Christopher Columbus set out on his epic voyage from **Palos de la Frontera**. Some 4 km (2.5 miles) to the west, the **Convento de la Rabida** was Columbus' home while he planned the trip, and the rooms he used are maintained as they were.

Mazagón, further down the coast, is a get-away-from-it-all family resort, surrounded by pine trees and lovely beaches. From here it's a straight shot to Torre de la Higuera, and the big hotel developments around the endless **Matalascañas Beach**, most international of Huelva's resorts. This is the dead end of the coastal highway; the only place you can go is the tiny village of **El Rocío**, which would not even be on the map were it not for the annual *Romería* at Pentecost, the biggest and perhaps the oldest in Spain. Every year hundreds of thousands of pilgrims bring their families for a few days of music and merry-making in the fields; it is traditional to arrive in a horse-drawn, covered wagon, decorated with flowers and streamers. Campfires burn all night, and the atmosphere is pure electricity.

Las Marismas

Add the water of the broad Guadalquivir to this flat coastal plain, and the result is southern Europe's greatest marshland wildlife preserve. Las Marismas is another world, a bit of the Everglades in a country better known for dry heated mountains. Hundreds of species of migratory birds pass through in the spring and autumn—storks among them—but the Marismas have a fantastically varied population of their own: rare golden eagles, snowy egrets, flamingoes, griffin vultures, tortoises, red deer, foxes and European lynx.

As in the Everglades, wildlife congregates around 'islands' among the wetlands; here they're called *corrales*, built of patches of dune anchored by surrounding shrubs and stands of low pines. Also like the Everglades, Las Marismas is threatened by development, from the growing resorts like Matalascañas. This has become Spain's top environmental concern, and the government has limited coastal development and also set aside a large slice of the area as the **Parque Nacional de la Coto Doñana**.

For visitors, the park conducts tours by Land Rover from a station about half-way between El Rocío and Matalascañas; check with the tourist offices in Huelva or Sevilla for details before you go. Keep in mind that the wetlands are largely dried up in the summer. Whenever you come, bring a few gallons of mosquito repellent and watch out for quicksand.

WHERE TO STAY (tel prefix 955)
In an attractive pine-tree setting and looking down onto Mazagón beach, the **Parador Cristobal Colón***** is the best option, with pleasant gardens, pool and air-conditioned rooms (8000–11,000 pts; Ctra Mazagón–Moguer, tel 37 60 00). There are a number of resort hotels at Matalascañas, predictably packed in high season. **El Cortijo**** is a pleasant alternative next to Coto Doñana and a 5-minute walk from the beach and there are facilities for horse-riding (suites 7500 pts, doubles 5000 pts; Parcelas 15/46, Ctra del Norte, tel 43 02 59).

EATING OUT
Mazagón hasn't a great choice , but try **El Faro** for a few unusual dishes such as broad beans with cuttlefish, and pigs' trotters (Av Fuente Piña 61, tel 37 61 77; 1500 pts; open weekends only out of season). Many people eat in their hotels down on Matalascañas Beach. **Da Pino** is a pricey Italian restaurant but the food is good, with pastas, excellent salads and good steaks (Av Adelfas 1, tel 43 02 03; 2500 pts, closed Mon and Christmas). **Los Galanes**, in the Edificio Las Begoñas, has a lovely terrace where you can enjoy your seafood at leisure (1500 pts).

Sanlúcar and Rota

Like those to the east, the beaches around Cádiz are popular mostly with Spaniards— more crowded, though, at least in July and August. Just the same, the beaches are lovely

96

and huge, the towns behind them relatively unspoiled; there may be few better places in Spain to baste yourself, with plenty of opportunities for exploring *bodegas*.

TOURIST INFORMATION

Sanlúcar de Barrameda: Calzada del Ejército s/n, tel (956) 36 61 10.
Rota: Plaza de Andalucía 3, tel (956) 81 01 00.
Puerto de Santa María: C. Guadalete, tel (956) 85 75 45.

Sanlúcar de Barrameda makes *manzanilla*, most ethereal of sherries. It is known as the port that launched Magellan on his way around the world, and Columbus on his second voyage to the Indies; and is the birthplace of the artist Pacheco, Velázquez's teacher. The town has a certain crumbling colonial charm and an exceptionally pretty main plaza. Worth a visit are the church of **Nuestra Señora de la O**, with its fine Mudejár portal and 16th-century coffered ceiling, and the 19th-century **Montpensier Palace**, with an extensive library and paintings by Murillo, El Greco, Rubens and Goya. Although its beaches are not major-league, this town has always been a popular summer destination with Spanish holidaymakers for its excellent cheap seafood. The Bajo de Guía is a particularly charming and run-down fishing district, and from here you can take the motor boat over to Coto Doñana. If you have an afternoon to spare, amuse yourself by visiting the public fish auction in **Bonanza**, 4 km away. **Chipiona** is a family resort, full of small pensions and *hostales*, with a good beach at **Playa de Regla** near the lighthouse. Next, on the edge of the bay of Cádiz, comes **Rota**, a bigger, flashier resort taking advantage of the best and longest beach on the coast; the town is pretty, though it's a bit overbuilt. It's also full of unpicturesque Americans from the largest naval base in the region, just outside town. This was the key base Franco gave up in the 1953 deal with President Eisenhower; in the recent dealings over the future of Spain's role in NATO, the Americans made it unpleasantly clear this base is not a subject of negotiations, although in the 1986 NATO referendum this region turned out the highest 'yes' vote in Spain.

Puerto de Santa María

Across the bay from Cádiz lies the traditional port of the sherry houses in Jerez, which has quite a few *bodegas* of its own—Osborne, Terry and Duff Gordon among other famous names. The town has some interesting churches, mansions of the Anglo-Spanish sherry aristocracy, and the fine, restored 13th-century Mudejár **Castle of San Marcos**. The century-old **bullring** ranks with those of Sevilla and Ronda in prestige. Puerto itself isn't a big resort, but it's a typical town of Cádiz province, with bright bustling streets, and some good beaches (**Puntilla** especially) on the edges of town.

WHERE TO STAY   (tel prefix 956)

It's no problem finding a place in any of the coastal resorts: especially in the high season, little old ladies meet the buses to drag you off to their *hostales*.

The loveliest and most unusual place to stay in Sanlúcar is the old house of **Medina Sedonia**, once the building from which the collecting of taxes on river traffic was organised. The palace is austere but comfortable; beautifully decorated and elegant, with wood-beamed ceilings and brightly painted rooms (4500 pts; Palace of Medina Sedonia, tel 36 01 61).

Other places worth mentioning are the **Andalucía***, in Sanlúcar (González Montero 8, tel 36 01 40; doubles, 3600 pts with bath), and the **Paquito*** in Chipiona (Francisco Lara 26, tel 37 02 06; doubles 3000 pts—no bath). Both are decent *hostales* near the beaches—but really typical of what you'll find in these modest resorts. **Del Sur**** in Chipiona is fancier, with a pool and garden, and still a bargain at the price (Avda. Sevilla 2, tel 37 03 50; doubles 5500 pts). Rota is more of the same, but has a few classy modern resort hotels: **Playa de la Luz**** is on the beach at Arroyo Hondo, a sports-oriented hotel with a lovely pool and gardens (tel 81 05 00; doubles 9000 pts). One place many people like in Puerto is the **Puertobahia****, also on the beach (Av. de La Paz 38, Urb. Valdelagrana, tel 86 27 21; doubles 8000 pts).

EATING OUT
Most of the restaurants in this area are open only during the summer; informal cafés where you can pick out the fish that catches your fancy. Famous throughout Andalucía, is **Casa Bigote** in Sanlúcar (at Bajo de Guía, tel 36 26 96) and rightly so; it serves delicious appetisers, classic dishes of the region, and the best and freshest of seafood in all its varieties; the crayfish are a must, and you can try the local *manzanilla* with the day's catch. You may find you'll need more than one visit, though, as the *tapas* selection is extensive and truly excellent. Get there early or you won't find a table (2000–3000 pts; closed Sun). Down on the beach front, Casa Bigote's main rival is the attractive **Mirador de Doñana**, a very popular restaurant on three levels with a panoramic view across to the bird reserve. Particularly delicious are: *cigalas* (crayfish), *angulas* (baby eels) and *Nido de rapé a la Sanluqueña*, a nest of straw potato chips, deep-fried with monkfish and parsley (2,500 pts; Bajo de Guía, tel 36 42 05). In Rota the cuisine is heavily influenced by the presence of the naval base—pizza and Chinese restaurants alongside the usual seafood. Apart from the excellent *bodegas* and simple beach cafés, Puerto has some deservedly popular restaurants. The most successful is **La Goleta** (Ctra Rota, tel 85 42 32), with simple but well-prepared seafood dishes, especially the fish cooked in salt, the *tosta de salmón* and the *porgy* in brandy (3000 pts; closed Mon and first two weeks in Nov). Down on the riverside quay, the reasonably priced menu at **Guadalete** attracts the crowds for its shrimps, sole and clams (2000 pts; Av. Bajamar 14, tel 86 02 98).

Jerez de la Frontera

The name is synonymous with wine—by the English corruption of Jerez into sherry—but besides the *finos*, *amontillados*, *olorosos* and other varieties of that noble sauce, Jerez also ships out much of Spain's equally good brandy. Most of the well-known companies, whose advertising is plastered all over Spain, have their headquarters here, and they're quite accustomed to taking visitors—especially English ones—through the *bodegas*. Don't be shy. Most are open to visitors 9–1 Monday–Saturday—but not in August, or when they're busy with the *vendimia* (harvest) in September.

Business is good, and Jerez is growing. Though not an attractive town, it has a few lovely buildings for you to squint at after you've done the rounds of the *bodegas*.

One of the most interesting *bodegas* to visit is that belonging to Gonzalez Byass. The tour includes the old sawdust-strewn *bodegas* that have held the sherry *soleras* for two centuries; the casks have been signed by many famous visitors over the years. The tour ends at the *degustacíon*, where the motto is, 'If you don't have a *copa* at eleven o'clock, you should have eleven at one', and cellarmen demonstrate their skill at pouring sherry from distances of a metre or more into the small *copitas*, in order to aerate the wine.

The Semana Santa (Holy Week) festival in Jerez is more intimate, but just as splendid as that in Sevilla. The nightly processions escorting the Saint and Madonna images create a city-wide pageant. Late in the night, as they return home through the back streets, they are serenaded by impromptu solo voices; for the finest singers, the whole procession halts in appreciation.

GETTING AROUND (tel prefix 956)

Cádiz is the base for visiting Jerez and the coasts. There is a regular bus service (Amarillo company) from Cádiz to all the coastal towns, and at least five daily to Jerez. Infrequent buses connect Jerez with Rota, Sanlúcar and Puerto. Almost all the Sevilla–Cádiz buses stop in Jerez and Puerto as do the trains. Frequent connections for Arcos de la Frontera and Ronda. One bus a day to Córdoba and Granada. Jerez stations for buses and trains are together on the eastern edge of town (tel 33 66 82). There's a regular ferry service from Puerto to Cádiz—more fun than the bus.

TOURIST INFORMATION

Alameda Cristina s/n, tel (956) 33 11 50/33 11 62. Check here for information on visiting the sherry *bodegas*.

La Colegiata (also called San Salvador), Jerez's landmark, is a curious pseudo-Gothic church with a separate bell-tower and Baroque staircase; though begun in the 13th century, its façade, largely the work of Vincente Acero, was not completed until 1750. Works inside include a Madonna by Zurbarán and sculptures by Juan de Mesa. Nearby, on the central Plaza de los Reyes Católicos, **San Miguel** (begun 1482) changes the scene to Isabelline Gothic—a fine example of that style, with a florid retablo inside. The 1575 **Ayuntamiento** is a lovely building that also houses a small archaeology museum. There is a Moorish **Alcazar** at the end of Calle Pérez Galdos, with a tower and some remains of the baths. Outside town, on the road to Medina Sidonia, is the **Cartuja de la Defensión**, a 15th-century monastery with the best Baroque façade (added in 1667) in Andalucía—a sort of giant retablo with sculptures by Alonso Cano and others. This is still a working monastery, and you'll need special permission to go inside. There is little reason to; the main attraction, a great altarpiece by Zurbarán, is scattered to the four winds—you can see panels in the museums of Sevilla and Cádiz.

Horses, Flamenco and Racing Cars

While in Jerez, look out for exhibitions scheduled at the **Escuela Andaluz del Arte Ecuestre** (School of Equestrian Art). Jerez's snooty wine aristocracy takes horsemanship very seriously; they have some of the finest horses you're likely to see anywhere, and they know how to use them. You can see them, proud as Tío Pepe bottles, at the annual **Horse Fair** during the first half of May. The origin of this fair can be traced back to the 13th century, and its events include jumping, classical riding, harness and Andalucían country riding. Being Andalucían, it is also the best excuse for attending the *corrida*, drinking plenty of sherry and of course joining in the *flamenco* extravaganza.

Another attraction is the recently opened **Museum of Flamenco-Flamencology**, a science you can delve into at Calle Quintos 1. Housed in one of the most beautiful buildings of the old part of the city, the Flamenco Foundation presents different kinds of activities throughout the year: concerts, exhibitions, seminars and video shows, in an effort to promote and prolong the art. Open Mon–Fri 10–2.

WHERE TO STAY   (tel prefix 956)
In Jerez, there are many unremarkable hotels. The two top hotels are close to the centre of town and provide convenient access to the fair and the Spanish Riding School. The luxury **Jerez*****, with a pool and tennis courts, is set in lovely tropical gardens, but is no bargain (23,000 pts; Avda Alvaro Domecq 35, tel 33 06 00). On the same avenue, but closer to town, the modern **Royal Sherry Park**** is surrounded by a park, and also has a pool (20,000 pts; Avda Alvaro Domecq 11 bis, tel 30 30 11). Almost opposite is the more affordable **Avenida Jerez***, a rather characterless modern place (9000 pts; Avda Alvaro Domecq 10, tel 34 74 11).

In the centre of town, with underground parking, the **Serit** has comfy rooms for 8000 pts (Higueras 7, tel 34 07 00). **Virt** (Higueras 20, tel 32 28 11) is a middle-range bargain with decent air-conditioned rooms with bath for 5500 pts.

There's a decent selection down the lower end of the price scale: **Las Palomas***, at 2600 pts (Higueras 17, tel 34 37 73); and **San Andrés*** (Morenos 12, tel 34 09 83), and **Sanvi*** (Morenos 10, tel 34 56 24), both with basic rooms for about 2000 pts.

EATING OUT
Jerez boasts one of Andalucía's loveliest restaurants, **El Bosque**, beautifully situated in the woods near the Parque González Montoria, yet only a short distance from the centre of town. The seafood is top-class; try *langostinos de Sanlúcar, gambas de Huelva*, hake cooked in salt, angler fish in shellfish sauce (3500 pts; Avda Alvaro Domecq 26, tel 30 33 33/30 70 30; closed Sun). Closer to town, by the bullring the **Tendido 6** (Circo 10, tel 34 48 35) has a covered patio with adjoining dining room, decorated on a *feria* theme, with bullfight memorabilia on the walls. Here the emphasis is on robust helpings of traditional food, and you can gorge to the full for 2000 pts (closed Sun eve, all day Sun in winter). A couple of streets behind the tourist office is one of the favourite dining places in town, **Gaitan** (Gaitan 3, tel 34 58 59), proud bearer of a gastronomy award in the 80s (2500 pts; closed Sun eve and first two weeks of Aug). Near the Avenida Jerez hotel, **La Mesa Redonda** is beautifully decorated with antique furniture and paintings, giving the impression of an old aristocratic Jerez home. It's home cooking here—sole with mushrooms, game dishes and fresh salads (2000–2500 pts; Manuel de la Quintana 3, tel 34 00 69; closed Sun and Aug). Naturally there are many street *bodegas* where you can try the whole spectrum of the area's produce. Try the **Alcazaba** (Medina 19) or **La Tasca** (C. Matadero s/n), both near the centre.

CÁDIZ

If Cádiz were a tiny village, the government would immediately declare it a National Monument and put up a sign. It's a big, busy seaport, though, and the tourist business generally leaves it alone. It's a pity, for Cádiz (if you pronounce it any other way but 'Caddy' no one will understand you) is one of the most distinctive Spanish cities, worth spending a few days in even if there are few 'sights'. The city is a small peninsula, resembling a sturdy galleon patiently waiting to put to sea, packed tightly and pounded by the rough Atlantic breakers on all sides. It comes in colours—a hundred shades of off-white, bleached and faded by sun and spray into a soft patina, broken only by the golden dome of a rambling Baroque cathedral that would be a civic misfortune anywhere else, but seems inexplicably beautiful here.

History

Cádiz modestly claims to be the oldest city in Western Europe. It's hard to argue; the Phoenician city of *Gadir* has a documented foundation of 1100 BC, and while other cities have traces of older settlements, it would be difficult to find another city west of Greece with a continuous urban life of 3000 years. Gadir served as the port for shipping Spanish copper and tin, and was undoubtedly the station for the now-forgotten Phoenician trade routes with west Africa and England—and possibly even for explorations to America. Cádiz, however, prefers to consider Hercules its founder, and he appears on the arms of the city between his famous pillars.

Under Roman rule, **Gades** as it was called, was a favoured city, especially under Julius Caesar who held his first public office here. The city was out of the spotlight until the 16th century, when the American trade and Spain's growth as a naval power made a major port of it once again. Sir Francis Drake came here to 'singe the King of Spain's beard' in 1587, and later British admirals followed the custom for a century, calling every decade or so for a fish dinner and an afternoon's sacking and burning. The years after 1720 when Cádiz controlled the American market shaped its present character. Street names like Calle Conde O'Reilly (an Irish-born royal governor who did a lot for Cádiz) and a statue of one José MacPherson y Hemas testify to the contacts the city enjoyed with the outside world—uniquely so for Spain in those dark years—and it became the most liberal and tolerant corner of Spain. Its shining hour came in 1812, when the Constitution was declared here, and the city became the capital of free Spain.

The Best Carnival in Spain

This took its present form in the 19th century; some claim there is a strong Cuban influence behind its masquerades and crazy music. It says something about Cádiz that under the dictatorship, theirs was the only carnival Franco failed to suppress, and if you ever experience it you'll know why. In the second week of February, if there were an instrument to measure atmosphere, it would glow red here; everyone, young or old, native or stranger, is roaming the streets, singing and dancing. Small food stalls spring up on every corner, and the bars, cafés and restaurants have a hard time keeping up with the constant flow of revellers.

GETTING AROUND

Cádiz isn't the big passenger port it used to be, but you can still take the weekly ferries to Almería, Genoa, Italy, Tenerife–Las Palmas–Arrecife in the Canary Islands, or to Palma de Mallorca with various stops along the way. They run a little more frequently in the summer. For all of them, see the Transmediterránea office on Av. Ramón de Carranza 26, tel (956) 28 41 62 or 28 41 63. There's also a regular ferry ride from the port to Puerto Santa María.

By train you can go only to Jerez (18 daily) and Sevilla (five) directly. The station is at the narrow landward end of the old city; just a few blocks from the Pl. San Juan de Dios (tel 23 43 01). Cádiz is served by two bus companies: Los Amarillos takes the route west to Rota and Sanlúcar de Barrameda (Av. Ramón de Carranza 31, tel 28 58 52 by the port) and Comes runs east to Tarifa and Algeciras (their terminal is on the Pl. de España). City bus 1 will take you from the Plaza de España to Cádiz's suburban beaches.

TOURIST INFORMATION
Pl. de Mina, C. Calderón de la Barca 1, tel (956) 21 13 13.

The approach to Cádiz is a dismal one, through marshes and salt pans cluttered with power lines and industrial junk. After this, you must pass through a long, narrow strip of land full of modern suburbs before arriving at the **Puerta de Tierra**, entrance to the old city on the peninsula. Almost everything about warfare in the 18th century had a certain decorum to it, and Cádiz's gates and formidable **land walls** (1757), all well-preserved, are among the most aesthetically pleasing structures in town.

It's a great city for exploring—streets as narrow as Toledo's, neither decaying nor prettified for the tourists. The old city lies behind the **Tierra** gate, its maze of lanes bathed in soft lamplight after dusk, when the numerous cafés fill up with young, exuberant *Gaditanos*. A walk through the myriad of cobbled streets, past solid doors carved from the trees of South American forests, and balconies spilling over with flowers, will take you back in history to the time when mighty Cádiz bustled with industry as the gateway to the Americas. Keep an eye out for the little plaques—for the birthplace of Manuel de Falla, of Miranda, the first president of Venezuela, and others—reminders of what an important role this little city has often played. Note the houses, too, in a style unique to Cádiz, with roof-terraces and little Moorish-looking turrets, from which the *Gaditanos* watch for ships coming in. In an hour or so you can walk entirely around Cádiz, on the coast road past parks like the pretty **Alameda de Apodaca**, and forts and bastions of the 18th century.

The Cathedral
From the Puerta de Tierra, the Cuesta de las Calesas leads down to the port and rail station, then around the corner to **Plaza San Juan de Dios**, the lively, palm-shaded centre of Cádiz, with most of the restaurants and hotels on the surrounding streets. Two blocks away is the **Cathedral**, on a small plaza. A recent thorough restoration of this ungainly bulk has not destroyed its ingratiating charm. It was begun in 1722, at the height of Cádiz's prosperity. Funds soon started running short, sadly enough; if original architect Vincente Acero had had his way, he might have made this as fanciful a work as his Cathedral in Guadix. Of the paintings within, Zurbarán's *Santa Ursula* stands out. The composer Manuel de Falla has his tomb in the cathedral crypt (open weekdays 5.30–7.30, Sat 9.30–10.30 am and 5.30–8, Sun 11–1). The **Museo de la Catedral** has a lot of religious gold and silverware, paintings by Murillo, Zurbarán, Alejo Fernández and painted panels and an ivory crucifix by Alonso Cano (open daily except Sun, 10–1). Continuing eastwards, the Plaza Topete was named for a *tophet*, the Phoenician temple

dedicated to that nasty habit of theirs—sacrificing first-born babies; remains of one were found here. Now this is Cádiz's almost excessively colourful **market district**, spread around a wonderful, dilapidated old market building.

The Constitution of 1812

A few more blocks east, the little church of **San Felipe Neri** on Calle Sacramonte is an unprepossessing shrine to the beginnings of Spanish liberty. On 29 March 1812, an assemblage of refugees from Napoleon's occupation of the rest of Spain gathered here and declared Spain an independent republic, guaranteeing full political and religious freedom. Though their Constitution, and their revolution, proved stillborn, it was a notable beginning for Spain's struggle towards democracy. Big marble plaques, sent as tributes, cover the church's façade. Inside is a beautiful *Immaculate Conception* by Murillo (open 12–2 and 5–7).

Around the corner, Cádiz's very good **Municipal Museum** has a huge Romantic-era mural depicting the event. In front of it, in the main hall, is the museum's star exhibit, a 15.4 m (50 ft) **scale model of Cádiz**, made entirely of mahogany and ivory by an unknown obsessive in 1779. Nearly every building is detailed—Cádiz hasn't changed much since. Among a collection of portraits of Spanish heroes is the Duke of Wellington, who in Spain carried the title of Duke of Ciudad Rodrigo. The best picture, though, also from that era, shows Hercules about to give Napoleon a good bashing with his club (open daily except Mon, 9–1 and 4–7, Sat and Sun 9–1).

Plaza de Mina

On this lovely square, in the northwestern corner of the peninsula, you'll find the **Tourist Information Office** and the **Museum of Fine Arts and Archaeology** (open daily except Monday, 9–2, 5–8). The museum has recently undergone a complete reconstruction; the archaeology section contains a Phoenician sarcophagus, Phoenician jewellery, Roman pottery and Greek ceramics; among the statues there's a dumb-looking Emperor Trajan with a big Roman nose. But best in the museum are the paintings: some Murillos and very good portraits of the Four Evangelists and John the Baptist by Zurbarán. On the top floor are unaffectedly charming puppets and stage sets from a Cádiz genre of marionette show called *Tía Norica*, still performed in these parts.

Around the corner, on Calle Rosario Ponce, the **Oratorio de la Santa Cueva**, with its three Goya frescoes (the only ones in Andalucía) has irregular opening times, but generally is safe to visit 10–1.

WHERE TO STAY   (tel prefix 956)

There is a good Parador in Cádiz, The **Atlántico***** (Parque Genovés 9, tel 22 69 05). It is a modern building with wonderful views over the Atlantic and a large outdoor swimming pool (14,000 pts for a double). The **Francia y Paris** *** is a quiet, elegant well-run hotel around the corner from Plaza Mina at a very reasonable 6500 pts for a double (Plaza San Francisco 2, tel 22 23 48). Nearby, the **Imares*** has comfortable rooms for 2600–4000 pts, depending on the plumbing (San Francisco 9, tel 21 22 57).

There will be no problem finding cheaper—lots of sailors pass through here. The **Hostal Manolíta*** (Benjumeda 2, tel 21 15 77), is clean and family-run and has doubles for around 2500 pts. For even cheaper establishments just look for the 'Camas' signs and take your pick. Don't hesitate to turn down anything that appears too run-down; some places appear as if they haven't had visitors for decades.

On the other side of the Tierra gate, in the new part of Cádiz, there's just as much choice. The Paseo Marítimo is lively, so don't feel you're missing out if you stay here. The **Isecotel***** (Avda Amilcar Barca 35, tel 25 54 01) is the best and sits directly over the popular Victoria Beach, slap in the middle of all the irresistible *tapas* bars, pubs and discos (7000–9000 pts). In the mid-range bracket, **San Remo**** has doubles for 5500–7500 pts with bath, and the rooms are adequately comfortable and overlook the beach (Paseo Marítimo 3, tel 25 22 02). In a side street off the Paseo is the more reasonable **La Playa***, with rooms going for 5500 pts with bath, about 3000 pts without (Dr. Herrera Quevedo 1, tel 25 84 00).

EATING OUT
Dining, of course, means more fish. **El Faro**, at C. San Felix 15, is a place that takes it seriously, where you can get to know all of the amazingly wide range of seafood—things that we don't even have names for in English like *mojarras* and *urtas*—that come out of this part of the Atlantic, but apart from these outlandish creatures you'll have no problem ordering the more recognizable varieties—steamed hake with asparagus, clams with spinach, fried fish *a la Gaditana*, as well as a selection of meat dishes (full-course dinners 2500 pts; tel 21 25 01). **El Anteojo** is by the Alameda Apodaca walls, and its rustically decorated upstairs dining room looks over to Puerto de Santa María. The menu is a mix of Cádiz, Galician and Basque kitchens (Alameda Apodaca 22, tel 21 36 39; 2500–3500 pts). A little further along, on the corner of Honduras and San German, the family-run **La Piconera** is a less expensive choice with a simpler, yet nonetheless wholesome menu (around 1500 pts; C. San German 5, tel 22 18 84)—but you don't get the view. **El Sardinero**, Plaza San Juan de Dios 4, is one of the oldest restaurants in the city, with a variety of Basque and Andaluz dishes, which you can enjoy at the outside tables (about 2000 pts; tel 28 25 05).

In newer Cádiz, along the Paseo Marítimo, there's a wide choice of restaurants, nearly all with terraces or outside seating. **Curro el Cojo** specializes in meats from the Sierra, pork and game in particular (full dinner 2500 pts; Paseo Marítimo 2, tel 25 31 86). **La Costera**, a few steps along and around the corner (C. Dr. Fleming 8, tel 27 34 88), specializes in fish and also has a good wine list, and dining on the terrace. Two smaller restaurants nearby are **Noray** and **Baro**, both predictably specializing in shellfish (2000 pts). The *tapas* bar **Savoy**, along from Curro's, is popular with the young crowd in the afternoon. Behind the sea front, (at Av. José León de Carranza 4, tel 25 77 59) **El Brocal** is a small restaurant serving meat with a North African and Greek bias (2000–2500 pts; closed Sun, Mon lunch and Nov).

From Cádiz to Algeciras

The green, hilly countryside of this region looks a lot like the parts of Morocco just across the Straits; the hills force the main road away from the sea, leaving a few villages with fine beaches relatively unspoilt and good places to take time out from your overactive holiday; the problem is they're hard to reach unless you have a car.

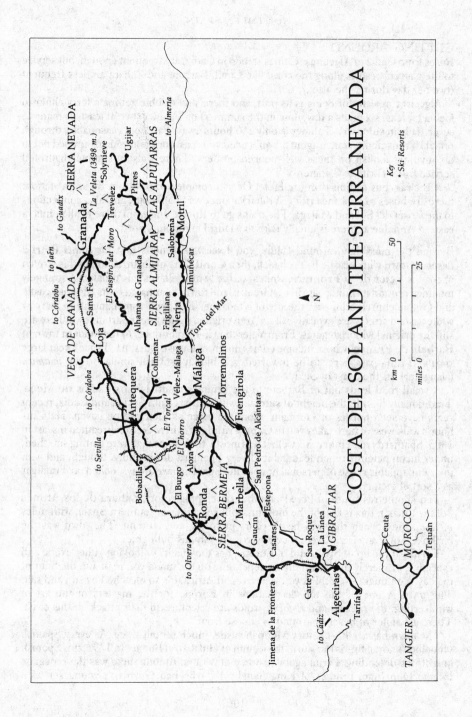

COSTA DEL SOL AND THE SIERRA NEVADA

Key
* Ski Resorts

km 0   25   50

miles 0

GETTING AROUND

Buses from Cádiz to Algeciras (Comes station in Cádiz) are frequent enough, but service to the nascent resorts along the coast like Conil, Barbate and Zahara are less frequent (two per day during the week).

Algeciras' reason for being is its port, and there's no trouble getting a ferry either to Ceuta (at least six boats a day, nine in the summer) or Tangier (two at least, as many as seven daily in summer). Tangier is only 2½ hours away. Fares are reasonable, through official Transmediterránea agents. You'll need your passport, and you are advised not to do anything foolish on these well-policed borders. There's also a summer hydrofoil service from Tarifa to Tangier.

Algeciras' bus station is in the Hotel Octavo complex across from the train station; there are buses to La Línea (for Gibraltar) about every half-hour, and also connections to the Costa del Sol and Málaga. The trains go to Ronda, and from there to all points in eastern Andalucía; there is a daily *talgo* to Madrid and points north.

Beyond the marshland around Cádiz, you'll see the turnoffs first for **Santi Petri** a deserted town with a castle by the beach, then **Conil**. The main attraction of this stretch of road is **Vejer de la Frontera**, whitest of the 'white villages' of Andalucía, strangely moulded around its hilltop site like a Greek island town, dominated by its Moorish castle and Gothic church built over the site of a mosque. The town's spanking clean, narrow whitewashed streets are evocative of its Arab origins. In the upper part of town there are still the original Moorish gates. From Vejer the C343 goes down to the modern town of **Barbate de Franco**, whose income comes not from tourists but tuna. Twice a year large shoals of tuna pass here, to be thwarted in a bloody ambush similar to the *matanza* (slaughter) off the coast of Sicily.

A small road leads out of Barbate to the summer resort of **Los Caños de Meca**. Traditionally busy in the height of summer with tourists from Sevilla and Cádiz, recent years have seen hordes of Germans adopt the place as their escape haven. Half-an-hour's walk west of here takes you to **Cape Trafalgar**, where Nelson breathed his last in 1805. Spaniards remember this well; it was mostly their ships that were getting smashed, under incompetent French leadership. Every Spaniard did his duty, though, and with their unflappable sense of personal honour the Spanish have always looked on Trafalgar as a sort of victory.

Ten kilometres south of here is another developing resort, **Zahara de los Atunes** ('of the tunas'); this is one of the most unspoilt coastlines in southern Spain, with miles of fine sandy beach that will be all yours in spring and autumn. The town was the birthplace of Francisco Rivera, or Paquirri, the famous bullfighter.

Tarifa, at the tip of Spain and of Europe, has the quality of looking either exotic and evocative, or merely dusty and drear, depending on the mood you're in and the hour of the day. You might even think you've arrived in Africa, it's so bleached by sun and salt. The town is one of the top destinations in Europe for the masters of the art of windsurfing; the *Levante* and *Poniente* winds are relentless in their attack on this coast. There are miles of beaches around to choose from.

The town has a 10th-century Moorish castle, much rebuilt since. As every Spanish schoolboy knows, this is the site of the legend of Guzman el Bueno. In 1292, this Spanish knight was defending Tarifa against a force of Moors. Among them was the renegade Infante Don Juan, brother of King Sancho IV, who had Guzman's young son as a prisoner, and threatened to kill him if Guzman did not surrender. Guzman's response was to toss him a dagger. His son was killed, but Tarifa did not fall; Fascist propaganda recycled this legend for the 1936 siege of the Alcazar in Toledo, with the Republicans in the villain's role. Outside Tarifa, along the beaches east of the town, there are ruins of a once sizeable Roman town, **Bolonia**, parts of which are currently undergoing restoration (visit by guided tour).

Algeciras

Ask at the tourist office what there is to see and you'll be told 'Nothing. Nobody ever stays here'. Nevertheless Algeciras has an interesting history, and an attractive setting opposite the Rock of Gibraltar. It played a significant role in the colonization of the eastern Mediterranean, becoming an important port in the Roman era. From AD 713 on, it was occupied by the Moors, and its name derives from the Arabic 'Al Djezirah al Hadra' (Green Island). Today, apart from its importance as a port with regular connections to Ceuta, Tangier and the Canary Islands, Algeciras is a sizeable industrial and fishing centre.

TOURIST INFORMATION
By the port, Juan de la Cierva s/n, tel (956) 60 09 11.

The bustling, seedy port area has little attraction for the visitor, although the small bazaars in the side streets, selling Moroccan leather goods, may whet your appetite for a trip across the straits—you can see Morocco's jagged, surreal peaks all along the coastal highway. It is also the centre of one of the busiest drug-smuggling routes in the world, and every stevedore and cab driver will be whispering little propositions in your ear if you look the type.

Inland, lying in a pleasantly wooded area is **Los Barrios**, settled by refugees when Gibraltar was lost to the British; archaeological finds indicate that it was inhabited from earliest times. The parish church of **San Isidro** dates from the 18th century. There are two fairly decent beaches nearby—Guadarranque and Palmones.

On the N340 heading north, the road passes **San Roque**, with exceptional views over the bay of Algeciras and Gibraltar. Here are the ruins of *Carteya*, the first Roman settlement in the south of the peninsula. The 18th-century parish church of **Santa María Coronada** was built above the ancient hermitage of San Roque, and is worth a visit. This pretty little town is a welcome relief after the more sordid quarters of Algeciras, and an added bonus are the nearby clean beaches of Puente Mayorga, Los Portichuelos and Carteya.

Ceuta

The ferry here takes only 1¹/₂ hours, and leaves you in one of Spain's two remaining enclaves on the North African coast. Every time the Spanish make self-righteous noises about getting Gibraltar back, someone reminds them of these two colonial leftovers. Morocco's King Hussein (a good friend of Juan Carlos) mentions them every year in his New Year's speech. Lately Colonel Gaddafi has also been heard from on the issue. Ceuta has a mainly Spanish population; that is why it was excluded from the 1955 withdrawal from the Spanish Moroccan protectorate. They are the stumbling-block, and some way will have to be found to accommodate them before the inevitable transfer of sovereignty.

TOURIST INFORMATION
Muelle Cañonero Dato 1, tel (956) 51 13 79.

Ceuta is a pleasant enough town, but there's little reason to go there: only the impressive 16th-century **walls** and moat, and a **museum** dedicated to Spain's Foreign Legion (a band of cut-throats who became notorious during the Civil War under a one-armed, one-eyed commander named Millán Astray; their slogan: 'Long live Death'). Like Andorra on the other end of Spain, Ceuta is a big duty-free supermarket. You can easily cross into Morocco from here, though it's better to take the ferry straight to Tangier.

WHERE TO STAY
(tel prefix 956)

In Tarifa, the recently 'discovered' resort along this coast, rooms are surprisingly and unnecessarily expensive; the same is true of Conil. The **Balcon de España*** is one of the better options, situated in a pretty spot by the Playa de los Lances between Tarifa and Punta Paloma to the west of town. It has a pool, tennis courts and horse-riding facilities (5500–7500 pts; Ctra Cádiz-Málaga Km 76, tel 68 43 26; closed Nov–Mar). Further along the coast, windsurfers stay (where else?) at the **Hurricane**, but they pay for the privilege (8000–12,000 pts; Ctra N340 Km 94, tel 68 49 19; closed Jan). Near Zahara de los Atunes, at the Bahía de la Plata, the big resort complex **Atlanterra**** is German-owned and offers a variety of sports and recreational activities (7000–10,000 pts, depending on the season; Urb. Cabo de Plata, tel 43 27 00 or 43 26 09; closed Nov–April).

Alternatively, there are two very popular *hostales*, the **Castro*** on the boulevard near the beach (Dres. Sánchez Rodríguez s/n, tel 43 02 48; 2500–4800 pts) and the **Nicholas**** María Luisa 13, tel 43 11 74; 4000–5000 pts, but both are packed through August.

The hotel of Algeciras' bygone elegance is the **Reina Cristina**** on Paseo Conferencia (all the luxuries for 11,000–14,000 pts; tel 60 26 22) where W. B. Yeats rested one winter. The convenient **Octavio****, borders the bus station and is within a few metres of the train station (C. San Bernardo 1, tel 65 24 61; 10,000 pts). Right on the seafront, above the busy arcades filled with cafés and ticket offices is the **Al Mar*** looking out over the port area (7000–8000 pts; Avda de la Marina 2, tel 65 46 61). Clustered in the back streets of the area behind the Avda de la Marina are a host of convenient little *hostales* in the 2000 pts range.

Finding a place to sleep in Ceuta can be a problem as there are only a few hotels. Within the walls, **La Muralla**** offers the most comfort and luxury, with a pool and gardens (9000–11,000 pts; Plaza Virgen de Africa 15, tel 51 49 40). The **Atlante*** is a good bargain in the middle of town (Pso. de las Palmeras 1, tel 51 35 48; 3600–5500 pts double with bath, 3000–3500 pts without).

EATING OUT
Tarifa: near the Hurricane hotel is one of the best restaurants in the area, in the hotel **Mesón de Sancho**, specializing in home-cooked dishes—favourites are the garlic soup,

bream *provençal, rabo de toro* (2500 pts; Ctra N340 Km 94, tel 68 49 00). In Zahara tourists flock to the beach restaurant **Antonio**, for high-quality fish and seafood (2000 pts; Ctra Atlanterra Km 1, tel 43 12 41). Inevitably, in Caños de Meca there had to be a **Trafalgar**. On the seafront with a pleasant terrace, the menu concentrates on international fare (1600–2200 pts; closed in winter). In Algeciras, just back from the Avda Virgen del Carmen (on the corner of Gomez Ortega and Trafalgar) is the **Marea Baja**, a fashionable restaurant specializing in seafood. Try their *lubina* (sea bass) (3000 pts for a full meal with wine; Trafalgar 2, tel 66 36 54). For a break from salty marine life, you may care to drive out on to the N340 and try some of the grilled meats on offer at **El Bosque**, charmingly situated in the woods at Pelayo 5, Bda. Pelayo (tel 67 91 13; 2000–25000 pts). Back in town, a popular place with working people is **Casa Montes**, where *urta* surfaces again, along with roast kid and poultry (1000 pts; San Juan 16, no tel). If you want to splurge, **El Copo** in Los Barrios is a good place for it. The restaurant serves a wide range of dishes, from delicately prepared fish to *rabo de toro* (bull's tail) and *solomillo* (fillet steak) (3500 pts; Bda. Palmones, tel 65 27 10). The most famous restaurant in the area is **Los Remos**, in an old house surrounded by lovely gardens, on the road out of San Roque to La Línea, at Villa Victoria, but carnivores beware—it serves mostly fish (3000–4000 pts; tel 76 08 12).

The best restaurant in Ceuta is **La Kasba**, serving besides Spanish dishes the requisite North African speciality, *couscous* (3000 pts; General Yague 12, tel 52 10 13). One place to meet the locals (and a strange bunch they are) is the **Restaurant Mar Chica** (Pso. Colón 9, tel 51 39 57) with decent fish dinners from 800 pts up. In Zahara, during the season, the **Bar Marisquería Porfirio** on Plaza Tamron serves excellent seafood.

An Excursion to Morocco

The ferries run regularly enough for you to do this conveniently. If you do it from Ceuta, you'll have to take a cab or city bus (the one marked 'frontera') to the border; after some cacophanous border confusion, you wait for the infrequent bus or carefully negotiate a taxi trip to **Tetuán**, 30 km (18.8 miles) away. Tetuán is a decent town, full of gleaming white, Spanish colonial architecture; it has a famous market in its *medina*, a historical museum, and it's a good place to purchase Moroccan crafts.

Buses (there's no train) to Tangier are cheap and regular, run by a number of companies from the central bus station. They'll take you right to Tangier's port (on the way note how the Moroccans have turned Tangier's old Plaza de Toros into flats). Once in the big square outside the port entrance, you may take your chances with the inexpensive hotels in the surrounding streets, or take a cab to fancier spots in the newer, Europeanized districts. Tangier may not be as romantic as you expect; the wares in the markets of the *medina* are fun to look at, but the quarter itself is down-at-heel and dusty. You may not enter mosques in Morocco, but in the old governor's palace are two fine **museums** of archaeology and Moroccan art.

Unfortunately the real treasures of Morocco are all far to the south—Rabat, Fez, and Meknes—but you can still get quite a good look at Morocco from the admittedly international city of Tangier.

SOME MOROCCAN PRACTICALITIES

Wait until you get into Morocco to change money. Spanish travel agents will do it, often at a dishonestly low rate, and the rates at the border crossings aren't much better. The currency is the *dirham*, lately averaging about 15 to the pound, 8 to the dollar.

This corner of Morocco, being the fullest of tourists, is also full of English-speaking hustlers and creeps. We do not exaggerate: around the bus stations and ports they're thick as flies and 10 times as persistent, sometimes weaseling, sometimes menacing. Entertain no offers, especially of drugs or guided tours, and do your best to totally ignore the scum. The Moroccans don't like them either. Beyond that, you'll need your wits to bargain, with merchants, taxi drivers, and even hotel-keepers. There's no reason why you can't do this firmly and gracefully. Also, crime is a problem after dark in these two cities.

On the good side, you'll have a chance to explore a fascinating society—and perhaps see a little reflection of the lost culture of al-Andalus. Hotels, restaurants, and everything also will be almost half as expensive as in Spain. The food has an international reputation; national dishes like *couscous* and *harira* are superb. Don't judge Morocco by Tangier and Tetuán, and don't even judge those places by first impressions. A little side-trip to Morocco may not be an epiphany, but think how much you'll regret it if you pass up the chance.

La Línea

GETTING AROUND

Two companies serve La Línea, the town on the Spanish side of the border with Gibraltar. Transportes Comes runs the service to Algeciras (every half-hour) and points west; and the Portillo company to the Costa del Sol, Málaga and Madrid. Both have offices on Avda. de España, just off La Línea's central square, and from here it's a 5-minute walk to the border with Gibraltar. The nearest railway station is at San Roque, 8 km away, from where trains go to Ronda and all destinations in Andalucía.

La Línea ('the line', named for Gibraltar's old land walls) is a lively, fun town that has built up dramatically since the re-opening of the Gibraltar border in 1985. Given its unique status as the only Spanish town to border with British territory, La Línea has almost taken on a split personality. Whilst retaining its Spanish essence, it takes in its stride the daily invasion of soldiers, day-trippers and smugglers (of tobacco especially), who have descended on the town since the barrier came down. Not that the people of La Línea are unhappy about the situation—the open frontier means they can scoot over in their coffee breaks to buy up tax-free goods and off-the-peg clothing, and hope that the Spanish customs' officers aren't too rigorous in their searches on the way back. But the *Liñense* are still guarded about their colonial neighbours, and not for reasons of politics. They have in the past had to suffer the jolly old British tradition of street brawls involving servicemen, although this practice is admittedly now in decline due to its lack of novelty and vigilant MPs.

La Línea's reputation is not exactly unblemished either—stray too far from the centre of town or the water-front after dark, and there are some exceedingly unpleasant seedy people skulking in dark doorways and hungry for your money, whether by selling you drugs or just stealing your wallet.

The centre of La Línea, however, is safe and tame, and worth an overnight stay for its sparkling, hybrid nightlife, if not for its monuments. There's only the 19th-century church of **La Inmaculada**, with its Baroque-style altar; and the **Cruz Herrera Museum**, tucked away in a modern dilapidated building 100 metres from the main square, Plaza de la Constitución, on C. Carbonn.

La Línea may be the best place to stay while you visit Gibraltar—you'll save money, and crossing the border regularly is no real inconvenience.

WHERE TO STAY   (tel prefix 956)
The **Rocamar***** has the most comforts (6500–8500 pts; Avda España 170, tel 76 79 23) but the best bargain in town is **La Campana***, just off the main Plaza. In the high season doubles with bath are 4200 pts, low season 3200 pts, and there's a good little restaurant downstairs with *menu del día* for 950 pts (Carboneros 3, tel 10 30 59). There are cheaper *hostales*, recommended only if you are on a budget. Heading the list is the **Sevilla***, for no other reason than its flamboyant, crumbling glass-and-stone building, and the cranky old folks who run it (2000 pts for a double, no bath; Duque de Tetuán 4, tel 76 47 96).

EATING OUT
Again, prices are a lot lower than in Gibraltar, particularly if you want to spoil yourself on fish. At **La Marina** on Paseo Marítimo the speciality is the favourite of the southern coast: grilled sardines on a spit (2500 pts). In an unfortunate postion opposite the cemetery, **Casa Manue** is nevertheless thriving. The menu is varied, but best are the *solomillo* and *entrecôte* steaks (1500–2000 pts). On the central pedestrian thoroughfare the **Jerez** is a bar more than a restaurant, serving simple, cheap *raciones* for 650 pts.

The Costa del Sol

At first glance, it doesn't seem the speculators and developers could have picked a more unlikely place to conjure up the Mediterranean's biggest holiday playground. The stretch of coast between Gibraltar and Málaga is devoid of beautiful or even attractive scenery, and its long beaches come in a uniformly dismal shade of grey. Spain's low prices are one explanation, and the greatest number of guaranteed sunny days in Europe another. The reason it happened here, though, is breathtakingly simple—cheap land. Forty years ago, all this coast had was fantastically poor fishing villages and malaria, and it was one of the forgotten backwaters of Spain.

After a few decades of holiday intensity, though, this unlikely strip, all concrete and garish signboards, is beginning to develop a personality of its own. Any hype you hear or read about the Costa, anything that employs flowery prose and superlatives, is utter nonsense; on the other hand, it has become almost fashionable to mock the Costa for its brash *turismo* exuberance, and that is uncalled for. The Costa does attract people who don't expect much from their holiday (or retirement) except good weather, like-minded companions, and places to play. Their presence, in such large numbers and from so many nations, has created a unique international community of everyday folks. It's easy to forget you're in Spain, but if you ever get homesick you can always take a break from Andalucía and have a noisy good time by the beach.

GETTING AROUND

The Portillo bus company has the franchise for this stretch of coast; and with the growth of tourism their service has become almost like a city bus-line, stopping every few hundred yards in the developed areas between Algeciras and Málaga. There's never too long a wait in either direction. San Pedro is where the buses branch off for Ronda, an easy destination from any town on the coast. You can also go directly to Sevilla or Madrid at least once daily from the bus station in Marbella.

TOURIST INFORMATION

Estepona: Paseo Marítimo, tel (952) 80 09 13.
Marbella: C. Miguel Cano 1, tel (952) 77 14 42.

ACTIVITIES ON THE COSTA DEL SOL

To discover what's on, take a quick look through the local publications—*Lookout*, a slick monthly magazine for the British on the Costa; a weekly English edition of Málaga's newspaper, *Sur*; and various local entertainment guides will show you all sorts of chances.

There are *bullrings* in Marbella, Fuengirola, Estepona, Mijas (a square one!) and Benalmadena Costa, though *corridas* are infrequent and the really serious action occurs in the big ring in Málaga. There are **concerts** at the Casa de Cultura and Salon Varietés in Fuengirola and the Mijas Arts Centre, among others; art exhibitions and guitar and dance courses; and, occasionally, movies in English at the Cine Puerto Banús.

For sports, there are over 14 major **golf courses** on the Costa, though green fees are a little dear (3000 pts and up); **tennis** at many of the hotels, most open to the public; even **snooker clubs** (in Fuengirola). Of course all the **water sports** are popular; you can always make arrangements for equipment or instruction through your hotel. There are **casinos** at Benalmadena Costa (the Torrequebrada, on the coastal highway) and quite a bit higher stakes, at Puerto Banús (the Casino de Marbella, at Torre del Duque).

For kids there's a Disneyland-style amusement park at Benalmadena called **Tivoli World** with a Wild West, Chinese pagodas, Cinerama and flamenco can-can shows. Also, a small **Zoo** in Fuengirola, Super Bonanza cruise boats for leisurely excursions between Torremolinos and Puerto Banús, and horseback riding from the El Castillo Salvador stables outside Fuengirola (1000 pts per hour). The **Aquapark** in Fuengirola has slides and rides to keep the little ones amused for an afternoon. For something out of the ordinary, get in touch with the Viajes CHAT travel agency in Torremolinos (tel 38 71 86) and they'll make arrangements for a hot-air balloon ride over the Costa, champagne included.

Estepona and San Pedro

Estepona, the first of the resort towns east of Gibraltar, is also the quietest, although the big developers are now moving in and concrete blocks are beginning to sprout all over. Its biggest attraction is a nudist beach. It hasn't entirely lost its fishing village simplicity, however, despite the highway which slices its way through. The old town is still a pleasant, quiet place, with narrow streets and whitewashed houses, a heritage of its Arab occupation. It has a marina, where you can grab a beer and a bite to eat while you study

112

the classy yachts. If you're staying here, a worthwhile side-trip would be **Casares**, 20 km (12.5 miles) northwest, up in the Sierra Bermeja, a typical white Andalucían village perched on a steep hill under the ruins of its castle. Nearby, outside the village of Manilva, there are ruins of a **Roman spa**. The old spring still pours out strange, sulphurous water, and the locals drop in to bathe for what ails them.

San Pedro de Alcántara down the coast, is a little fancier, and probably the most attractive resort on the Costa del Sol—its developers get credit for learning at least a little from past mistakes. Most of the town is a good walk from the beaches. From here the only good road through the mountains will take you to Ronda and its surrounding villages—the best excursion you can make from the Costa.

Marbella

This is the poshest and most expensive resort in Spain. When you arrive, you'll find yourself asking why: Marbella has no visible attraction whatsoever. Its recently trendy old village, with a square full of orange trees, has been swallowed up by look-alike developments; it's nothing more than a high-rise suburb by the sea. The answer is simple: rich people come here because other rich people do, and it's really people who make Marbella; a heady mixture of adventurers, celebrities, executives, tycoons and the ordinary man, coming from every corner of the globe.

This is said to be the fastest-growing area in Europe, but it is not without its growing pains. Until recently zoning laws were permissive to the point of being totally ineffective, and developers, eager to make a quick profit, threw up one unattractive building after another. But for every ugly development there is a stunningly beautiful one, carefully preserving Andaluz tradition and delightfully landscaped with trees, lawns and flowering shrubs. So, despite her limited charm, Marbella continues to thrive, and the fun-loving teenager she was is now slowly but surely turning into a respectable matron. Wild parties, eccentric ways and a live-for-today attitude have given way to serious business, fuelled by the property boom on the Costa del Sol in the 80s.

Nonetheless, for the earnest tourist there wouldn't be a great deal of point in spending time in the town. You'll pay jet-set prices without getting in on the action, which takes place in a score of private clubs, private villas and very private yachts. The top crust have already forsaken Marbella for **Puerto Banús**, a new development 6 km to the west, with a yacht harbour full of crystal chandelier gin palaces, though you shouldn't pass up the chance of spending an afternoon here in one of the many waterside cafés, sipping chilled rosé and observing how the other half live.

WHERE TO STAY   (tel prefix 952)
In Estepona, there are more real bargains to be found than elsewhere on the coast. For a modicum of concrete splendour near the beach, the **Buenavista**** is the best bet (Pso Marítimo, tel 80 01 37; doubles 3500–5000 pts). Estepona isn't a place to spend money, though; there are plenty of inexpensive *hostales* (like **El Pilar***, Plaza de las Flores 22, tel 80 00 18; 3600–4200 pts a double, in a pretty setting), both in the town and on the beach.

San Pedro doesn't yet have a wide choice. **El Pueblo Andaluz**** is one of the outstanding bargains on the coast, a pretty place near the beach built around an old Andalucían home with a pool, playground, restaurant and garden (on the coastal highway, tel 78 05 97; 6000 pts for a double). There are some *hostales* in the town: **Bamar*** (San Antonio 3, tel 78 41 92) and **Marta*** (Lagasca 24, tel 78 33 36); both have rooms in the 2400–3000 pts range.

If you want to brush shoulders with gossip-mag personalities, eastern princes or western tycoons, check into Marbella's most expensive hotel, **Los Monteros*******, and enjoy all the luxuries that 36,000 pts will buy (Ctra Cádiz, Km 188, tel 77 17 00). The **Meliá Don Pepe******* is another mega-luxury hotel facing out over the sea. It has a large tourist and sports complex, including an 18-hole golf course, 11 tennis courts, 5 squash clubs, riding school, heated pool, gym and sauna (24,000–32,000 pts; Finca Las Merinas, tel 77 03 00) but these are not the only top-price luxury hotels here. **Puente Romano******* is one of the most beautiful, if not the most expensive, and its name comes from the genuine Roman bridge incorporated into its lovely surroundings (33,000 pts; Ctra Cádiz, Km 178, tel 77 01 00). Ideally placed next to the Marbella shopping centre, at the end of the promenade overlooking the sea, **El Fuerte****** is more affordable at 14,000 pts for a double (Avda El Fuerte s/n, tel 77 15 00).

On Marbella's main street is the reasonably priced **Alfil**** with rooms for 4200 pts (Avda Ricardo Soriano 19, tel 77 23 50). Surprisingly, there is a wide selection of *hostales* in the 2500–3500 pts range, most of them in the old town, like the pleasant **Hotel Paco****, C. Peral 16, tel 77 12 00 (doubles 3500 pts with bath) and a dozen other places in the 2000–3000 pts range around C. Peral, C. San Francisco and other streets nearby. If you do want to splurge here, the best buys among the luxury hotels will be found on the less-crowded beaches outside the town, like **Las Chapas*****, a nearly self-sufficient holiday complex with opportunities for tennis, golf and water sports—it's right on the beach on the coastal highway, 8 km (5 miles) to the east (Ctra Cádiz, Km 192, tel 83 13 75; 11,000 pts for a double). Don't count on finding a room at any price during the season; package tours have taken over just as in the resorts to the east, and most places are booked pretty solid.

EATING OUT

In Estepona, the best bet when you're tired of seafood is to try the Moroccan couscous at the **Restaurant del Paseo** on the coastal highway (1500–2000 pts). Eating with the ocean as a backdrop on a warm summer night is an experience at **Belmondo**, an Italian restaurant located at Playa D'Or on the N340 (Km 165). Authentic Italian dishes head the menu, including home-made pasta; follow this with turbot in cream, mustard and white wine sauce, tender fillets of beef or other meats grilled by the poolside (4000 pts; tel 78 05 00). Otherwise head to **El Vagabundo**, a few kilometres up the road, where a choice of international dishes, including seafood pancakes and roast duck, awaits you (2500 pts; Urb. Monte Biarritz, Ctra Cádiz Km 168, tel 78 66 98).

Two km west of San Pedro, at Benavista, **Le Soufflé** serves excellent soufflés, from starters through to desserts, and classic French dishes. The sole *Le Soufflé* is especially recommended, served with a béchamel and shrimp sauce (4000 pts; Urb. El Pilar, Benavista, tel 78 62 89; evenings only, closed Tue).

Dining in Marbella can empty your pockets quickly enough, and there's a wealth of places to choose from. **Hosteria del Mar** has summer dining on the patio looking onto the swimming pool, and in winter is cosy inside. Specialities include: chicken and shrimp Catalan style, stuffed quail, roast duck in a sauce of *Cassis* and candied figs (4000 pts;

Avda Canovas del Castillo 1A, tel 77 55 81; open evenings only). Next to the Marbella Club, **Villa Tiberio** is a palatial restaurant with affordable prices, soft music and luxurious surroundings. Superb antipasta dishes—*bresola con aguacate* (thinly sliced cured beef with avocado), delicious pasta. Main courses are good too, although less adventurous (4000–5000 pts for dinner with wine; Ctra Cádiz Km 178.5, tel 77 17 99). A favourite, even in competitive Marbella, **La Meridiana** offers international cuisine and unusual dishes such as salad of angler fish marinated in dill, or braised veal sweetbreads with grapefruit (4000–5000 pts; situated just behind the mosque, on Camino de la Cruz s/n, tel 77 61 90; open evenings only in summer). The Marbella Hill Club has now been transformed into the restaurant **La Camargue**, but still attracts the same, select clientele. Its setting in beautiful gardens with lovely views and a flexible, interesting menu, assure its continued popularity. The menu includes a medley of shrimp and lobster in a delicate sauce, poached salmon with fresh basil sauce, *solomillo* with two pepper sauces, and a selection of desserts, mostly based on fresh fruit (4000–5000 pts; tel 82 40 85; open every evening in summer). One special outing in Marbella is to the restaurant **Toni Dalli**, housed in a Moorish mansion with a central courtyard and a magnificent view of the beach. Dalli, a retired Italian opera singer, often entertains his customers personally with the odd aria; otherwise there's the regular lively showbiz band to tap your toes to. Italian food is obviously the order of the day (4000 pts; The Oasis Club, Ctra Cádiz Km 176, tel 77 00 55). In town, on the Pl. de los Naranjos, the **Crêperia Marbella** offers crêpes and a wide choice of other dishes (2500 pts). Many less expensive places, mostly specializing in seafood, can be found in the area around C. Aduar.

In Puerto Banús the **Silhouette** commands an attractive panorama over the town itself and the Mediterranean. Its elegant interior is complete with piano bar and dance floor. The menu is international: wild partridge mousse, breast of duck with fresh raspberry and butter sauce, and *parfait* of pistachio in chocolate sauce (3500 pts; First floor, Cristamar Centre, tel 81 56 02). In the heart of Puerto Banús you'll find more cuisine with a French bias; **Michel** serves terrific *bouillabaisse* in modern, plush surroundings (3000 pts; tel 81 55 19).

East of Marbella on the N340 in Las Chapas, **La Hacienda** is frequently described as the best restaurant on the Costa del Sol. It prides itself on its super-fresh ingredients. Try the hake in wine sauce, river crab and mushroom salad, fresh pasta, home-made ice cream. Dining out on the terrace here will set you back around 6000 pts (Ctra Cádiz, Km 193, Urb. Las Chapas, tel 83 11 16; closed Mon). It would be hard to imagine a more agreeable spot to spend an evening, complete with live music and dancing, than at **Club Miraflores**. Consistently good food: fresh spinach with onions and cream, *croquettes de crevettes*, fresh grilled salmon with Hollandaise sauce, beef Stroganoff, or baby chicken casseroled in white wine (3500 pts; on the Urbanización Miraflores, Ctra Cádiz Km 199, tel 83 01 02).

Fuengirola

Thirty years ago, Fuengirola was a typical whitewashed, Spanish fishing village. It's still white, but hardly typical, and even less Spanish. With the miles of speculative *urbanizaciónes* that surround it, it would be easy to be unkind to Fuengirola except that everyone there seems to be having such a good time. The town, and its adjacent community of **Los Boliches** may be the only place in Spain where you'll see a sign in a shop-window reading '*Se habla Español*'; the laid-back international community appreciates a good joke. The shops of the old village have been transformed into pubs, English bookshops, travel agencies and Swiss–Chinese–Belgian–Italian–Moroccan, and even Spanish, restaurants, but there's something genuine in the atmosphere of this casual European village—now grown into a fair-sized city. Today the Spaniards live mostly in town, picnicking and sunbathing on their flat roofs or balconies; the foreigners drive in from the *ubanizacónes* for pub-hopping or to shop the vast hypermarkets. The centre is becoming ever more determinedly multinational and multilingual, while upwardly-mobile Spaniards are buying their way into the *urbanizaciónes*. Try to imagine Fuengirola in another 20 years—it should be quite an interesting place.

GETTING AROUND
Besides the Portillo buses that ply the coastal highway towards Málaga and Marbella, there's also a suburban railway regularly connecting Fuengirola and Málaga. It stops at most points in between, and it's the best way to get in and out of Málaga airport.

TOURIST INFORMATION
Plaza de España, tel (952) 47 95 00.

Fuengirola's weekly event is the Tuesday outdoor **market**, the best place to observe this curious community. Unlike other resorts on the Costa, there are some things to see—the Moorish **Sohail Castle** above town (currently being restored), a bullring, even the brand new façade of a **Roman temple**. In Roman times there were important marble quarries in the mountains here, and recently divers discovered a wreck off the coast with these stones, bound for somewhere else; they've been salvaged and assembled on a spot near the beach.

Visitors from Fuengirola totally overwhelm the village of **Mijas**, 3 km (1.9 miles) up in the hills above town but at dusk it returns to the hands of the foreign residents, who count for 70% of the village's population. To escape the coastal sprawl, visitors drive up here by the coachload to find 'real Spain', and a typical Andalucían village. Yet it's still a pretty place with a promenade offering a view out to sea, a votive shrine to the Virgin, lots of pine woods, dozens of photogenic souvenir shops and 'officially licensed burro taxis' to take you around. The munchkin-sized whitewashed **bullring** sees its fair share of action throughout the year, but the town's museum of miniature curiosities is hard to take, even as a joke.

Torremolinos

TOURIST INFORMATION
Bajos de la Nogalera, Local 517, tel (952) 38 15 78.

All sources agree about Torremolinos, one of the oldest and biggest resort towns on the Costa: it is a ghastly, hyperactive, unsightly holiday inferno. In other words, it has character. Torremolinos isn't at all interested in our opinion, though, or yours either; it's doing quite well with its endless screaming blocks of bars, shopping centres and concrete hotels. For those who want to spend their holiday in the fast lane, in a raucous, international, entirely synthetic environment, this is the place.

In the summer the tourists, hustlers, gypsies, drug-pushers, sailors and an assortment of others mingle in the streets and the movement is fast and frantic between the bars. The predominant language is English, but a dozen others can be heard in the space of a few steps. To escape this Babylonian horde, step down to one of the beach cafés, popular day and night; if your luck is in you'll be treated to some of the local street performers sharing their talents: an anís-soaked troubadour mangling an aria, cigarette dangling from his lower lip, or a transvestite flamenco dancer, whirling between the passing cars, his grim-looking mother handing round the hat. This is all treated with good humour by the Spaniards, even if some of the tourists look a bit non-plussed.

Part of Torremolinos' character arises from its status as capital of what the newspapers like to call the 'Costa del Crime'. Literally thousands of clever bank-heisters, cons and embezzlers, mostly from Britain, add to the local colour, courtesy of Spain's traditional unwillingness to conclude extradition treaties with other nations. However, an agreement with Britain has finally been reached, and the crooks will have to move along when their visas run out. There will still be plenty of other types left—smooth operators of uncertain nationality, religious cult agents, hedonists of all shapes and sizes, and other European detritus. They're only the surface though, the most noticeable segment of an enormous permanent and transient population made up of gawking sun-seekers from every corner of Europe. The welcome signs on the outskirts of town proclaim 'City of Tourists'.

WHERE TO STAY   (tel prefix 952)

You really should come on a package tour if you find Fuengirola and Torremolinos to your taste. That's what these places are for, and you would get a better deal. If you're just passing through and want to rest in anonymity by the beach, there are some possibilities.

It's difficult to tell one new holiday hotel from the next, but two places do stand out as the best deals in Fuengirola: the **Florida***** in town on the Pso. Marítimo (tel 47 61 00; 5000–6500 pts for a double), with a pool and gardens, though not luxurious is still a comfortable enough place; and the **Cendrillon****, just outside town on the coastal highway is much the same as the Florida, only with tennis courts, for 6000 pts a double (Ctra Cádiz Km 213, tel 47 53 16). Both are on the beach and popular with families. There are also plenty of inexpensive *hostales* around the centre of Fuengirola, and especially in its suburb of Los Boliches on the eastern end.

At Torremolinos and its neighbouring stretch of tourist sprawl at Benalmadena Costa, the possibilities are endless, though these, too, will probably be packed with package tours. They come in all price ranges, from about 9000 pts to rock-bottom *hostales*. There are several golfers' hotels on the Costa, but the one that stands out is the **Parador del Golf****** on the road to Málaga, tel 38 12 55, with tennis courts and a pool, right on the beach, attracting an active crowd to some of the best rooms in Torremolinos. The price is average for a *parador*, 9000–12,500 pts. One of the finest of the beach hotels (though it's hard to tell from the outside) is the **Don Pablo******, in the centre of the action (Pso. Marítimo, tel 38 38 88; 6500–10,000 pts with nice beds, fancy salons, even a billiards room). In a quiet corner of the Playamar area, 2 km from the centre, the **Sol Principe*****

is a comfortable hotel with three pools and a good restaurant (9000 pts; Paseo Colorado 26, tel 38 41 00). Some of the good bargains can be found out towards Carihuela, along Avda Carlota Alessandri. Also in the Sol chain of hotels, the **Las Palomas*** is of a high standard in this price category, and although catering mostly to package tours the independent traveller will find it perfectly amenable here. It's a few minutes' walk from the centre of town and Carihuela, with pool and tennis courts (8000 pts; C. Carmen Montes 1, tel 38 50 00). The **Carihuela Palace-Park** *** offers many of the amenities of the larger hotels for a nicer price—7000 pts. One of its advantages is that it doesn't have a restaurant, in a town where tourists are often dragooned into full pension during the busy season (Avda Alessandri 31, tel 38 02 00). Whether staying a few days or just passing through, opposite the bus station the *hostal* **Victoria** is pleasant, conveniently placed and reasonably priced (3200–4500) pts for double with bath (Los Naranjos 103, tel 38 10 47). The **Miami*** is special, built around an old mansion and beautifully furnished (C. Aladino 14 in Carihuela, tel 38 52 55, doubles 3000–5000 pts; you'll need to book). Carihuela is also the place to look for inexpensive accommodation, such as the spartan but acceptable **Hostal Pedro*** (C. Bulto 1, tel 38 05 36; 1500 pts a double).

EATING OUT   (tel prefix 952)
Dining in Fuengirola is an experience; you can choose from any sort of restaurant from Indonesian to Belgian without going broke. The **Raj** is an attractive Indian restaurant and a welcome addition to Fuengirola's already cosmopolitan culinary scene. Decorated with charming *objets d'art* brought back from India, the cuisine is from the north of the sub-continent (2500 pts; C. Asturias 3, tel 46 94 70). If you've ever tried an Indonesian *rijstafel* in the Netherlands, you'll be glad to know there are plenty of such places on the Costa; the Dutch wouldn't live without it. Long famous for these delectable dishes is **Bali Mas**, Sol Playa, C. Martinez Catena, (tel 47 19 94; 2000 pts; closed Wed). At the western end of the Paseo Marítimo, in the Edificio Saturno, you'll find **La Baraka**, serving good simple French and Italian food (tel 47 14 95; 2000–3000 pts; closed Wed in winter). Also on the Paseo Marítimo, in the Edificio Perla, **Portofino**, is a popular restaurant where Italian specialities head the list (tel 47 06 42; 3000 pts; closed Mon, Jun–Aug dinner only). **Mesón El Castellano** serves authentic Castilian food: roast meats, especially pork and lamb, and the service is fast and friendly (2000 pts; Camino de Coin 5, tel 46 27 36; closed Sun lunch).

If you want to keep up with what's happening, drop into **La Cepa**, the English bar on Plaza Constitución, run by Diane and her brother-in-law Manolo. It serves as a substitute consulate for the community and questions are answered with a smile. Take a *tapas* from the bar, sit outside at one of the tables and observe the plaza, core of all life here.

Just outside Fuengirola on the road to Mijas is one of the most attractive and popular restaurants in the area, **Valparaiso**, with bars, terrace, swimming pool and an extensive menu with international cuisine. It's a favourite haunt of the foreign communities in particular (3000 pts; Ctra de Mijas Km 4, tel 48 59 75; closed Sun). Spanish cuisine from Navarre is on the menu at the nearby **Casa Navarra**: huge steaks and delicious fish that you can choose yourself. Try the *merluzo* in shrimp and parsley sauce (2000 pts; Ctra de Mijas Km 4, no phone; closed Tues). Up in Mijas there's a fair selection of eating places, **Blanco** is a family-run restaurant with reasonably priced Basque fish specialities (2500 pts; Plaza de la Constitución 13, tel 48 57 00).

Dining in Torremolinos is much like Fuengirola—a lot of choice. **Dana's** has long been one of the best restaurants, both for international cuisine and some classy Spanish dishes (4000 pts; on the main Fuengirola road, Avda Carlota Alessandri 25, tel 38 22 88; closed Sun). In the Eurosol complex, the **María de Valladolid** presents an alternative to Andalucían cuisine. Its dishes are mainly Castilian; especially good are the stews, rabbit with rice, suckling lamb and, for more wholesome appetites, tripe with chick peas (2500 pts; tel 38 95 25; closed Sun).

A short walk from the bus station, and on the main road, **Mesón Gallego Antoxo** is a typical Spanish restaurant with beautiful interior and charming little courtyard. There's a wide choice of fish, many dishes cooked to Galician recipes. Your wine will be served in the traditional Galician ceramic jug, and the drinking vessels resemble large finger bowls (1500–2000 pts). On the main Carretera, next to Los Alamos petrol station, **Frutos** is a popular restaurant, with high quality food at reasonable prices, and the portions are generous: leg of lamb, suckling pig, Málaga fry, *tocino de cielo*—not a hint of *nouvelle cuisine*! (2500 pts; Ctra Cádiz Km 235, tel 38 14 50; closed Sun eve in the off season).

For fine Moroccan cuisine and charmingly garish decor, try the **Restaurant Marrakesh**, Avda Juan Miró 7, tel 38 21 69, for a big full-course dinner with a choice of *couscous*, kebabs and stuffed pastries (2500–3000 pts). If you've never had the Vietnamese variations on Chinese cuisine so popular in France, try **Vietnam Sur**, Paseo del Colorado, Urb. Playamar, 'Bloque 9, where they serve delicious food at affordable prices (1500 pts; tel 38 67 37). The best seafood restaurants are in Carihuela, and the **Casa Guaquin** is very good indeed (C. Carmen 37, tel 38 45 30; 2500 pts), where you can try such specialities of the Costa as 'fish baked in salt'. It's better than it sounds. Another good place on the beach here is **La Jabega**, with fish, of course, and a wide variety of starters and shellfish (2500 pts; Mar 15, tel 38 63 75; closed Mon).

If you want to escape the bedlam of Torremolinos, head up into the hills to the rambling, ranch-type restaurant run by a Spanish-German couple, **Venta Los Pinos del Coto**. The spacious, attractive interior has stained-wood ceilings and a log fire for cold winter evenings. The menu is devoted to meat in large quantities (2500 pts; a 10-minute drive from town, behind the airport at Cañada de Ceuta s/n, Churriana, tel 43 58 00; closed Sūn eve and Mon). Back in town, for a cheap aperitif, sit out at the **Bodega Quitapeñas** on the central steps down to the beach—everybody passes this way.

Finally, if you are bursting at the seams with superfluous cash and want to lighten the load, head a few kilometres south to Hotel Torrequebrada, with its casino, nightclub and **Café Royal** restaurant. In attractive surroundings, and with a fine view over the curve of the coastline, they offer mouth-watering international cuisine: pheasant with sour oranges, sea scallops in cider, smoked salmon between veal scallops with truffles. Once you've paid your 3500 pts for the meal, you can join the high-rollers and spend some real money (Ctra Cádiz Km 220, Benalmadena-Costa, tel 44 16 43).

MÁLAGA

Much-maligned Málaga, capital not only of the Costa del Sol, but also of crime and sleaze in southern Spain, is making a determined effort to improve her reputation and attract more tourists. In the past, a visit to the swish department store *El Corté Inglés* may have been the only reason a tourist considered spending any time here at all.

To miss Málaga, however, means to miss the most Spanish of cities, certainly on the Costa del Sol. Whatever you may think of the place, it is alive and real: ungainly cranes and elegant palm trees compete for dominance of the skyline; police helicopters roar over the Plaza de la Constitución as pretty Spanish girls toss their skirts and stamp their heels to *flamenco* music, to a private audience in a public square; elegant old Spanish ladies, scented with *Maja* soap, sit and reminisce, and dark-eyed tattooed gypsy boys flash their double-edged smiles to lure you into a shoeshine. From its tattered billboards and walls splashed with political slogans, to its public gardens overflowing with exotic fauna, Málaga is a jamboree bag of colours, aromas and sounds. Admittedly she cannot compete with Sevilla or Granada for sheer wealth of cultural distractions, but the Málagueños are proud of their fun-loving metropolis. To experience real local *juerga*, treat yourself to an afternoon ramble through her many and famous *tapas* bars, where you will encounter more Spaniards in one afternoon than in a week in Torremolinos.

Unfortunately, the old quarters of Málaga have been treated ruthlessly by town planners, and *El Perchel*, once the heart of Málaga's flamenco district, has lost a lot of its personality and charm. The Avenida de Andalucía cuts through this old district and then becomes the Alameda Principal and the Paseo del Parque. The essence of Málaga is within this limited area, from the elegant Avenida de Andalucía to the seedy, teeming neo-Moorish market on the Calle Atarazanas.

You will find it difficult to decide whether you love or loathe this city—will you notice the two snarling drivers impatient for the green light; or the two old gentlemen sipping sherry in the doorway of a cool, dark *bodega*, hung with Serrano hams and lined with wine casks?

GETTING AROUND

As the main port of entry to the Costa del Sol and southern Andalucía, you'll probably pass through Málaga either coming or going.

By air: Málaga's often frenetic airport connects the city to Madrid, Valencia, Almería, Sevilla, Melilla and Tangier, besides being the charter-flight gateway to the Costa. Currently under construction is a new larger terminal, which will relieve the congestion and baggage delays that so frequently occur in summer months. The easiest way to get into the city, or to Torremolinos or Fuengirola, is the suburban railway line (separate stops at the airport for the regular and charter terminals). These trains and local buses stop running before midnight. After that you'll have to get a taxi (about 1000 pts to Málaga centre or Torremolinos).

By train: There's a daily *talgo* to Madrid (7 hours), plus four normal trains ($7\frac{1}{2}$–$9\frac{1}{2}$ hours), two trains a day to Valencia and Barcelona. Direct connections also to Sevilla and Córdoba; for all other destinations in Andalucía you'll have to make a change at that inescapable Bobadilla Junction. The station is on C. Cuarteles (city office C. Strachen 2, tel 31 25 00 for information).

By Bus: The new main bus station is by the train station at Paseo de los Tilos, south of the Avenida Andalucía (tel 35 00 61), and is used by a number of companies. Connections for local destinations run ¹/₂ hourly; for destinations in other provinces, generally every 1–2 hours. **Portillo** operate buses for the Costa, Sevilla, Granada, Ronda, Algeciras and towns and villages in the interior (tel 36 01 91); **Bacoma** buses to Alora and Ronda (tel 32 12 62). **Los Amarillos** for Antequera, Carratraca (tel 31 59 78). **Alsina Graells** for Granada, Nerja and Almería (tel 31 04 00) and also for Alicante and Barcelona.

TOURIST INFORMATION
Pasaje Chinitas 4, just north of the Alameda, tel (952) 21 34 45/22 89 48, and also at the airport, tel (952) 23 04 88).
Melilla: C. General Aizpuru 20, tel (952) 68 40 13.

As the Avenida de Andalucía, the main road from the west, crosses the dry rocky bed of the Guadalmedina river, it becomes the **Alameda Principal**, a majestic 19th-century boulevard. North of the Alameda is the **Plaza de la Constitución**, in the heart of the commercial centre, and the Pasaje Chinitas, an all-and-sundry shopping arcade. One of the clothes shops bears a commemorative plaque—it's the original site of the *Café Chinitas*, where bullfighters and flamenco singers would gather in the old days; the spirit of it was captured by García Lorca.

The Alameda continues into the Paseo del Parque, a tree-lined promenade that runs along the port area, and leads to the city's **bullring**, built in 1874 with a capacity for 14,000, and very much in use today. Nearby is the **English cemetery**. William Mark, the 19th-century consul, so loved Málaga that he described it as a 'second paradise', and encouraged his fellow countrymen to join him here. In 1830 he founded this cemetery, allowing a decent burial to Protestants who had previously been buried on the beach. Hans Christian Andersen declared he could 'well understand how a splenetic Englishman might take his own life in order to be buried in this place'. Its sea views, however, have long since been blocked by concrete buildings.

Just off the Paseo del Parque, the steps lead up to the Moorish **Alcazaba** (open 11–1 and 5–8 summer, 10–1 and 4–7 winter). Under the Moors, Málaga was the most important port of al-Andalus, and from contemporary references it seems also to have been one of its most beautiful cities. King Ferdinand thoroughly ruined it in the conquest of 1487, and after the expulsion of the Moors in 1568, little remained of its ancient distinction. Little too remains of the Alcazaba, except a few Moorish gates, but the site has been restored to a lovely series of terraced gardens with an **Archaeological Museum** at the top, containing relics from the Phoenician necropolis found on the site, and lists of Moorish architectural decoration salvaged from the ruins (open 10–1 and 4–7, Sun 10–2). The top of the Alcazaba also affords fine views over Málaga.

There is a half-ruined **Roman theatre**, recently excavated on the lower slopes of the hill, and from the Alcazaba you may climb a little more to the **Gibralfaro**, the ruined Moorish castle that dominates the city (open summer 11–2 and 5–8; winter 10–1 and 4–7, Sunday 10–2).

Back on the Paseo, note the chunky Art-Nouveau **Ayuntamiento**, one of the more unusual buildings in Málaga. On the opposite side of the Alcazaba, on Calle San Agustín 8 is Málaga's **Museo de Bellas Artes**, in a restored 16th-century palace (open summer

10–1.30 and 5–8; winter 10–1, 4–7, closed Monday and Sun afternoon in winter). It's worth a look for some good medieval polychrome icons, two strange paintings by Luis de Morales (c. 1580) and a small collection of Picassos on the first floor. Picasso was a native of Málaga, though once he left it at the age of 14, he never returned. Much of the museum is given over to the works of other late-19th century Malagueño painters who make up in eccentricity for what they lack in genius; one of them, Muñoz Degrain, was Picasso's first teacher. Also present are works of Zurbarán, Murillo and Ribero.

Málaga's **Cathedral** is a few blocks away on Calle Molina Lario. It's an ugly, unfinished 16th-century work, immense and mouldering. Known as *La Manquita*, the one-armed lady, the only interesting feature is the faded, gaudy façade of the **Sacristy**, left over from the earlier Isabelline Gothic church that once stood here. Also on the cathedral square is the **Museo de Arte Sacro** (open 10–1 and 4–7, closed Sun afternoon). Next to the dry river bed, the **Museo de Artes Populare** (Pasillo de Santa Isabel 10), occupies a restored 17th-century inn with a collection of household bric-à-brac from days gone by (open 10–1.30 and 5–8 in summer, 4–6 in winter; closed Sun afternoon and Mon). Now open for visits, Picasso's birthplace—**Casa Natal Picasso**—is on Plaza de la Merced, where occasional exhibitions are held (tel 28 39 00). An old farm, the **Finca de la Concepción**, 7 km (4½ miles) north of Málaga on the new road to Granada, is now owned by the municipality, and has been turned into botanical gardens, with occasional summer shows of folklore and Andalucían dance; there are also some Roman remains on the site (enquire at tourist office for details).

Melilla

Nobody ever goes to Melilla, the more obscure of Spain's two remaining *presidios* on the North African coast. It's a long boat ride from Málaga, or a slightly shorter one from Almería, and onward destinations are severely limited. Morocco's big towns are far away, though you may consider Melilla as a quieter, less exasperating way to slip into Morocco than Tangier or Tetuán, with their hustlers and aggravations. The town itself is prettier than Ceuta, hiding behind stern-looking fortifications over the water's edge, and a 1.6 km (1 mile) long beach spreads awkwardly from the walls. Melilla has had its problems lately; the Spanish papers regularly report the local police bullying the Moroccan minority during protests over discrimination and citizenship.

WHERE TO STAY   (tel prefix 952)
Málaga looks deceptively good from the **Parador de Gibralfaro*****, up in the old Moorish castle above the city; the small hotel offers few luxuries (there are only 12 rooms), but the quality and the view make it a better bet than the more expensive modern hotels around the port (Apdo. de Correos 274, tel 22 19 02; doubles 9000–10,500 pts). For about the same price you can stay at **Los Naranjos***** (Paseo de Sancha 35, tel 22 43 17; 9900 pts) out at the eastern end of Málaga, 1 km (½ mile) from the beach, such as it is.

There are some acceptable middle-range and inexpensive places. Try the **Avenida**** at Alameda 5, tel 21 77 29 (2600–3300 pts, double with bath). South of here is the small **Alameda**** (Casas de Campos 3, tel 22 20 99; 3000–3600 pts). The **Castilla*** (2600 pts a double with bath; tel 21 86 35) and the **Guerrero*** (same price, same tel) are well-run

122

establishments in the same building at C. Cordoba 5, also south of the Alameda. Any place on or around the Alameda will be decent, but avoid the cheap dives around the train station.

In Melilla, the **Anfora**** is a reliable, unremarkable hotel (C. Vallesca 8, tel 68 33 40; 5000–5500 pts) and there are quite a few modest *hostales* scattered all over.

EATING OUT

If you've exhausted yourself shopping at the swish department store **El Corté Inglés**, stroll up to the top floor for their **buffet** lunch: meat and fish dishes, pastas and salads (Avda de Andalucía, tel 30 00 00; 2000 pts, closed Sun). North of Picasso's house is the **Café de la Opera**, C. Ramos Martín 3, tel 22 38 78, a popular place to people-watch and especially interesting on theatre nights (Andalucían specialities, imaginative decor, 1500 pts; closed Sun eve, Mon and Sept). In the Cervantes Edificio Horizonte, **El Figon de Bonilla** attracts a trendy crowd for its excellent fish and pork dishes; particularly good are the fish soup, lobster, swordfish and *cola de toro* (2000 pts; tel 22 32 23; closed Sun and last 2 weeks of Feb). Popular with young people and reasonably priced is **La Taberna del Pintor** by the bullring (Maestranza 6, tel 21 53 15), deserving its reputation as one of the best places to eat meat in Málaga (soups, salads and steaks done to your liking; 1600–2000 pts). Málagueños flock to the Paseo Marítimo and the El Palo district east of town on Sunday especially, to fill up the many restaurants that line the beaches in what was once a simple fishing community. A favourite is **Antonio Martín**, out on the Paseo Marítimo right next to the sea. Fish and rice dishes are the basis of the menu; scrambled eggs with baby eel and salmon, gilthead cooked in salt (2500 pts; tel 22 21 13; closed Sun eve in winter). Also in this area are: **El Cabra** (Calle Copo 21, Pedregalejo, tel 29 15 95), which has a more expensive range of seafood; **Casa Pedro** (Quitapenas 4, El Palo, tel 29 00 13), where you may well be deafened by the din while you tuck into skewered sardines or Sierra-style angler fish (2000–2500 pts; closed Mon eve and Nov). At **Tintero** (Playa del Dedo, tel 29 00 01) you don't order your food—fish are 'auctioned off' as they appear from the kitchen. If heading south from Málaga, pop into **Casa Pepe** on the Carretera de Cádiz. It's an honest-to-goodness family-run place with local goodies on the menu (1500 pts).

East of Málaga

For some reason the tourist industry has neglected the areas east of the city. There are a few resorts strung out along the coastal highway, notably **Torre del Mar**, but they are all grim-looking places, little bits of Málaga that escaped to the beach. Nearby are some scanty remains of a Greek-Phoenician settlement called **Mainake**.

GETTING AROUND

The Portillo and Alsina Graells buses from Málaga or Motril serve Nerja, Almuñécar and Salobreña, and connections can be made from these towns to the interior villages. Note that long-distance buses along the coast do not usually stop at these towns.

TOURIST INFORMATION
Nerja: Puerto de Mar 1, tel (952) 52 15 31.

Vélez Málaga and Alhama de Granada

From Torre del Mar you can make a short detour inland to **Velez Málaga**, lying in a fertile valley at the foot of the Axarquía mountain area. The new town holds no particular charm, but the old part tells of its Moorish past; above the town, the castle (of which a restored tower remains), was one of the last Moorish outposts to fall to Christian forces during the purge by Isabella and Ferdinand. Below it, the church of **Nuestra Señora de la Encarnación** has had a chequered career—first as a Visigothic church, then a mosque, then a church again when the town was recaptured by Christian forces in 1487.

For a further detour into the mountains, you can tackle the 50 km (31 mile) drive up on the C335, (becoming the C340 at Ventas) over the Sierra to **Alhama de Granada**. The road winds its way up through the serene surroundings of olive trees, trickling streams and rocky gulches; but pay close attention—the road has some helter-skelter turns. Alhama balances precariously on a rocky lip and looks down to the deep grassy-banked gorge, through which runs the river bed of the Alhama. Up here you're away from it all. 'Oh for my Alhama' was the lament of Boabdil el Chico, who had to abandon this beauty-spot to the Christians in 1482. The town's 17–18th-century church of **El Carmen** has a terrace from which you can enjoy the panorama. No prizes for guessing the town's other attractions—the remains of a Moorish castle, in the main square, and a 15th-century parish church, a gift to the town from Ferdinand and Isabella. The Catholic Kings' Granada architects, Enrique Egas and Diego de Siloe, both worked on it. Alhama has been famous since Roman times for its spa waters; ask at the modern spa, the Hotel Balnearia, to see the Roman and Moorish baths below.

Another detour, one that will eventually bring you back to the coast, is to take the twisting MA 117 to Archez, and continue on to **Cómpeta**, a truly lovely old village known principally for its sweet wines; the grapes are sun-dried to sweeten and fortify them. The big wine fiesta is held on 15 August in the main square. Like many Andalucían villages near the coast, new northern invaders have discovered its charm, Brits and Danes particularly. Beyond Cómpeta begin the wilds of the **National Reserve of the Sierra de Tejeda**; you'll have to leave your car to explore it, though, and strong comfortable shoes are recommended. To get back to the coast, take the MA137 through beautiful vine-clad slopes to **Torrox**, another Nordic enclave, and continue down to **Torrox Costa**, an expanding resort, 8 km (5 miles) from Nerja.

Nerja

Approaching this town, the scenery becomes impressive as the mountains grow closer to the sea. Sitting at the base of the Sierra de Tejeda, Nerja itself is pleasant and quiet for a Costa resort. In Moorish times the town was a major producer of silk and sugar, an industry that fell into rapid decline after their departure. An earthquake in 1884 partially destroyed Nerja, and from then to the early 60s it had to eke a living from fishing and farming.

Its attractions are the **Balcón de Europa**, a promenade with a fountain overlooking the sea, and a series of secluded beaches under the cliffs—the best are a good walk away on either side of the town. A few kilometres east, the **Cueva de Nerja** is one of Spain's fabled grottos, full of Gaudiesque formations and needle-thin stalactites—one, they claim, is the longest in the world. The caves were discovered only in 1959, just in time for the tourist boom, and they have been fitted out with lights and music, with photographers lurking in the shadow who'll try to sell you a picture of yourself when you leave. The caves were popular with Cro-Magnon man (first found in a cave of that name in France), and there are some Paleolithic artworks (not open to visitors at this time). Occasionally, this perfect setting is used for ballet and concerts.

A scenic 7 km (4¹/₂ mile) drive north of Nerja on the MA105 finds pretty **Frigiliana**, a pristine whitewashed village of neat houses and cobbled streets, with great views down to the eastern coast, especially from the ruins of the Moorish fort. This was the site of one of the last battles between Christians and Moriscos in 1569; the story of the battle is retold on ceramic plates around the village's old quarter. Nowadays Frigiliana is like an English colony, rather than an inland Andalucían village.

Almuñécar and Salobreña

The coastal road east of Nerja, bobbing in and out of the hills and cliffs, is the best part of the Costa, where avocado pears and sugarcane keep the farming community busy; the next resort, however, **Almuñécar**, is better left alone; a nest of dreary high-rises around a beleaguered village. Its only interesting feature is the **Moorish castle**, which houses the local cemetery. Outside the town are the remains of a Roman aqueduct. **Salobreña** is much better, though it may not stay that way. The village's dramatic setting, slung down a steep, lone peak overlooking the sea, is the most stunning of any on the coast, and helps to insulate it just a little from the tourist industry. The beaches, just starting to become built up, are about 2 km (1¹/₂ miles) away.

From here, the next town is **Motril**, a large settlement set back from the sea with little to attract visitors; it's the centre of the coastal sugarcane production, thanks to the gin family Larios. There isn't much Costa left further east, and the only real choice for a destination is the spectacular mountain road through the Sierra Nevada towards Granada.

WHERE TO STAY   (tel prefix 952)
Nerja has two fine hotels: the **Parador Nacional de Nerja****** (just outside town at El Tablazo; tel 52 00 50; 10,500–12,500 pts a double) and the **Balcón de Europa***** (Paseo Balcón de Europa, tel 52 08 00; 6000–8500 pts, doubles). The latter is probably the better bet, though not quite as luxurious as the *parador*; the beautiful location on the 'balcony of Europe' in the town centre and the reasonable rates make the difference. Both hotels have lifts down to the beaches under Nerja's cliffs. Another good bargain on the beach is the **Portofino*** (Puerta del Mar 2, tel 52 01 50; 5500 pts a double with bath). There are a few more inexpensive places about town, notably the **Florida*** (C. San Miguel 35, tel 52 07 43; 3000 pts a double with bath, 2400 pts without) but Nerja is notoriously tight during the high season. You will have serious trouble finding a place without a reservation.

In Salobreña, you have a choice between the **Salobreña*****, outside the town on the coastal highway (tel 61 02 61; 6000–7500 pts doubles; both beach and pool, and a garden) and a number of *hostales* both on the beach and in the alleys. **Mari Tere*** has doubles with bath for 3200 pts (Ctra de la Playa 94, tel 61 01 26).

EATING OUT
A popular restaurant in Nerja is the **Rey Alfonso**—nothing special about the cuisine but the view is superb, on cliffs directly under the Balcón de Europa (2000–2500 pts). You can dine in genuine old Spanish surroundings in the restaurant at the hotel **Cala Bella**, complete with wrought ironwork, ceramics and cool tiled floors, and views of Calahonda Bay and the Balcón; *salmón con salsa de anchoa* (salmon in anchovy sauce), *perdiz a la Almijara* (partridge with local herbs), plus a selection of meats (3000 pts; Puerta de Mar 2, tel 52 07 00). In Almuñécar **Los Geranios** is a cheerful place, full of geraniums. Owned by a Spanish-Belgian couple, the menu is international with a Spanish bias (about 2,000 pts; Plaza Rosa 4a, tel 63 07 24; closed Wed). Salobreña has one good restaurant, the **Mesón Duran**, specializing in meat and some Andalucían dishes (2500 pts; Ctra Málaga Km 341; closed Wed). If you're in the Motril area and hungry, head for Gualchos, 17 km (10½ miles) away inland, to **La Posada** (Plaza Constitución 9, tel 64 60 34), where they serve spinach rolls with fish mousse, red mullet with Andalucían mayonnaise, sword fish with garlic, cream and wine, duck in Jerez vinegar and raisins (2000–3000 pts; closed Mon).

East of Motril to Almería

The coastal road cuts between the sea and the plastic—not coastal development, but agricultural plastic covering a good percentage of Europe's winter vegetables. At **Adra** you enter the province of Almería, the sunniest, driest and hottest little corner of all Europe. What they call winter here lasts from the end of November to March; scores of films (most famously, *Lawrence of Arabia*) have been shot here, taking advantage of the light and the scenery. Until the 1970s the **Costa de Almería**, difficult of access and bereft of utilities and water, was untouched by tourism. Now, charter flights drop in from northern Europe, and hotels are sprouting up here and there—but compared to the region further west, it's pleasantly underwhelming.

Adra was an ancient Phoenician town, and the last spot in Spain surrendered by the Moors, at the moment Boabdil sailed from here to Africa. Though it's still basically a fishing and agricultural village, it has spawned **Almerimar**, a large new development of mostly villas and flats, with a new marina and one of Spain's best golf courses. From here you can dip into the eastern Alpujarras to the pretty 'city' of **Berja**, with its palatial country homes or **Canjáyar**; this area supplies most of northern Europe's Christmas grapes. The resorts at **Roquetas de Mar** (more golfing) and **Aguadulce** (oldest and biggest course on the Almería coast) are easily reached from Almería capital by bus.

Almería

GETTING AROUND
By air: Almería's airport is 8 km (5 miles) from the city on the road to Níjar, tel 22 19 54. Besides charters from London, Iberia has regular connections with Madrid, Barcelona and Melilla—its offices are at Pso. de Almería 32, tel 23 84 11.

By boat: Transmediterránea runs car ferries from Almería to Melilla on the North African coast at 2 every Tuesday, Thursday, and Saturday; the voyage takes 6¹/₂ hours. Ticket office is at Parque Nicolás Salmerón 28, tel 23 63 56.

By train: Almería's RENFE station is a block from the bus station, on Ctra. Ronda, easy walking distance from the centre, tel 25 11 35—there's an office as well at C. Alcalde Muños 1, tel 23 12 07. There are daily trains and *talgos* to Madrid, Barcelona and Valencia; you can go to Granada twice a day; or daily at 11 pm take an all-night journey across Andalucía, arriving at Córdoba at 7 am, or Sevilla at 8.30 am.

By bus: The bus station, in the new part of town on the Pl. Barcelona, tel 22 10 11, has a daily service to the major cities of the Levante up to Barcelona; also to Madrid, Granada, Sevilla, Cádiz, Málaga and Algeciras. There are seven buses daily to Adra; hourly connections to Aguadulce and Roquetas; five buses daily to Berja; and two each to Cabo de Gata, Mojacár, Nijár and Tabernas, and weekday connections to Jaén and Guadix.

TOURIST INFORMATION
Calle Hermanos Machado 4, in the big ministries building, tel (951) 23 08 58.

Almería has been a genial, dusty little port since its founding by the Phoenicians, though for a short time in the 11th century, after the fall of the Caliphate, it dominated this end of al-Andalus, rivalling Córdoba and Sevilla. The upper city, with its narrow streets, tiny pastel houses and whitewashed cave dwellings hugging the looming walls of the **Alcazaba**, has retained a fine Moorish feel to this day. Built by the Caliph Abd ar-Rahman II in the 10th century, the Alcazaba was the most powerful Moorish fortress in Spain; today its great curtain walls and towers defend mostly market- and flower-gardens—nothing remains of the once-splendid palace. It has recently been restored (open 10–2 and 4–9). Behind the fortress, by the wall of Jayrán, you can visit the **Centre of Rescue of Animals of the Sahara**: before going up, get permission from the centre's headquarters near the tourist office—they'll give you a note letting you wander through the cages and enclosures of a wide variety of endangered animals, in an environment that must feel just like home.

Almería's **cathedral**, begun in 1524, was seemingly built for defence with its four mighty towers. Prettier, and boasting a fine carving of St James Matamoros and a minaret-like tower, is **Santiago El Viejo**, just off the Puerta Purchena near the top of the Paseo de Almería. It's a bit unusual to find a pilgrimage church, complete with St James' cockleshells, so far off the main routes.

Almería has a small **archaeological museum** on Calle Javier Sanz, with remains from the remarkable Neolithic culture of *Los Millares* that flourished here about 3500–3000 BC. You'll learn more about it here than at the sites themselves, but determined Neolithic fans will want to see Los Millares itself, in stark, barren mountains about 25 km (15¹/₂ miles) north on the N324. Five thousand years ago this was rich farmland, and the people who lived here had the leisure to create one of the most advanced prehistoric civilizations in Spain. The burial mounds here are almost true temples, with interior passages and surrounding concentric stone circles, broken by concave semicircular entrances. Five millennia of erosion have made these difficult to make out, and you'll have an even harder time distinguishing the remains of the walled town that once stood nearby.

East of Almería

The **Sierra Alhamilla** —one of the driest, most rugged and lunar of Spanish sierras—occupies this most southeastern corner of Spain. The coastal road struggles out to the **Cabo de Gata**, with a pretty beach, solitary lighthouse and crystal-clear waters, popular with divers. Inland, the white village of **Níjar** is a charming oasis in an arid setting where potters actively carry on a craft introduced by the Phoenicians. Lorca's play *Blood Wedding* was based on incidents that occurred here around the turn of the century.

The main road east winds through the northern flanks of the sierra, passing through a lush *huerta* of country estates before rising into a weirdly beautiful but perfectly desolate region, where even in the springtime green is a foreign colour. Here in **Tabernas** are a couple of spaghetti-western sets. At **Mini Hollywood**, the town built by Sergio Leone for such classics as Clint Eastwood's first vehicle, *A Fistful of Dollars*, cowboy shoot-ups and bank robberies are staged for the benefit of visitors. **Sorbas**, with its hanging houses, is most impressively seen from the highway; between the two, the government has decided to exploit the province's greatest natural resource—sunlight—with the country's largest solar energy installation.

Mojácar

Isolated amidst the rugged mountains, on a hill 2 km (1.3 miles) from the beach, trendy Mojácar has often been compared to a pile of sugar cubes. No town in Spain wears such a Moorish face—its little, flat-roofed, white houses stacked almost on top of one another. Before the equally white hotels were added to the scene a couple of decades ago, the women covered their faces with their veils when passing a stranger; a plaque by the fountain tells how the townspeople valiantly defended themselves against the army of the Catholic Kings. Most unusually, it was the practice of the old women in the village to paint a symbol known as the *indalo* (a stick figure with outstretched arms, holding up an arc) on their doors as a charm against the evil eye and thunderbolts. No one knows when the practice originated, though in the nearby caves of Vélez-Blanco, Neolithic drawings of *indalos* dating from 3000 BC have led anthropologists to the conclusion that this is one of the few, if only, cases of a prehistoric symbol being handed down in one place for thousands of years.

East of Mojácar, there's nothing but empty spaces as far as the Andalucía–Murcia border (and well beyond it, for that matter). The nondescript village of **Palomares** may ring a bell; it occupied all the world's headlines for a while in 1966, when an American B-52 crashed nearby and littered the countryside and sea with live hydrogen bombs.

WHERE TO STAY   (tel prefix 951)
In Adra you can spend an economy beach holiday at the **Delfin***, Natalio Rivas 106, tel 40 00 50, with doubles with bath for 1800–2500 pts; or splurge and golf nearby at Ejido in the **Gran Hotel Almerimar****, tel 48 09 50, a plush 38-room refuge, with tennis courts, pool, recreational activities in an attractive setting (open all year; doubles 9000–11,000 pts). If you'd prefer peace and quiet to comfort and facilities, try the little **Isleta del Moro***, a hostel near Níjar, with a simple restaurant and rooms with bath for 2000 pts; open all year (tel 36 63 13).

When on location in Almería, Hollywood denizens have traditionally checked into the

Gran Hotel Almería****, in town at Avda Reina Regente 8, tel 23 80 11. Rooms are plush and air-conditioned, and among the available diversions are a pool and bingo hall; breakfast only (doubles 10,000–11,500 pts). On the beach similar smart lodgings are available at **Playalúz******, Bahia del Palmer, tel 34 05 04, located in a lovely setting, and offering golf, tennis, sauna, indoor and oudoor pools, and children's facilities (open all year; doubles 8000–12,500 pts). Another comfortable and air-conditioned choice in town is the **Torreluz****, Pl. de Flores 6, tel 23 47 99, with doubles for 5000–6000 pts. There are a number of inexpensive *hostales*. The **Maribel*** is within easy walking distance of the bus and train stations on Avda Lorca 153, tel 23 51 73, offering simple but adequate doubles for 2000–2500 pts with bath.

In Mojacár there's the modern beach-side **Parador Reyes Católicos******, tel 47 82 50, with a pool and air-conditioning; doubles 7500–9500 pts. In the village there are a couple of new, trendy hotels at lovely Mirador de la Puntica; **El Moresco***** has the advantage of being open all year, and indoor, outdoor and children's swimming pools (7000–7500 pts). There's little in the budget category; you'll spend less at **El Puntazo** on the beach (tel 47 82 29), where a nondescript double will set you back 2800–3200 pts with bath (open all year).

EATING OUT
The best restaurant in Almería is the **Anfora** (G. Garbín 25, tel 23 13 74; closed Sun), specializing in the freshest of local ingredients—vegetables and seafood (2500 pts). This is off the Pl. S. Sebastián, near the Puerta de Purchena and another good seafood restaurant, the **Imperial**, with good seafood soups and mixed fish platters (2000 pts; Puerta de Purchena 13, tel 23 17 40, closed Wed). On the seafront, facing the gardens, are a couple of inexpensive choices, **La Cartuja** and the **Canoe**, the latter with a 750 pts set menu.

In Mojacár seafood and couscous on Fridays are served at **Mamabel's** on Embajadores—open only in the evening (1500 pts); less expensive and overlooking the sea, **Mediterráneo** at Cueva del Lobo has more seafood for 1200–1500 pts. **Palacio** in Pl. del Caño is the best restaurant in town, with excellent chocolate truffles (2500 pts).

THE INTERIOR
Guadalquivir to the Coast

For some, this will be the best of Andalucía. It doesn't have beaches, and it doesn't have famous buildings or museums. Tourists are in short supply too—mostly young Germans and British with backpacks, along with day-trippers from the Costa and a few examples of that beloved but endangered species, the serious British traveller, with nose in a Latin chronicle or a bird-watcher's guide. What this region does have is a chain of peaceful white villages, draped along hillsides under their castles, their steep streets lined with pots of geraniums. Some are prosperous, some quite poor; some have a reputation for friendliness, others can seem silent and introverted. None of them is really different from the others—except to their natives, of course—and they all share some of southern Spain's most delightful scenery. It is a region of rolling hills broken by patches of grey mountains, well-tended lands devoted to the traditional Mediterranean staples of wheat, vines and olives, coloured in the spring by orange and almond blossom in the lower areas.

The big town of Ronda, and the curiosities around Antequera are the main attractions, but if you're like many of the travellers who come here you won't worry too much about destinations, but lazily pick your way from one pretty village to the next, get to know the land and its people, and look for the little surprises that make the trip worthwhile.

GETTING AROUND
In this region, you'll be depending on buses. Arcos de la Frontera has regular connections to Jerez, Cádiz and Ronda; less frequently to Sevilla. From Ronda you can go directly to Jerez, Cádiz, Málaga, and most of the towns along the Costa del Sol; there are also four daily buses to and from Sevilla. Arcos and Ronda have connections to the villages in their hinterlands—usually only once a day, so if you're day-tripping, make sure there's a return. Ronda's new bus station is in the new town, on the Paseo de Andalucía.

Ronda has trains, too; the station is just a few blocks down Paseo de Andalucía (tel (952) 87 16 73 for information). There are at least 3 a day for Algeciras and Málaga, with connections at Bobadilla Junction for Madrid and the other cities of Andalucía. Some trains stop at Gaucin and Setenil.

Arcos de la Frontera

Starting from the west, near Jerez, **Arcos de la Frontera** is the first and one of the most spectacular of the towns, hung on a steep rock with wonderful views over the valley of the Guadalete from the *mirador* near the Plaza del Ayuntamiento. The narrow streets twist and turn like an oriental maze, an inheritance from its Moorish past. Follow the long street up to the castle and you'll be rewarded with panoramic views in all directions. The older sections of town under the castle contain some ancient palaces and the Isabelline Gothic **Santa María de la Asunción**, next to which is a rectangular esplanade hanging over the cliff above the Guadalete. Way below stretches the river and its fertile valley. Arcos was an important fortress for the Moors, a seemingly impregnable eyrie that Alfonso the Wise was smart enough to take in 1264.

Further east, **Grazalema** is a lovely village, full of flowers and surrounded by pine woods. It is considered by many to be the most representative of the Sierra towns, and its peaceful beauty is in perfect accord with its surroundings. It has been famous for hand-woven blankets since Moorish times, and they still make them here on big old, wooden looms. The surrounding area is a national park; details of walks, horse-trekking, etc., can be found at the campsite office just above the village. Nearby **Benaocaz** has a small museum of local archaeology. To the south, **Ubrique** hangs dramatically over the Rio Majaceite; though a growing industrial town, best known for its leather-craft work, it still manages to retain some of its medieval charm. Further east is **Setenil**, an odd village with some of its few streets lining the walls of a gorge. The houses are tucked under the overhanging rock, and their front doors overlook a stream. **Zahara** and **Olvera** have memorable silhouettes, their castles and churches sticking bravely up over the white-washed houses. Zahara ('desert' or 'flower' in Arabic) is a quiet town perfumed by orange groves, at the foot of a hill crowned by a medieval castle which the Christians captured from the Moors towards the end of the 15th century. Once a famous bandits' hideout, Olvera has the ruins of a 12th-century Moorish castle, from which there is a heady view down to the village; and a very dignified 17th-century church, **La Encarnación**.

Ronda

The Serrania de Ronda is a region of difficult topography, and it made life difficult for most would-be conquerors. A band of southern Celts gave the Romans fits in these mountains; various Christian chieftains held out for centuries against the Moors, and to return the favour the Moors kept Castile at bay here until 1485, just 7 years before the conquest of Granada. **Ronda**, the only city in the Serrania, is a beautiful place, blessed with a perfect postcard shot of its lofty bridge over the steep gorge that divides the old and new towns. Because of its proximity to the Costa del Sol, it has lately become the only really tourist-ridden corner of the interior. Its monuments are few; what Ferdinand the Catholic didn't wreck in 1485, the French finished off in 1809. Ronda saw plenty of trouble in the Civil War, with hundreds of bodies being tossed into the gorge (the exact numbers, and who was doing the tossing, depend on who is telling you the story).

TOURIST INFORMATION
Ronda: Pl. de España, by the bridge, tel (952) 87 12 72.

Don't be discouraged, though; the views alone are worth the trip. One of the best places to enjoy them is the **Alameda del Tajo**, a park on the edge of the **Mercadillo**, as the new town is called. Next to it, Ronda has one of Spain's oldest and most picturesque bullrings. The 1785 **Plaza de Toros**, the 'cathedral of bullfighting', gets only about three *corridas* a year, but it still has great prestige; the art of bullfighting was developed here. There's a small museum inside. The **Puente Nuevo**, as the bridge to the *Ciudad* (old town) is called, was built on the second try in 1740—the first one immediately collapsed. The bridge's two thick piers descend almost 92 m (300 ft) into the bottom of the narrow gorge.

In the Ciudad
From the bridge, a steep path heads downwards to two 18th-century palaces: the

Palacio de Salvatierra and the **Casa del Rey Moro**, built over Moorish foundations. From its garden there is a stairway—365 steps cut out of the rock, called the **Mina**—that takes you down to the bottom of the gorge. Here there's a Moorish bridge and well-preserved remains of a **Moorish bath**. Back on top, if you survive the climb back up, there is the town's main church, **Santa María La Mayor**, still retaining the mihrab and minaret of the mosque it replaced, and the ruins of the **Alcazar**, blown up by the French.

Besides the opportunities for walks in and around the valleys under Ronda an interesting excursion can be made to an area of curiosities 15–20 km (9–12 miles) west of town. The hills around the hamlet of Montejague are full of caves. Two, the **Cueva del Gato** and **Cueva del Hundidero**, both full of stalactites and odd formations, are connected. The little stream called the Gaduares disappears in one and comes out in the other. Five kilometres (3.1 miles) south, past the village of Benaoján, the **Cueva de la Pileta** has some 25,000-year-old art—simple drawings in black of animals and magic symbols (the caretaker lives in the farmhouse near the entrance if no one's around). Twelve km (7.5 miles) west of Ronda, off the road to Grazalema, are the Roman ruins of **Aciupo** known locally as 'Ronda la Vieja', with a theatre and stage building like Mérida's. And finally, from the ancient isolated village of **Gaucin**, 25 km (15.6 miles) southwest of Ronda, you can see Gibraltar and the African coast over the peaks of the Serrania.

WHERE TO STAY (tel prefix 956)
The **Parador Nacional Casa del Corregidor***** in Arcos has recently been reopened after a thorough restoration of the old palace that houses it; it's a lovely place, and quite popular, so book ahead (Pl. de España, tel 70 05 00; doubles 10,000–11,500 pts). More reasonable is **Los Olivos***** (San Miguel 2, tel 70 08 11), where rooms with bath go for 5000–6000 pts. Apart from that, in Arcos and the other 'white villages' there are only the simplest of places to stay and eat.

(tel prefix 952)
Ronda has a wider choice. The **Reina Victoria****** is a fine old hotel, built by the British around the turn of the century, with lovely views over the cliffs. The German poet, Rainer Maria Rilke, stayed here for a season and wrote some of his best-known works (C. Jerez 25, tel 87 12 40; doubles 7500–10,000 pts). Less expensive, near the old town, is the **Royal*****, C. Virgen de la Paz 42, near the bullring, tel 87 11 41; doubles 3500–4000 pts). There are dozens of small *hostales* and *camas* over bars—most of them quite agreeable—in the Mercadillo (new town) on all the side streets of C. Jerez. In Benaoján, near the Pileta caves, the **Molino del Santo***** is a converted water mill beside a mountain stream. It's friendly and intimate (10 rooms, all with bath), and offers excursions each week—hiking, cycling and mini-bus nature tours in the Grazalema National Park There's a spring-fed swimming pool, and the kitchen serves Andaluz cuisine (Benaoján, tel 16 71 51; 6500 pts).

EATING OUT
Arcos has one reputable restaurant, **Mesón del Brigadier**, serving mostly pork and game dishes (2000 pts; Lago de Arcos, tel 70 10 03). The best meals Ronda can offer, with a view to match, are at the **Don Miguel**, overlooking the gorge next to the famous bridge; they also have a bar built into the bridge itself (2000–3500 pts for a full-course

dinner; Villanueva 4, tel 87 10 90). Otherwise, stick to the restaurants in the Mercadillo like the **Mesón Santiago** (C. Marina 3, tel 87 15 59) or the **Cafe Doña Pepa** next door. Quite a few really inferior tourist restaurants have been opening in conspicuous places to take advantage of day-trippers from the Costa: watch out.

Málaga to Córdoba

The heart of Andalucía, a vast tract of bountiful hills covered in olives and vines, this area is more densely populated, and a bit more prosperous than most of the region's rural districts. The towns are closer together; all white, and all punctuated by the warm sandstone of their palaces and towers. Some did well even in Andalucía's grim 18th century: Osuna under its haughty dukes, and Priego de Córdoba with its once-famous textiles; others haven't had a break since the passing of the Moors. Some inspired poets and novelists, others are famous for leather or barrels. Along the way, on what we hope will be a properly Spanish picaresque journey through a region few tourists enter, there will be flamingoes, dolmens, rococo frippery, memorabilia of Julius Caesar, a cask of *amontillado*, a pretty fair canyon, and 139 gargoyles.

GETTING AROUND
Antequera is on the rail line from Algeciras to Granada, and there are easy connections to all points from nearby Bobadilla Junction (station on Av. de la Estación, tel (952) 84 23 30). The bus station is on C. Alameda, with lots of buses to Málaga and Sevilla, less frequently to Granada and Córdoba, as well as Olvera, Osuna and the other villages of the region.

TOURIST INFORMATION
Antequera: Pl. Coso Viejo, tel (952) 84 21 80.
Osuna: Plaza Major s/n, tel (954) 481 16 17.
Estepa: Plaza del Carmen 1, tel (954) 482 10 00.
In the *ayuntamiento* (town hall) of: Priego de Córdoba, Plaza de la Constitución 3, tel (957) 54 01 34; Lucena, Plaza Nueva 1, tel (957) 50 03 27; Cabra, Plaza de España 11, tel (957) 52 21 11.

For a complete contrast to urban life in Málaga, take the MA423 north out of the city to visit some of the remote villages and take in some spectacular scenery as almond trees, cactus and olive groves replace apartment blocks and the mountains drop steeply away to the silver ribbon of a stream down below. Thirty km northwest from Málaga lies **Almogia**, presenting a dramatic spectacle overlooking a high ridge. From 15–18 August this place comes to life with dancing in the streets in celebration of San Roque and San Sebastian. The best views are from the ruined tower. The MA424 continues north from here, to **Villanueva de la Concepción**, the closest town to the rock formations at **El Torcal**. A natural park has been laid out around this tall but hikeable mountain with unusual, eroded red limestone crags around it. Several paths are marked out.

Heading east from Ronda, turn north at the town of Alora and in about 15 km (9.3 miles) you'll come to one of Andalucía's natural wonders, **El Chorro Gorge**, in the deep rugged canyon of the Río Guadalhorce, with sheer walls of limestone tossed about at crazy angles. Thrill-seekers can cirumnavigate it on an old concrete catwalk called **El Camino del Rey**, gradually crumbling into a ruin though, amazingly, they still keep it open.

If you have time to explore this region, around three separate artificial lakes of a big government hydroelectric scheme, seek out the **Church of Bobastro**, just west of El Chorro on the little road north from Alora. Bobastro is a 9th-century basilica cut out of bare rock that supposedly contains the tomb of ibn-Hafsun, the (possibly) Christian emir who founded a short-lived independent state in the mountains around 880. Some remains of the city and fortress he built can be seen on the heights nearby. The lake shores themselves, surrounded by gentle hills, make an ideal place to have a lazy picnic.

From Bobastro follow the road to **Ardales** and **Carratraca**. Carratraca has been a spa town from Greek and Roman times, but its heyday was in the 19th and early 20th centuries. Visitors included Byron, Dumas, Rilke and Napoleon II's wife, the Empress Eugènie, who gadded about everywhere else in Europe, and lived to the ripe old age of 94. The baths have been restored and can be visited by would-be cure-seekers from June to October. This town also attracts many visitors for its passion play *El Paso*, performed in Holy Week by 140 of the villagers in the bullring. From here the road twists its way to **Alora**, once a Roman settlement, later owned by the Moors until 1484. From here it's a 38 km drive down to Málaga. Some 30 km (18.8 miles) west of Antequera, off the road to Sevilla, the **Laguna de Fuente de Piedra** is one of Europe's largest breeding grounds for flamingoes. You can see them from March to September; the rest of the year you'll have to look them up in Senegal.

Antequera

Known in Roman times as *Antikaria*, later history saw it as the first of the Granadan border fortresses to fall to the Reconquista, in 1410, although subsequently it was retaken by the Moors and lost again. The centre of a leather-tanning industry, it is not an especially interesting city, though it's as large as Ronda. There is, however, quite an impressive ensemble of 16–18th-century buildings. The 17th-century Nerja Palace houses the **Municipal Museum**, with many religious works including a wonderful St Francis by Alonso Cano and a Roman bronze of a boy that dates back nearly 2000 years (open 11–1 and 4.30–6.30). Up the Cuesta Zapateros, at the top of the hill, is the 16th-century **Arco de los Gigantos** meant as a sort of triumphal arch for the seldom-victorious Philip II, and incorporating ancient fragments; next to it, the ruins of a Moorish fortress offer views over the town. Nearby is the *plateresque* church of **Santa María La Mayor**, attached to which is an art restoration centre, teaching stone masonry, woodwork and ironwork.

The Romans may have given Antequera its name—'old town', and there was probably a settlement here some centuries before the arrival of the Phoenicians. Another possibility is that the name is related to *anta*, the local word for dolmen. Some 5 km (3.1 miles) north of the town are the Neolithic monuments known as the **Cuevas de Menga** 'first real architecture in Spain'. They are hardly as impressive the *talayots* and *taulas* of the island of Menorca, but there's nothing like them in mainland Spain. Le Corbusier came here in the 50s, as he said 'to pay homage to my predecessors'. There are three, dating from anything between 4500 and 2500 BC. The two largest, the Menga and Viera dolmens (open 10–1:30 and 5–7), are covered chambers about 21.5 m (70 ft) long, roughly elliptical and lined with huge, flat stones; other monoliths support the roof-like pillars. At El Romeral nearby, under a mound and in the grounds of a sugar factory, the third of these temples has two chambers with domed ceilings. Originally the mound would have been about 300 feet in diameter, as big as Newgrange in County Meath, Ireland. All three have etchings of figures and symbols around their walls.

Fifteen kilometres east of Antequera on the N342 is **Archidona**. The town overlooks acres of olive trees, but its main feauture is the unique, octagonal Plaza Mayor, the **Ochavada**, one of the loveliest plazas in Andalucía, built 1780–86 by Francisco Astorga and Antonio Gonzalez. Nearby **Loja** had a 9th-century **Alcazaba** and the 16th-century church of **San Gabriel** has a cúpula attributed to Diego de Siloé.

WHERE TO STAY
If you're not on a budget, then *the* hotel in the area is **La Bobadilla***** near Loja, 12 km east of Archidona. It's an honest attempt at reconstructing the typical Andaluz *pueblo*, complete with Moorish touches, and covers a large area of land on a hilltop. Luxuries like this don't come cheaply, though—about 32,000 pts a night in high season, 30,000 pts otherwise (Finca La Bobadilla, Loja, tel (958) 32 18 61).

(tel prefix 952)
In Antequera the **Parador de Antequera*** is a plain, modern building but has the most comforts here, and is reasonably priced at 7000–9000 pts for air-conditioned doubles (García del Olmo s/n, tel 84 00 61). In the town centre, the best choice is the **Manzanito***, nine rooms in a pretty location at C. Calvo Sotelo 5, tel 84 10 23 (doubles with bath 3500–4200 pts). The management also runs a good restaurant (800–1000 pts) next door. Alora's only hotel, the **Alondra II***, has only four rooms (C. Mola 56, tel 49 63 71; 2800 pts with bath, 2200 pts without) and it is typical of the small *hostales* around these villages. The place to stay in Carratraca is **El Principe***, but in season it's always advisable to book beforehand (4000 pts; Antonio Riobo 9, tel 45 80 20). Archidona only has small one star *hostales*. Of them, **Las Palomas*** is the best bet, on the main Jerez–Granada road (km 177, tel 71 43 26; 3000 pts without bath).

EATING OUT
Andaluz and international dishes are on the menu of **La Finca**, the restaurant in La Bobadilla Hotel; 6000–7000 pts for a full dinner). Other than in the hotels the roadside *ventas* are probably the best bet.

North of Antequera

In the gentler hills to the north, approaching the valley of the Guadalquivir, a few more towns are worth mentioning if you're passing that way. **Osuna** , founded by a busy, go-ahead governor named Julius Caesar, was an important Roman military centre for the south of Spain, and survives as an attractive little city of white houses with characteristic *rejas* (grilles) over every window. Osuna was an aristocratic town after the Reconquista, home of the objectionable Dukes of Osuna who lorded it over much of Andalucía. Their 'pantheon' of tombs may be seen in the fine Renaissance **Colegiata Church** on a hill on the west side of town. Inside is a memorable *Crucifixion* by José Ribera, and four other of his works in the high altar retablo. Behind the church is the old university building, founded in 1548 and now serving as a school. Several decorative façades of 16th-century mansions can be seen along the **Calle San Pedro**. Osuna has a little **archaeology museum** in the **Torre del Agua**, part of the old fortifications, and a museum of dubious art in **La Encarnación** convent, a Baroque work of the late 18th century; the cloister is done out in ceramic tiles (both open daily except Monday, 10–1.30 and 4–7.30).

Further east, on the Osuna–Antequera road, **Estepa** is a smaller but not so neat version of Osuna. It's known for its Christmas biscuits *polverones* and *mantecado*, along with the mass suicide of its inhabitants who preferred not to surrender to the Roman enemy in 208 BC. Above the town are the remains of a castle with a well-preserved Almohad keep; the two Baroque showpieces are the churches of **El Carmen**, in the main square, with a spectacular façade, and the 18th-century *Virgen de los Remedios*.

The Cordobés Subbética and La Campiña

Here in the heartland of Andalucía lies the grandly titled **Parque Natural de las Sierras Subbéticas de Córdoba**—a succession of wooded hills that dip into the valleys of the rivers Zagrillo, Salado and Caicena. The landscape of oak trees, olive groves and much shrubland is home to eagles, falcons and vultures, rabbit and partridge, the odd adder, field mice, bats and badgers; the rivers and small lakes dotted around brim with bass, perch and trout. Most tourists miss these corners of Andalucía that seem untouched by the passing of time, where the people are god-fearing and industrious, and where the visitor is welcomed but watched carefully.

Twenty km north of Estepa on the C338 at **Puente Genil** an old Moorish-style mill still turns in a pretty setting along the Río Genil. In the town is the 15th-century church of **La Concepción**, but the town's latter-day claim to fame is its local importance as a food manufacturing centre. *Semana Santa* here is a big affair, and people come from all over the province to see the very colourful procession in Roman costume and biblical dress.

Further east on the C338, **Lucena** is one of the centres of a great wine-growing region. The town is not known for its beauty, but for making the biggest wine barrels in Andalucía, and as the birthplace of the Baroque architect Hurtado Izquierdo. He produced the incredible Cartuja chapel in Granada, though he is not responsible for Lucena's wonderful Baroque **Sagrario** chapel in the church of **San Mateo**. Before the Reconquista Lucena seems to have been for a time an autonomous Jewish republic, and a major trading centre. Its small industries still thrive today; notably furniture-making, the manufacture of brass and copperware, and barrels. Nearby are the remains of the **Tower of Moral**, where Granada's last king Boabdil was imprisoned by Ferdinand in 1483. Twenty km south of here, the town of **Rute** produces the potent elixir *anís*. Right at the centre of Andalucía, fittingly set in a sea of olive groves and vineyards, is **Cabra**, 10 km north of Lucena on the C327. From here you get a sweeping view of the Sierra Nevada to the southeast and the Guadalquivir valley to the north.

Priego de Córdoba lies at the foot of the highest mountain in the province, **La Tiñosa**, and has a famous ensemble of Baroque churches, monasteries and fountains; the best is the **Asunción** Church with a beautiful dome over its Sagrario chapel and a sumptuous stucco interior. The town's other pride is the Baroque **Fuente del Rey**:

three connecting fountain pools lined with 139 gargoyles, and a centrepiece of Neptune and Aphrodite on a horse drawn carriage—it wouldn't look out of place in a *piazza* in Rome. In the church of **San Pedro** is an image of the *Immaculada*, a work attributed to Alonso Cano. The town is typified by its fancy window grillwork and ornate front doors, as on display in the Calle Río.

From Cabra the C327 heads northeast to **Baena**, a town of major importance in Moorish times, now squeezing out olive oil in remarkable quantities. A clean, tightly packed town with narrow, whitewashed streets and the ruins of a Moorish castle, Baena sees most of its visitors arrive for the Holy Week celebrations, when a deafening drum-rolling competition is held to see who can play the longest and the loudest; it lasts *two days*. Twenty two km northwest from Cabra is **Aguilar de la Frontera**, another attractive wine town (producing *solera fina*, mostly). It has an unusual octagonal plaza, a copy of the one in Antequera, and the Renaissance church of **Santa María del Sorerraño**.

From Aguilar it's a short hop up the road to the prince of the wine-producing towns, **Montilla**, sitting on a rise amidst endless acres of vines. Although the name for pale dry sherry *amontillado* takes its name from this town, the wine produced here is not a sherry, in that no extra alcohol is added to fortify it, unlike in Jerez. The town is refreshingly short of Baroque churches, but its wine bodegas can be visited to sample the good stuff. A small **museum** is dedicated to Garcilaso de la Vega, Spanish-Inca son of a *conquistador* and chronicler of the Inca civilisation in the 16th century. The 1512 Gothic convent of **Santa Clara** is worth a visit for its *mudejár* roof and Baroque altarpiece. The town is believed to be the site of the Battle of Munda, where former governor Caesar's men finally put paid to the Spanish followers of Pompey.

WHERE TO STAY AND EAT   (tel prefix 954)
In Osuna, the best is the **Cinco Puertas*** (also the only one with heating; doubles 3000 pts with bath, 2000 pts without; C. Franco 79, tel (954) 481 12 43). In Estepa, **Los Angeles**** is adequate (2200 pts without bath; Avda Andalucía 21, tel (954) 482 09 84).

(tel prefix 957)
Puente Genil has only one *hostal*, the **Xenil****, where doubles with bath are 4000–4800 pts (Garcia Lorca 3, tel 60 02 00). Priego de Córdoba: the **Río-Piscina**** has a small pool and tennis court, and reasonable rates for its doubles with bath (3400 pts; Ctra Monturque–Alcalá la Real Km 44, tel 70 01 86). Aguilar has a number of places, but none offering any luxury. **San José** is the best (2200 pts for basic room; Pescaderia 6, tel 66 02 22). Montilla is the only place with sophisticated accommodation: **Don Gonzalo***** on the main road with gardens, swimming pool and tennis court (5500 pts; Ctra Madrid–Málaga Km 447, tel 65 06 58). Montilla also has a decent restaurant, again on the main road, **Las Camachas**, where you can accompany the tasty fish dishes with a glass or two of the local brew (2000 pts; no phone).

137

GRANADA AND THE SIERRA NEVADA

The Alhambra

Granada

The first thing to do upon arrival is to pick up a copy of Washington Irving's *Tales of the Alhambra*. Every bookshop in town can sell you one in just about any language; it was Irving who put Granada on the map, and established the Alhambra as the necessary romantic pilgrimage of Spain.

Granada, in fact, might seem a disappointment without Irving. The modern city underneath the Alhambra is a stolid, remarkably unmagical place, with little to show for the 500 years since the Catholic Kings put an end to its ancient glory. As the Moors were expelled, the Spanish Crown replaced them with Castilians and Galicians from up north, and even today Granadinos are thought of as a bit foreign by other Andalucíans. Their Granada has never been a happy place. Particularly in the last 100 years it has been full of political troubles. Around the turn of the century even the Holy Week processions had to be called off for a few years because of disruptions from the leftists, and at the start of the Civil War the reactionaries who always controlled Granada made one of the first big massacres of Republicans.

One of their victims was Federico García Lorca, the Granadino who, in the decades since his death, has come to be recognized as the greatest Spanish dramatist and poet since the 'golden age'. If Irving's fairy tales aren't to your taste, consider the works of Lorca, in which Granada and its sweet melancholy are recurring themes. Lorca once wrote that he remembered Granada 'as one should remember a sweetheart who has died'.

The Nasrid Kingdom of Karnattah

First Iberian *Elibyrge*, then Roman *Illiberis*, the town did not make a name for itself until

138

the era of the *taifas* in the early 11th century, when it emerged as the centre of a very minor state. In the 1230s, while the Castilians were seizing Córdoba and preparing to polish off the rest of the Almoravid states of al-Andalus, an Arab chieftain named Muhammad ibn-Yusuf ibn-Nasr established himself around Jaén. When that town fell to the Castilians in 1235, he moved his capital to the town the Moors called *Karnattah*. Ibn Nasr (or Muhammad I, as he is generally known) and his descendants in the Nasrid dynasty enjoyed great success at first in extending their domains. By 1300 this last Moorish state of Spain extended from Gibraltar to Almería, but this accomplishment came entirely at the expense of other Moors. Muhammad and his successors were in fact vassals of the Kings of Castile, and aided them in campaigns more often than they fought them.

Karnattah at this time is said to have had a population of some 200,000—as many as it has now—and both its arts and industries were strengthened by refugees from the fallen towns of al-Andalus. Thousands came from Córdoba, especially, and the Albaicín quarter was largely settled by the former inhabitants of Baeza. Although a significant Jewish population remained, there were very few Christians. In the comparatively peaceful 14th century, Granada's conservative, introspective civilization reached its height, with the last flowering of Arabic-Andaluz lyric poetry and the architecture and decorative arts of the Alhambra.

This state of affairs lasted until the coming of the Catholic Kings. Isabella's religious fanaticism made the completion of the Reconquista the supreme goal of her reign; she sent Ferdinand out in 1484 to do the job, which he accomplished in eight years by a breathtakingly brilliant combination of force and diplomacy. Karnattah at the time was suffering the usual curse of al-Andalus states—disunity founded on the egotism of princes. In this fatal feud, the main actors were Abu al-Hasan Ali (Mulay Hassan in Irving's tales), King of Karnattah, his brother El Zagal ('the valiant') and the king's rebellious son, Abn abd-Allah, better known to posterity as Boabdil el Chico. His seizure of the throne in 1482 started a period of civil war at the worst possible time. Ferdinand was clever enough to take advantage of the divisions; he captured Boabdil twice, and turned him into a tool of Castilian designs. Playing one side against the other, Ferdinand snatched away one Nasrid province after another with few losses. When the unfortunate Boabdil, after renouncing his kingship in favour of the Castilians, finally changed his mind and decided to fight for the remnants of Karnattah (by then little more than the city itself and the Sierra Nevada), Ferdinand had the excuse he needed to mount his final attack. Karnattah was besieged, and after two years, Boabdil agreed to surrender under terms that guaranteed his people the use of their religion and customs. When the keys of the city were handed over on 2 January 1492, the Reconquista was complete.

Under a gentlemanly military governor, the Conde de Tendilla, the agreement was kept until the arrival in 1499 of Cardinal Cisneros, the most influential cleric in Spain and a man who made it his personal business to destroy the last vestiges of Islam and Moorish culture. The new Spanish policy—planned, gradual genocide (see History)— was as successful in the former lands of Granada as it was among those other troublesome heathens of the same period, the Indians of Central and South America. The famous revolt in the Alpujarras (1568) was followed by a rising in the city itself, in the Albaicín. Between 1609 and 1614, the last of the Muslims were expelled, including most of those who had converted to Christianity, and their property confiscated. It is said that

GRANADA

Key

1. Tourist Information
2. Train Station
3. Bus Station
4. Post Office
5. Telephones
6. Audiencia
7. Sta Ana
8. Alcazaba
9. Gate of Justice
10. Moorish Palace
11. Palacio de Carlos V
12. S. José
13. Archaeological Museum
14. S. Juan de los Reyes
15. Casa Chapiz
16. S. Miguel
17. S. Nicolás (Mirador)
18. Sta Isabel la Real
19. Elvira Gate
20. La Cartuja
21. Hospice Real
22. S. Juan de Dios
23. S. Jerónimo
24. University (New Campus)
25. Royal Chapel
26. Alcaicería
27. La Madraza
28. Corral del Carbón
29. S. Domingo
30. Diputación

even today, there are old families in Morocco who sentimentally keep the keys to their long-lost homes in Granada.

Such a history does not easily wear away, even after so many centuries. The Castilians corrupted Karnattah to *Granada*; just by coincidence that means 'pomegranate' in Spanish, and the pomegranite has come to be the symbol of the city. With its associations with the myth of Persephone, with the mysteries of death and loss, no symbol could be more suitable for this capital of melancholy.

GETTING AROUND   (tel prefix 958)

By air: There are two flights daily to Madrid (except Sun), twice daily to Barcelona (weekdays only) and three times a week to the Balearics and Canaries.

By train: Granada has connections to Guadix and Almería (three daily), to Algeciras, Sevilla, and Córdoba by way of Bobadilla Junction (they are sometimes complicated) and two daily to Madrid and Barcelona; three daily to Alicante, one a day to Valencia. The station is on the northern end of town, about a mile from the centre, on Av. de los Andaluces (city ticket office is on C. Reyes Católicos, off Pl. Nueva, tel 22 34 97 for information).

By bus: The main bus station, run by the Alsina Graells company, is equally inconveniently located on the Camino de Ronda (tel 25 12 58) with service to Madrid, and all points in Andalucía. For other buses to Madrid, Murcia, Alicante, Valencia and Barcelona, the services are run by the Bacoma and Nevamar lines, in front of the train station at Av. de los Andaluces (tel 23 18 83).

In the city, one very useful bus to know is the no. 11, a route that passes the train and bus stations, the Gran Vía and C. Reyes Católicos (take it in either direction since it's circular). A good way to see the Albaicín is to take the no. 7 bus from C. Reyes Católicos to the top of the hill (get off at C. Pages) and walk down. And the no. 2 from the Pl. Nueva will save you the trouble of climbing up to the Alhambra.

TOURIST INFORMATION

Provincial Tourist Office at Plaza Mariana Pineda 10, tel 22 66 88. In addition, there's a Municipal Tourist Office near the Cathedral on C. Libreros 2, tel 22 59 90. You can hire personal stereos from these places for audio-guides to the Alhambra and the Cathedral.

A Sentimental Orientation

In spite of everything, more of the lost world of al-Andalus can be seen in Granada than even in Córdoba. Granada stands where the foothills of the Sierra Nevada meet the fertile 'Vega de Granada', the greenest and best stretch of farmland in Andalucía. Two of those hills extend into the city itself. One bears the **Alhambra**, the fortified palace of the Nasrid kings, and the other the **Albaicín**, the most evocative of the 'Moorish' neighbourhoods of Andalucían cities. Parts of old Karnattah extended down into the plain, but they have been largely submerged into the new city. How much you enjoy Granada will depend largely on how successful you are in ignoring the new districts, in particular three barbarically ugly streets that form the main automobile route through Granada: the **Gran Vía Colón** chopped through the centre of town in the 19th century, the **Calle Reyes Católicos** and the **Acera del Darro**. The latter two are paved over the course of the Río Darro, the little stream that ran picturesquely through the city until the 1880s.

Before these streets were built, the centre of Granada was the **Plaza Nueva**, a square

THE ALHAMBRA

1 Puerta de las Granadas
2 Puerta de la Justicia (Gate of Justice)
3 Puerta del Vino
4 Ticket booths
5 Torre de la Vela
6 Patio del Mexuar
7 Patio de las Arrayanes (Court of the Myrtles)
8 Sala de la Barca (Hall of the Boat)
9 Salon de Embajadores (Hall of the Ambassadors)
10 Patio de los Leones (Court of the Lions)
11 Sala de Abencerrajes (Hall of the Abencerrajes)
12 Sala de las Dos Hermanes (Hall of the Two Sisters)
13 Sala de los Reyes (Hall of the Kings)
14 Patio de Lindaraja
15 Royal Apartments
16 Palace of Charles V
17 Chapel and Crypt
18 Church of Santa Maria
19 Convento de San Francisco (Parador)

that is also partly built over the Darro. The handsome building that gives it its character is the 1584 **Audiencia**, built by Philip II for the royal officials and judges. **Santa Ana church**, across the plaza, was built in 1537 by Diego de Siloe, one of the architects of Granada's cathedral. From this plaza the ascent to the Alhambra begins, up a narrow street called the **Cuesta de Gomerez**, past guitar-makers' shops, gypsies and vast displays of tourist trinkets, ending abruptly at the **Puerta de las Granadas**, a monumen: :l gateway erected by Charles V.

The Alhambra

The grounds of the Alhambra begin here with a bit of the unexpected. Instead of the walls and towers, not yet even in view, there is a lovely grove of great elms, the **Alameda**; even more unexpectedly, they are the contribution of the Duke of Wellington, who took time off from chasing the French to plant them during the Peninsular War. Take the path to the left—it's a stiff climb—and in a few minutes you'll arrive at the **Gate of Justice**, entrance of the Alhambra. The orange tint of the fortress walls explains the name *Al-hamra*: 'the vermilion', and the unusual style of the carving on the gate is the first clue that here is something very different. The two devices, a hand and a key, carved on the inner and outer arches, are famous. According to one of Irving's tales, the hand will one day reach down and grasp the key; then the Alhambra will fall into ruins, the earth will open, and the hidden treasures of the Moors be revealed.

From the gate, a path leads up to a broad square. Here are the **Puerta del Vino**, so called from a long-ago Spanish custom of doling out free wine here to the inhabitants of the Alhambra, and also the ticket booth. To the left you'll see the walls of the **Alcazaba**, the fort at the tip of the Alhambra's narrow promontory, and to the right the huge **Palace of Charles V**; signs point your way to the entrance of the **Royal Palace** (Casa Real), with its splendidly decorated rooms that are the Alhambra's main attraction. The entire complex is open daily 10–6, 10–5.30 in winter. The steep admission—475 pts—gets you into everything except the museum in Charles V's palace, and is also good for the Generalife gardens on the adjacent hill. Everything's free Sundays after 2.30. If you don't care to see everything in one day, your ticket will still work for the sections you miss on the following day. The Alhambra is also open Tuesday, Thursday, and Saturday night from 10–12 in the summer or 8–10 in mid-season; seeing it under the stars is the treat of a lifetime.

The Alcazaba

Not much remains of the oldest part of the Alhambra. This citadel probably dates back to the first of the Nasrid kings. Its walls and towers are still intact, but only the foundations of the buildings that once stood within it have survived. The **Torre de la Vela** at the tip of the promontory has the best views over Granada and the Vega. Its big bell was rung in the old days to signal the daily opening and closing of the water gates of the Vega's irrigation system; the Moors also used the tower as a signal post for sending messages. The Albaicín, visible on the opposite hill, is a revelation: its rows of white, flat-roofed houses on the hillside, punctuated by palm trees and cypresses, provide one of Europe's most exotic urban landscapes.

The Royal Palace

Words will not do, nor will exhaustive descriptions help, to communicate the experience of this greatest treasure of al-Andalus. This is what people come to Granada to see, and it is the surest, most accessible window into the refinement and subtlety of the culture of Moorish Spain—a building that can achieve in its handful of rooms what a work like Madrid's Royal Palace cannot even approach with its 2800.

It probably never occurs to most visitors, but one of the most unusual features of this palace is its modesty. What you see is what the Nasrid kings saw, and your imagination need add only a few carpets and tapestries, some well-crafted furniture of wood inlaid with ivory, wooden screens and grilles, and big round braziers of brass for heat or incense, to make the picture complete. Most of the actual building is wood and plaster, cheap and perishable, like a World's Fair pavilion; no good Muslim monarch would offend Allah's sense of propriety by pretending that these worldly splendours were anything more than the pleasures of a moment (much of the plaster, wood, and all of the tiles, are the products of careful restorations over the last 100 years). The Alhambra, in fact, is the only substantially intact medieval Muslim palace—anywhere.

THE MEXUAR

Like so many old royal palaces (those of the Hittites, the Byzantines or the Ottoman Turks, for example), this one is divided into three sections, one for everyday business of the palace and government; the next, more secluded, for the state rooms and official entertainments of the kings; and the third, where few outsiders ever reached, with the private apartments of the king and his household. Of the first, the small **Mexuar**, where the kings would hold their public audiences, survives near the present-day entrance to the palace complex. The adjacent **Patio of the Mexuar**, though much restored, is one of the finest rooms of the Alhambra. Nowhere is the meditative serenity of the palace more apparent (unless you arrive when all the tour groups do) and the small fountain in the centre provides an introduction to an important element of the architecture—water. Present everywhere, in pools, fountains and channels, water is as much a part of the design as the wood, tile, and stone.

COURT OF THE MYRTLES

If you have trouble finding your way around, remember the elaborately decorated portals never really lead anywhere; the door you want will always be tucked unobtrusively to the side; here, as in Sevilla's Alcazar, the principle is to heighten the sense of surprise. The entrance to the grand Court of the Myrtles, with its long goldfish pond and lovely arcades, is one of these. This was the centre of the second, state section of the palace; directly off it, you pass through the **Hall of the Boat**, so called from its hull-shaped wooden ceiling, and into the **Hall of the Ambassadors**, where the kings presided over all important state business. The views and the decoration are some of the Alhambra's best, with a cedarwood ceiling and plaster panels (many were originally painted) carved with floral arabesques or Arabic calligraphy. These inscriptions, some Koranic scripture (often the phrase 'Allah alone conquers', the motto of the Nasrids), some eulogies of the kings, and some poetry, recur throughout the palace. The more conspicuous are in a flowing script developed by the Granadan artists; look closely and you will see others, in the angular Kufic script, forming frames for the floral designs.

145

In some of the smaller chambers off the Court of the Myrtles, you can peek out over the domed roofs of the baths one floor below; opposite the Hall of the Ambassadors is a small entrance (often closed) into the dark, empty **crypt** of Charles V's palace, with curious echo effects.

COURT OF THE LIONS

Another half-hidden doorway leads you into the third section, the king's residence, built around the **Court of the Lions**, the most spectacular of the three. Here the artistic sensibility of Granada reached its limits of expression. The plaster and stucco work is the most ornate, the columns and arches the most delicate, with little pretence of any structural purpose; balanced on their slender shafts, the façades of the Court seem to hang in the air. As in much of Moorish architecture, the almost overripe arabesques of this patio conceal a subtle symbolism. The 'enclosed garden' that can stand for the attainment of truth, or paradise, or for the cosmos, is a recurring theme in Islamic mystical poetry. Here you may take the 12 endearingly preposterous lions who support the fountain in the centre as the months, or signs of the zodiac, and the four channels that flow out from the fountains as the four corners of the cosmos, the cardinal points, or on a different level the four rivers of paradise.

The rooms around the patio have exquisite decorations: to the right, from the entrance, the **Hall of the Abencerrajes**, named after the legend of the noble family that Boabdil supposedly had massacred at a banquet here during the civil wars just before the fall of Granada; to the left, the **Hall of the Two Sisters** (*las dos Hermanas*). Both of these have extravagant domed 'stalactite' ceilings. The latter chamber is also ornamented with a wooden window grille, another speciality of the Granadan artists; this is the only one surviving in the Alhambra. Adjacent to the Hall of the Two Sisters is the **Hall of the Ajimeces**, so called for its doubled windows. The **Hall of the Kings** (Sala de los Reyes), opposite the court's entrance, is unique for the paintings on its ceiling, works that would not be out of place in any Christian palace of medieval Europe. The central panel may represent six of Granada's 14th-century kings, those on the side are scenes of a chivalric court. The artist is believed to have been a visiting Spanish Christian painter, possibly from Seville.

From the Hall of the Two Sisters, steps lead down to the **Patio of the Lindaraja** (or Daraxa), with its fountain and flowers, Washington Irving's favourite spot in the Alhambra. Originally the inner garden of the palace, it was remodeled, along with the surrounding rooms, for the royal visits of Charles V and Philip V. Irving actually lived in the **Queen's Chamber**, decorated with frescoes of Charles V's expedition to Tunis—in 1829 apartments in the Alhambra could be had for the asking! Off the ground floor of this chamber is the beautifully decorated **Hammam**, the palace baths.

Follow the arrows, out of the palace and into the outer gardens, the **Jardines del Partal**, a broad expanse of rose terraces and flowing water. The northern walls of the Alhambra border the gardens, including a number of well-preserved towers: from the west, the *Torre de Las Damas*, entered by a small porch, the **Torre del Mihrab**, near which is a small mosque, now a chapel; the **Torre de los Picos**; the **Torre de la Cautiva**, one of the most elaborately decorated; and the **Torre de las Infantas**, one of the last projects in the Alhambra (c. 1400).

Palace of Charles V and the Museums
Anywhere else, this elegant Renaissance building would be an attraction in itself. Here it seems only pompous and oversized, and our appreciation of it is lessened by the mind-numbing thought of this Emperor, with a good half of Europe to build palaces in, having to plop it down here—ruining much of the Alhambra in the process. Once Charles had smashed up the place, he lost interest, and most of the still unfinished palace was not built until 1616.

The original architect, Pedro Machuco, had studied in Italy, and he took the opportunity to introduce into Spain the chilly, Olympian High Renaissance style of Rome. At the entrances are intricately detailed sculptural **reliefs** showing scenes from Charles' campaigns and military 'triumphs' in the antique manner; armoured torsos on sticks amidst heaps of weapons. This is a very particular sort of art, arrogant and weird, and wherever it appears around the Mediterranean it will usually be associated with the grisly reign of the man who dreamt of being Emperor of the World. Inside, Pachuco added a pristinely classical circular courtyard, based perhaps on a design by Raphael. For all its Doric gravity, the patio was used almost from its completion for bullfights and mock-tournaments.

On its top floor has been installed Granada's **Museo de Bellas Artes** (open daily 10–3) a largely forgettable collection of religious paintings and polychromes from Granada churches. Downstairs, the **Museo Nacional de Art Hispano-Musulman** contains perhaps Spain's best collection of Moorish art, including some paintings, similar to those in the Moorish palace's Hall of the Kings. Also present are original *azulejo* tiles and plaster arabesques from the palace, and some exceedingly fine wooden panels and screens. There is a collection of ceramic ware with fanciful figurative decoration—elephants and lady musicians—and some lovely astronomical instruments. Tucked in a corner of the museum are four big copper balls stacked on a pole, an ornament that once stood atop a Granada minaret. These were a typical feature of Andalucían minarets (as on La Giralda in Sevilla) and similar ones can be seen in Morocco today.

Behind Charles' palace a street leads into the remnants of the town that once filled much of the space within the Alhambra's walls, now reduced to a small collection of restaurants and souvenir stands. In Moorish times the Alhambra held a large permanent population, and even under the Spaniards it long retained the status of a separate municipality. At one end of the street, the 1581 **church of Santa María**, designed by Juan de Herrera, architect of El Escorial, occupies the site of the Alhambra's mosque; at the other, the first Christian building on the Alhambra, the 1495 **Convento de San Francisco**, has been converted into a Parador.

The Generalife
Many of the trillions of visitors the Alhambra receives each year have never heard of it, and pass up a chance to see the finest garden in Spain. The Generalife (**Djinat al-Arif**: high garden) was the summer palace of the Nasrid kings, built on the height the Moors called the 'Mountain of the Sun'. To get there, it's about a 5-minute walk from the Alhambra along a lovely avenue of tall cypresses.

The buildings, currently under restoration, hold few surprises if you've just come from the Alhambra. They are in fact older than most of the Royal Palace, probably begun

147

around 1260. The gardens and the view over the Alhambra and Albaicín are transcendent. They are built on terraces, on several levels along the hillside; in the centre, a long pool under sprays of water passes through beds of roses and an infinite variety of other blooms. A lower level, with a promenade on the hill's edge, is broken up into secluded bowers by cypress bushes cut into angular shapes of walls and gateways. There is no evidence that the original Moorish gardens looked anything like this; everything here was done in the last 200 years.

If you're walking down from the Alhambra, you might consider a different route, across the Alameda and down through the picturesque streets below the **Torres Bermejas**, an outwork of the Alhambra's fortifications built on foundations that may be as old as the Romans. The winding lanes and stairways around Calle del Aire and Calle Niño del Rollo, one of the most beautiful quarters of Granada, will eventually lead you back down near the Plaza Nueva.

Albaicín

Even more than the old quarters of Córdoba, this hillside neighbourhood of white-washed houses and tall cypresses has successfully preserved some of the atmosphere of al-Andalus. Its difficult site and the fact that it was long the district of Granada's poor, explains the lack of change, but today the Albaicín looks as if it is becoming fashionable again.

From the Plaza Nueva, a narrow street called the **Carretera del Darro** leads up the valley of the Darro between the Alhambra and Albaicín hills; here the little stream has not been covered over, and you can get an idea of how the centre of Granada looked in the old days. On the Alhambra side, old stone bridges lead up to a few half-forgotten streets hidden among the forested slopes; here you'll see some 17th-century Spanish houses with curious painted *esgrafiado* façades. Nearby, traces of a horseshoe arch can be seen where a Moorish wall once crossed the river; in the corner of Calle Baruelo there are well-preserved **Moorish baths**. Even more curious is the façade of the **Casa Castril** on the Darro, a flamboyant 16th-century mansion with a portal carved with a phoenix, winged scallop shells and other odd devices that have been interpreted as elements in a complex mystical symbolism. Over the big corner window is an inscription 'Waiting for her from the heavens'. The house's owner, Bernando de Zafra, was once a secretary to Ferdinand and Isabella, and he seems to have got into some trouble with the Inquisition.

Casa Castril has been restored as Granada's **Archaeological Museum** (open daily except Monday, 10–2) with a small collection of artefacts from the huge number of caves in Granada province, many inhabited since Paleolithic times, and a few Iberian settlements. There is a Moorish room, with some lovely works of art, and finally, an even greater oddity than Casa Castril itself. One room of the museum holds a collection of beautiful alabaster burial urns, made in Egypt, but found in a Phoenician-style necropolis near Almuñécar. Nothing like them has ever been discovered in Spain, and the Egyptian hieroglyphic inscriptions on them are provocative in the extreme (translations given in Spanish), telling how the deceased travelled here in search of some mysterious primordial deity.

Further up the Darro, there's a small park with a view up to the Alhambra; after that you'll have to do some climbing, but the higher you go the prettier the Albaicín is, and the better the views. Among the white houses and white walls are some of the oldest

Christian churches in Granada. As in Córdoba, they are tidy and extremely plain, built to avoid alienating a recently converted population unused to religious imagery. **San Juan de los Reyes** (1520) on Calle Zafra and **San José** (1525) are the oldest; both retain the plain minarets of the mosques they replaced. Quite a few Moorish houses survive in the Albaicín, and some can be seen on **Calle Horno de Oro**, just off the Darro, and **Calle Daralhorra** at the top of the Albaicín, the remains of a Nasrid palace that was largely destroyed for Isabella's **Convento de Santa Isabel la Real** (1501).

Here, running parallel to Calle Alcahaba is a long-surviving stretch of Moorish wall. There are probably a few miles of walls left, visible around the hillsides over Granada; the location of the city made a very complex set of fortifications necessary. In this one, about halfway up, you may pass through at **Las Pesas Gate**, with its horseshoe arches. The heart of the Albaicín is here, around the pretty, animated **Plaza Larga**; only a few blocks away the **Mirador de San Nicolás** in front of the church of that name, offers the most romantic view imaginable of the Alhambra with the snow-capped peaks of the Sierra Nevada behind it. Note the brick, barrel-vaulted fountain on the mirador, a typical Moorish survival; fountains like this can be seen throughout the Albaicín and most are still in use. Granada today has a small but growing Muslim community, and they have cleared the ground just off the mirador to build a mosque. Construction hasn't started yet; apparently they are facing some difficulties with the city government.

On your way back from the Albaicín you might take a different route, down a maze of back streets to the **Elvira Gate**; this area is one of the most picturesque corners of the neighbourhood.

Sacromonte

For something completely different, you might strike out beyond the Albaicín hill to the **Gypsy Caves of Sacromonte**. Granada has had a substantial gypsy population for several centuries now. Some have become settled and respectable, others live in trailers on vacant land around town. The most visible are those who prey on the tourists around the Alhambra and the Capilla Real, handing out carnations with a smile and then attempting to extort huge sums out of anyone dumb enough to take one (of course, they'll tell your fortune, too). The biggest part of the gypsy community, however, still lives around Sacromonte in streets of some quite well-appointed cave homes, where they wait to lure you in for a little display of flamenco. For 100 years or so, the consensus of opinion has been that the music and dancing are usually indifferent, and the gypsies' eventually successful attempts to shake out your last peseta make it an unpleasantly unforgettable affair. Nevertheless, if you care to match wits with the experts, proceed up the Cuesta del Chapiz from the Rio Darro, turn right at the **Casa del Chapiz**, a big 16th-century palace that now houses a school of Arab studies, and keep going until some gypsy child drags you home with him. Serious flamenco fans will probably not fare better elsewhere in Granada except during the festivals, though there are some touristy flamenco night-spots—the **Reina Mora** by Mirador San Cristobel is the best of them. On the third Sunday of each month, though, you can hear a **flamenco mass** performed in the San Pedro Church on the Carretera del Darro at 9 am.

Central Granada

The old city wall swung in a broad arc from Elvira Gate to the 'Puerta Real', now a small plaza full of traffic where Calle Reyes Católicos meets the Acera del Darro. Just a few blocks north of here, in a web of narrow pedestrian streets that make up modern Granada's shopping district, is the pretty **Plaza Bibarrambla**, full of flower stands and toy shops, with an unusual fountain supported by leering giants at its centre. This was an important square in Moorish times, used for public gatherings and tournaments of arms. The narrow streets leading off to the east are the **Alcaiceria**. This was the Moorish silk exchange, but the buildings you see now, full of tourist souvenir shops, are not original; the Alcaiceria burned down in the 1840s and was rebuilt in more or less the same fashion with Moorish arches and columns.

The Cathedral
The best way to see Granada's **cathedral** is to approach it from Calle Marques, just north of the Plaza Bibarrambla; the unique façade, with its three tall, recessed arches, is a striking sight, designed by the painter Alonso Cano (1667). On the central arch, the big plaque bearing the words 'Ave Maria' commemorates the exploit of the Spanish captain who sneaked into the city one night in 1490 and nailed this message up on the door of the great mosque this cathedral has replaced. The other conspicuous feature is the name *José Antonio Primo de Rivera* carved on the façade. Son of the 20's dictator Miguel Primo de Rivera, José Antonio was a mystic fascist who founded the Phalangist Party. His thugs provoked many of the disorders that started the Civil War, and at the beginning of the conflict he was captured by the Loyalists and executed. Afterwards his followers treated him as a sort of holy martyr, and chiselled his name on every cathedral in Spain. That you can still see it here says a lot about Granada today.

The rest of the cathedral isn't up to the standard of its façade, and there is little reason to go in and explore its cavernous interior or dreary museum. Work was begun in 1521, after the Spaniards broke their promise not to harm the great mosque. As in many Spanish cathedrals, the failure of this one stems from artistic indecision. Two very talented architects were in charge: Enrique de Egas, who wanted it Gothic, like his adjacent Capilla Real, and 5 years later Diego de Siloe, who decided Renaissance would look much nicer. A score of other architects got their fingers in the pie before the completion in 1703. Some features of the interior: the grandiose **Capilla Mayor**, with statues of the apostles, and of Ferdinand and Isabella, by Alonso de Mena, and enormous heads of Adam and Eve by Alonso Cano, whose sculptures and paintings can be seen all over the cathedral; the **Retablo de Jesús Nazareno** in the right aisle, with paintings by Cano and Ribera, and a *St Francis* of El Greco; the Gothic **portal** leading into the Capilla Real (now closed) by de Egas. The memorable work of the **museum**, at the foot of the bell tower, is a common subject of the degenerate art of the 1700s—a painted wooden head of John the Baptist.

Capilla Real
Leaving the Cathedral and turning left, you pass the outsized **Sacristy**, begun in 1705 and incorporated in the Cathedral façade. Turn left again at the first street, Calle de los Oficios, a narrow lane paved in charming patterns of coloured pebbles—a Granada speciality; on the left, you can pay your respects to *Los Reyes Católicos*, Ferdinand and Isabella, in the **Capilla Real** (open daily 11–1 and 4–7, Sunday 11–1). The royal couple had already built a mausoleum in Toledo, but after the capture of Granada they decided to plant themselves here. Even in the shadow of the bulky cathedral, Enrique de

Egas' Chapel (1507) reveals itself as the outstanding work of the Isabelline Gothic style, with its delicate roofline of traceries and pinnacles. Charles V thought it not nearly monumental enough for his grandparents, and only the distraction of his foreign wars kept him from wrecking it in favour of some elephantine replacement.

Inside, the Catholic Kings are buried under a pair of Carrara marble sarcophagi with their recumbent figures, elegantly carved though not necessarily flattering to either of them. The little staircase behind them leads down to the crypt, where you can peek in at their plain, lead coffins and those of their unfortunate daughter Juana the Mad and her husband Philip the Handsome, whose effigies lie next to the older couple above. Juana was Charles V's mother, and the rightful heir to the Spanish throne. There is considerable doubt as to whether she was mad at all; when Charles arrived from Flanders in 1517, he forced her to sign papers of abdication, and then locked her up in a windowless cell for the last 40 years of her life, never permitting any visitors. The interior of the chapel is sumptuously decorated—it should be, considering the huge proportion of the crown revenues that were expended on it. The iron reja by Master Bartolomé de Jaén and the retablo are especially fine; the latter is largely the work of a French artist, Phillipe de Bourgogne. In the chapel's sacristy you can see most of Isabella's personal art collection—works by Van der Weyden, Memling, Pedro Berruguete, Botticelli (attributed), Perugino and others, mostly in need of some restoration—as well as her crown and sceptre, her illuminated missal, some captured Moorish banners, and Ferdinand's sword.

Across the narrow street from the Capilla Real, an endearingly garish, painted Baroque façade hides **La Madraza**, a domed hall of the Moorish university (*medrese*); though one of the best Moorish works surviving in Granada, it is hardly ever open to visitors (just walk in if the building is open). The Christians converted it to a town hall, whence its other name, the Casa del Cabildo.

Across Calle Reyes Católicos

Even though this part of the city centre is as old as the Albaicín, most of it was rebuilt after 1492, and its age doesn't show. The only Moorish building remaining is also the only example left in Spain of a *khan* or caravanserai, the type of merchants' hotel common throughout the Muslim world. The 14th-century **Corral del Carbón**, just off Reyes Católicos, takes its name from the time, a century ago, when it was used as a coal warehouse. Under the Spaniards it also served time as a theatre; its interior courtyard with balconies lends itself admirably to the purpose, being about the same size and shape as a Spanish theatre of the classic age, like the one in Almagro (La Mancha). Today it houses a government handicrafts outlet, and much of the building is under restoration.

The neighbourhood of quiet streets and squares behind it is the best part of Spanish Granada and worth a walk if you have the time. Here you'll see the Mudejár **Casa de los Tiros**, a mansion built in 1505 on Calle Pavaneras, with strange figures carved on its façade. It presently houses a **museum** of the city's history, closed indefinitely for restorations. **Santo Domingo** (1512), the finest of Granada's early churches, is just a few blocks to the south. Ferdinand and Isabella endowed it, and their monograms figure prominently on the lovely façade. This neighbourhood is bounded on the west by the Acera del Darro, the noisy heart of modern Granada, with most of the big hotels. It's a little discouraging, but as compensation, just a block away the city has adorned itself with a beautiful string of wide boulevards very like the Ramblas of Barcelona, a wonderful spot for a stroll. The **Carretera del Genil** usually has some sort of open-air market on it, and further down, the **Paseo del Salon** and **Paseo de la Bomba** are quieter and more park-like, joining the pretty banks of the Rio Genil.

Northern Granada

From the little street on the north side of the Cathedral, the Carcel Baja, Calle San Jerónimo skirts the edge of Granada's markets and leads you towards the old **University** district. Even though much of the university has relocated to a new campus a half-mile to the north, this is still one of the livelier spots of town, and the colleges themselves occupy some fine, well-restored Baroque structures. The long yellow College of Law is one of the best, occupying a building put up in 1769 for the Jesuits; a small botanical garden is adjacent. Calle San Jerónimo ends at the Calle del Gran Capitán, where the landmark is the church of **San Juan de Dios**, with a Baroque façade and a big green-and-white tiled dome. **San Jerónimo**, a block west, is another of the oldest and largest Granada churches (1520); it contains the tomb of Gonzalvo de Córdoba, the 'Gran Capitán' who won so many victories in Italy for the Catholic Kings; adjacent are two Gothic cloisters.

Here you're not far from the Elvira Gate, in an area where old Granada fades into anonymous suburbs to the north. The big park at the end of the Gran Vía is the **Jardines del Triunfo**, with coloured, illuminated fountains the city hardly ever turns on. Behind them is the Renaissance **Hospice Real**, designed by Enrique de Egas (1504–22). A few blocks southwest, climbing up towards the Albaicín, your senses will be assaulted by the gaudiest Baroque chapel in Spain, in the **Cartuja**, or Carthusian monastery on Calle Real de Cartuja (open daily except Monday, 10–1 and 4–7). Gonzalvo de Córdoba endowed this Charterhouse, though little of the original works remain. The 18th-century chapel and its sacristy, done in the richest marble, gold and silver, and painted plaster, fairly oozes with a froth of twisted spiral columns, rosettes and curlicues. It has often been described as a Christian attempt to upstage the Alhambra, but the inspiration more likely comes from the Aztecs, via the extravagant Mexican Baroque.

Lorca

Under Franco, any mention of Spain's greatest modern poet was forbidden (under-standably so, since it was Franco's men who shot him). Today the Granadinos are coming to terms with Lorca, and seem determined to make up for the past. Lorca fans may pay their respects at two country-houses, now become museums, where the poet spent much of his early years: the **Huerta de San Vincente**, on the outskirts of town at Virgen Blanca, and the **Museo Lorca** at Fuente Vaqueros, a village just to the west on the Córdoba road (both open for guided tours every hour, 10–1 and 6–8, daily except Monday).

WHERE TO STAY   (tel prefix 958)
The city centre, around the Acera del Darro, is full of hotels, and there are lots of inexpensive *hostales* around the Gran Vía—but the less you see of these areas the better. Fortunately, you can choose from a wide range around the Alhambra and in the older parts of town if you spend the time to look. Right in the Alhambra itself, the **Parador**

Nacional San Francisco **** is perhaps the most famous of all paradors, housed in a convent where Queen Isabella was originally interred. It's beautiful, expensive, and small—you'll always need to book well in advance (doubles 16,000 pts; tel 22 14 40). Alternative choices very near the Alhambra would be the outrageously florid, neo-Moorish **Alhambra Palace** ****, where most rooms have terrific views over the city (C. Peña Portida 2, tel 22 14 68; doubles with TV, air-conditioning 14,000 pts) or the old **Washington Irving** ***, a little faded but still classy (Paseo del Generalife 2, tel 22 75 50; doubles 8000 pts). On the slopes below the Alhambra, the **Kenia** *** is a nice hotel recently installed in an old mansion with a garden (in a very quiet area, C. Molinos 65, tel 22 75 06; doubles 7500 pts). In the same area you can get a pool and air-conditioning at the **Los Angeles** ***, Cuesta Escoriaza 17, tel 22 14 24 (doubles 7400 pts). There's one other hotel in the Alhambra, the **Hostal America** *, with simple, pretty rooms for 7000 pts, but like the *parador*, book well in advance (Real de la Alhambra 53, tel 22 74 71).

For inexpensive *hostales*, the first place to look is the Cuesta de Gomerez, the street leading up to the Alhambra from Plaza Nueva. Besides the **Britz** ** (at no. 1; 3500 pts with bath, 2400 pts without, tel 22 36 52) and the **Gomerez** * (at no. 10; 1800 pts no bath), both nice, there are plenty of other spots nearby. Just a few blocks north of the Plaza Nueva, with the prettiest location in Granada, overlooking the Río Darro, is the **Huéspedes Santa Ana** (1800 pts, no bath; on C. Puente de Espiñosá, across the river). Off C. San Juan de Dios, in the university area, there are dozens of small *hostales* used to accommodating students. The **San Joaquin** * is one, with a pretty patio (tel 28 28 79, on C. Mano de Hierro; 3000 pts double with bath). Centrally placed on Plaza del Carmen (no. 29) is the immaculate *hostal* **Lisboa** ** (3000 pts; tel 22 14 13).

EATING OUT (tel prefix 958)

Granada isn't known for its cuisine. There is an infinity of touristic places around the Plaza Nueva, with little to distinguish between them. The *Granadinos* trust dining out at **Cunini**, where the menu depends on availability (2000–3000 pts; Plaza de Pescaderia 14, tel 25 07 77, closed Sun eve). Best known and best loved is the famous **Sevilla**, where García Lorca often met fellow poets and intellectuals. The character of the restaurant has been preserved and the specialities remain the local dishes of Granada and Andalucía (2000 pts; C. Oficios 12, tel 22 12 23, closed Sun eve). Both are near the cathedral. One of the touristy places, the **Abenhamar** on C. Abenhamar off C. Reyes Católicos, has good *paella* and a decent 800 pts *menú del día*. For agreeable dining in an intimate family-run restaurant, there is none better in Granada than **Mesón Antonio**, serving international dishes of meat and fish (2500 pts; Ecce Homo 6, tel 22 95 99; closed Sun, July and Aug). You should try to get up to the Albaicín for dinner on at least one night. In summer, **El Ladrillo**, on C. Pages on the northern end of the hill, fills a whole plaza with tables and serves up vast quantities of fish and beer at bargain rates—this place is the most popular in the area. Everyone's favourite rock-bottom, filling 400 pts menu is served up at the tiny **Cepillo** on C. Pescaderia, near the Cunini—order fish or squid.

Sierra Nevada and the Alpujarras

From everywhere in Granada, the mountains peer over the tops of buildings. Fortunately, Spain's loftiest peaks are also its most accessible; from the city centre you can be riding on Europe's highest mountain road in a little more than an hour. Even if you're without a car, there's a daily bus from town that makes the Sierra Nevada an easy day-trip.

Dress warmly, though. As the name implies, the Sierra Nevada is snowbound nearly all year, and even in late July and August, when the road is clear and you can travel right over the mountains to the valley of the Alpujarras, it's as chilly and windy as you would expect it to be, some 3390 m (11,000 ft) above sea level. These mountains, a geological curiosity of sorts, are just an oversized chunk of the Penibetic System, the chain that stretches from Arcos de la Frontera almost to Murcia. Their highest peak, **Mulhacen**, is less than 40 km (25 miles) from the coast. From Granada you can see nearly all of the Sierra: a jagged snowy wall without really distinctive peaks. The highest expanses are barren and frosty, but on a clear day they offer a view to Morocco. Mulhacen and especially its sister peak **Veleta** can be climbed without too much exertion; the road goes right by Veleta, and in August you can even drive to the top.

GETTING AROUND   (tel prefix 958)
For the Sierra Nevada, there is a daily bus from the Bar El Ventorrillo, in Granada'a Paseo del Violon, to the Albergue Universitario some 12 km (7.5 miles) from the peak of Veleta. Departures are at 9 am, returns at 5. If you're driving, call 48 01 53 for road reports in Spanish and English. For the Alpujarras: some buses on the Granada–Motril route stop in Lanjarón, but to penetrate the more isolated sections of the valley, you'll have to take a bus from Granada to Orgiva, the base for connecting buses to the other villages. The weekly Alpujarras tour bus from Granada on Sundays at 8 am departs from the Acera del Darro. Some 20 km (12.5 miles) before you reach Veleta, you'll enter the **Solynieve** ski area, beginning at its main resort, **Pradollano**, and continuing up to Veleta. From Pradollano there are cable cars up to the peak itself.

If you're adventurous and the road is clear, you can continue onwards from Veleta down into the **Alpujarras**, a string of white villages along the valley of the Rio Guadalfeo, between the Sierra Nevada and the little Contraviesa chain along the sea-coast. In Moorish times this was a densely populated region, full of vines and orchards. Much of its population was made up of refugees from the Reconquista, coming mainly from Sevilla. Under the conditions for Granada's surrender in 1492, the region was granted as a fief to Boabdil el Chico, but with forced Christianization and the resulting revolts, the entire population was expelled and replaced by settlers from the north.

Though often described as one of the most inaccessible corners of Spain, this region has attracted growing numbers of visitors since Gerald Brenan wrote *South from Granada*. The roads wind past stepped fields, cascades of water, high pastures and sudden drops, and when the almond trees are in blossom it is at its most appealing. Unlike the rest of Andalucían villages with their red-tiled roofs, the *pueblos* of the Alpujarras are flat-roofed. Far from the beaten track, you won't be alone if you visit the Alpujarras. Nevertheless, they're hardly spoiled; and with the villages relatively close to each other, and plenty of wild country on either side, it's a great spot for hiking or just finding some well-decorated peace and quiet.

Most visitors don't chance the Sierra Nevada route to Capileira, but use the Alpujarras' front door, off the main road from Granada to Motril. On the way, just outside the city, you'll pass the spot called **Suspiro de Moro**, where poor Boabdil sighed as he took his last look back over Granada. His mother was less than sympathetic—'Weep like a woman for what you were incapable of defending like a man,' she told him. The last 33 km (20.6 miles) of this route, where the road joins the Guadalfeo valley down to Motril, is one of the most scenic in Spain, but if you want to see the Alpujarras, you'll have to take the turnoff for **Lanjarón**, the only real tourist centre of the region. Lanjarón has long attracted visitors as a spa, and today it ships out most of the mineral water drunk in Spain. At **Orgiva**, the biggest town of the Alpujarras, is the **castle** of the Counts of Sástago, and a Renaissance church with a carving by Martinez Montañes. One other feature is the **Benizalte** mill, just outside the town.

From here you'll have a choice of keeping to the main road for **Ugijar**, or heading north through the highest and loveliest part of the region, with typical white villages climbing the hillsides under terraced fields. **Soportújar**, the first, has one of the Alpujarras' surviving primeval oak groves behind it. Next comes **Pampaneira**, a pretty little town of cobbled streets and flowers. In the Plaza Mayor there's a **museum** dedicated to the customs and costumes of Las Alpujarras. **Bubion** is a Berber-style village with an old textile mill.

All these villages are within sight of each other on a short detour along the edge of the beautiful (but walkable) ravine called **Barranco de Poqueira**. **Capileira**, the last village on the mountain pass route over Mulhacen and Veleta, sees more tourists than most. North from here the road takes you up across the Sierra Nevada and eventually to Granada. In winter this pass is snowbound, and even in summer you need to take extra care—it's steep and dangerous with precipitous drops down the ravines. However the beautiful scenery makes the risks worthwhile. Alternatively, continue on the GR421 to **Pitres**, centre of a Japanese-Spanish joint venture that produces and exports hand-crafted ballet shoes—of all things.

The road carries on through the villages of **Portugós** and **Busquistar** before arriving in **Trevelez**, on the slopes of Mulhacen. Trevelez likes to claim it's the highest village in Europe. It's also famous in Andalucía for its snow-cured hams. From there the road slopes back downwards to Juviles and **Berchules**, one of the villages where the traditional art of carpet-weaving has been maintained since Moorish times. **Yegen**, some 10 km (6.3 miles) further, became temporarily famous as the long-time home of British writer Gerald Brenan. After that come more intensively farmed areas on the lower slopes, with oranges, vineyards and almonds; you can either hit Ugijar and the main roads to the coast and Almería, or detour to the seldom-visited villages of **Laroles** and **Mairena** on the slopes of La Ragua, one of the last high peaks of the Sierra Nevada. Further east, through countryside that rapidly changes from healthy green to dry brown, the village of **Fondón** is of particular interest; an Australian architect Donald Grey and his Spanish partner José Antonio Garvayo have set up a school to teach the traditional crafts of ironwork, carpentry, tile- and brick-making, and by 1992 Fondón should be a model village with most of the old buildings restored.

East from Granada

GETTING AROUND

Daily buses from Granada to Murcia and Alicante stop in Guadix (Bacoma line, from Av. de los Andaluces, in front of the train station).

It's a better road on the way to Granada than leaving it. Between the city and Murcia are some of the emptiest, bleakest landscapes in Spain. The first village you pass through is **Purullena**, long famous for its pretty ceramic ware; the entire stretch of highway through it is lined with enormous stands and displays. The poverty of this region has long forced many of its inhabitants to live in caves, and nowhere more so than in **Guadix**. Several thousand of this city's population, most of them gypsies, have homes complete with whitewashed façades built into the hillsides, and chimneys and television aerials sticking out of the top. The cave dwellings have their advantages: they're warmer in the winter and cooler in summer than most Andalucían homes, relatively spacious and well-ventilated—and when the time comes to build a new room, all you need is a pick and shovel.

The centre of Guadix is dominated by a Moorish **Alcazaba**, largely rebuilt in the 16th century; near the arcaded central **Plaza Mayor** stands the huge **cathedral**, begun by Diego de Siloe, builder of Granada's cathedral, and given its magnificent façade in the 1700s by Andalucía's great rococo eccentric, Vincente Acero. The ornate traceries of the church, and the imposing castle, appearing together out of the empty, queerly eroded hills make a striking sight.

There's not much else to distract you in this corner of Spain. If you're headed for Almería and the coast (N324), you'll pass through **Calahorra**, with an unusual Renaissance castle with domed turrets, and **Gergal**, whose equally singular, perfectly preserved castle was built by the Moors. They claim you can see the stars more clearly here than anywhere in Europe, and Spain has built its national observatory outside town. The N342 from Guadix west to Murcia is even lonelier; here the surprisingly elegant, little whitewashed villages of **Vélez Blanco** and **Vélez Rubio** will provide a pleasant break in your travels. There are several caves in the neighbourhood where a wealth of 4000-year-old rock paintings of abstract patterns and symbols have been found.

WHERE TO STAY   (tel prefix 958)
In the Sierra Nevada, most of the ski hotels close from June to December. Ask at the tourist office in Granada for what's available, or contact the Cetursa Reservation Centre in Pradollano, tel 24 91 11. An exception, staying open year round, is the **Parador Nacional Sierra Nevada*****, on the main highway, tel 48 02 12 (doubles 6000–8500 pts), one of the smaller and newer *paradores*. Among the five modern hotels in the ski resort of Pradollano, none particularly stands out; in the skiing season accommodation at these places means a week's stay on half board for 80,000–110,000 pts per person (instruction extra). In summer months the very pleasant hostal **Telecabina**** in Plaza de Pradollano has double rooms with bath for 4200 pts, breakfast included (tel 48 12 00). Cheaper accommodation can be had at Peñones de San Francisco, at the end of the bus route. The **Albergue Universitario** there has rooms for 3000 pts half-board (tel 48 01 22). In the Alpujarras, Lanjarón has most of the rooms; a score of good bargains in the 2000–3000 pts range on or near the central C. Generalísimo Franco. Elsewhere, you'll find minimal though acceptable accommodation and food in Orgiva, Pampaneira, Capileira, Portugos (the **Mirador de Portugos***, tel 76 60 14; 3400–4000 pts, doubles with bath) and Ugijar.

156

EATING OUT
Most restaurants are open only in the skiing season, and most are a little pretentious.
Rincón de Pepe Reyes in Pradollano has good Andalucían cooking for 1500–2000 pts.
You can take the cable car up to the **Borreguiles** café/restaurant half-way up Veleta,
and sit out on the terrace to take in the view (tel 48 00 79). Granada's **Cunini** restaurant
has opened another premises with the same name, serving fish and some Castilian meat
dishes (2500 pts; Edificio Bulgaria, Prado Largo, tel 48 01 70; closed May–Nov).

Part V

GIBRALTAR

... a cosy smell of provincial groceries. I'd forgotten how much the atmosphere of home depended on white bread, soap and soup squares.

—Laurie Lee, *As I Walked Out One Midsummer Morning*

In 3½ hours, you can experience the ultimate culture shock: sailing from the smoky souks of Tangier to Algeciras, Spain, with time for *churros* and chocolate before the bus takes you off to a mysterious enclave of red phone booths, warm beer and policemen in silly hats.

The Spanish bus will really take you only as far as **La Línea** ('the Line', named for Gibraltar's old land walls), a lively, fun town that has built up dramatically since the re-opening of the Gibraltar border in 1985. Prices in Gibraltar are outrageous by Spanish standards, and La Línea may be the best place to stay while you visit. It's just a short walk through the **neutral zone** into Gibraltar, where immediately you'll be confronted with one of the Rock's curiosities: as you enter British territory you find yourself looking down the noses of 737s and Tridents. Nowhere else, perhaps, has a busy street crossing an airport runway. The airport, built on landfill at right angles to the narrow peninsula, symbolizes British determination to hold on during the years Franco was putting the squeeze on Gibraltar, and also points up the enclave's biggest problem— lack of space.

As well as large numbers of cigarette-smugglers who cross the border with regularity, British residents living on Spanish soil cross in droves to stock up with life's comforts: items either unobtainable in Spain, or just too expensive—baked beans and Christmas crackers, cheddar cheese and headache pills, pickled onions, liver salts. Other more

158

discreet visitors come over to bank their 'black' (undeclared) money made in Spain, and take advantage of the no-questions-asked, tax-free offshore banking. Needless to say, this gets the goat of the Spanish tax man. The Spanish government is trying to prevent another money-spinner slipping through their hands: nearly a quarter of all real estate investment in southern Spain comes from Gibraltar (mostly commercial companies), but because of Gibraltar's peculiar legal and off-shore economic status, they escape paying Spanish capital gains tax and death duties. A new law is presently going through the Spanish parliament to put an end to all this.

The other gripe, of course, is the political status of the Rock itself. Spain is like the little boy who kicks his ball into nextdoor's garden; Britain, the grouchy old bachelor who says 'I'm keeping it.' The question of the Rock's sovereignty comes up annually; Spain asks for concessions, Whitehall merely smiles and says, 'Sorry, old chap,' even to the question of joint access to the airstrip, so jealously eyed by Spain, for a new airport in the south is desperately needed. This contention should, in theory, disappear with the coming of 1992; but the problem is intrinsically emotional, not political.

You'll soon find that Gibraltar has a unique mixture of people—mostly Genoese (who have been around for centuries), along with Maltese, Indians, Spaniards, Jews and Moroccans, all as British as Trafalgar Square; when a referendum on joining Spain was held in the 1960s, they voted it down by 99.6 per cent. The dissenters were tagged *Las Palomas* (the White Doves), and some of these subsequently flew to Spanish climes; they are not missed in Gibraltar. With English as the official language, most Gibraltarians are, however, bi-lingual. For many Gibraltarians Spanish is used in everyday situations and particularly in moments of high emotion and anger; English is reserved for more formal situations.

History

At first sight it looks like a sphynx, crouching at the water's edge, her hindquarters resting in Europe, her head gazing over the sea and her forepaws stretching in front of her to form the most southerly part of our continent.

—Alexander Dumas, 1846

The Rock's location, where the continents of Europe and Africa rub noses and the Atlantic Ocean and Mediterranean Sea meet, is one of the world's most important crossroads; as a consequence it has been fought over for centuries. 'Calpe', as the Greeks knew it, was of course one of the Pillars of Hercules, beyond which the jealous Phoenicians would permit no other nation's ships to trade. The other, less dramatic pillar is Mount Abyle in Morocco (visible across the Straits on clear days). The Phoenicians could well have been the first people to pass through the Straits into the Atlantic and it is believed they reached England; though they used the Rock solely as a naval base and never seriously entertained the thought of settling there, preferring the more hospitable land near the Bay.

Similarly, under Roman rule from 190 BC onwards there was no permanent settlement on the Rock, which was regarded as the end of the road as far as safe exploration was concerned. Six hundred years later the Vandal and Gothic tribes surged through the

159

Iberian Peninsula on their way to North Africa, followed by the Visigoths, who remained as the most powerful local force until the late 7th century AD.

At that point the Arabs arrived, under the new and forceful banner of Islam. As they swept westward from Arabia, they forcibly converted the local population, and by the beginning of the 8th century were poised to invade the Iberian peninsula. In 711 they took the first step and under Tarik ibn-Zeyad, a Berber leader subordinate to the Arab governor of North Africa, they took Gibraltar as a prelude to their conquest of Spain. From this leader the Rock gained its name 'Jebel Tarik' (Tarik's Mountain), and for the following six centuries Gibraltar remained under Moorish rule. As the Moors moved further north, Gibraltar remained a vital camp, but it was not until 1160 that any sort of permanent settlement was established, under the orders of Abdul Mamen, Caliph of Morocco. The Tower of Homage, which survives to this day, was part of his Moorish castle. Other relics of the Moorish days are few and far between, but near the Shrine of Our Lady of Europe fragments of a Moorish pavement can still be seen. Its conversion to a Catholic chapel took place in 1462, after which a flame was kept continuously alight—a predecessor to the present lighthouse at Europa Point. In the Gibraltar Museum Moorish baths have been partially uncovered, and below the Signal Station the ruins of the upper part of the wall built by the Moors still stand.

Throughout the Moorish occupation of Andalucía, Gibraltar faced a number of sieges, at the hands of Moorish caliphs fighting amongst themselves over its control, and Christian Spaniards trying to win it back. Guzman el Bueno seized it for Castile in 1309, and in the centuries that followed it was one of the major battlegrounds of the Mediterranean. It was not until 1462 that the Rock was finally wrested from the Moorish grasp in the name of the King of Castile. In 1469 a royal decree proclaimed the son of the Duke of Messina as the rightful owner. (The day of liberation was 29 August, the feast day of St Bernard, the patron saint of Gibraltar.) Grateful Queen Isabella granted the Rock a coat of arms, still used today, with the inscription 'Seal of the Noble City of Gibraltar, the key of Spain'.

During this time of Spanish occupation the city was divided into three districts: *Villavieja* (the old town), *Barcina* ('wicker basket'—one was used to display the remains of the captured Count of Niebla) and *Turba*, which can be translated as 'mob', but these names have now disappeared. This was a fairly tranquil period by Gibraltar standards, until one fine autumn day in 1540 when, as the cityfolk were going about their daily business, a tremendous fleet of 16 galleys, manned by 2000 men, took them by surprise. These were the hordes of the infamous Barbarossa, who operated out of north African bases, raiding ships for goods and slaves; they had decided to break with tradition and sack Gibraltar, having heard of the great booty to be gained. The horror of that day stands out in Gibraltar's chequered history—a day of slaughter, rape and looting. Some were lucky enough to escape the carnage in the safety of the castle, but most were either killed or taken into slavery. The pirates headed straight for the Shrine of Our Lady of Europe at Europa Point and the Franciscan convent in the town (both well stocked with gold, jewels and precious coins) and stripped them bare, before making off across the bay for further pillaging and merry-making. Over-confidence proved to be their undoing, for the Christian fleet anchored in Tarifa had time to sail down the coast and cut off their escape route. A bloody battle ensued, and what was left of Barbarossa's mob fled back to the sanctuary of their north African ports with just 75 captives in tow, but leaving Gibraltar in ruins.

From this time on the Rock was heavily fortified and became an important naval base for Spain's explorations to the Americas, but life was far from peaceful, as a pirate of a different ilk, Sir Francis Drake, would drop in occasionally to 'singe the King of Spain's beard'.

The beginning of the 18th century brings us to the War of the Spanish Succession, with Britain on the side of Spain against the French. Admiral Sir George Rook, commanding the Anglo-Dutch fleet, tried to take Toulon and Barcelona, and having failed on both counts decided to take Gibraltar instead, as it was held by forces loyal to the French claimant to the Spanish throne. This accomplished, he offered the inhabitants of the Rock two choices—to pack their bags and leave, or swear allegiance to the Hapsburg claimant. Most opted for the former, probably hoping that the tide of war would change fairly soon; also, they may have heard of the Royal Navy's reputation— 'valiant at sea, horrendous on shore'.

By 1704, therefore, Gibraltar was in British hands, and the grateful Hapsburgs handed it over 'in perpetuity' as a reward, in the 1715 Treaty of Utrecht. It was a crucial acquisition; Britain's imperial expansion across the Mediterranean would have been inconceivable without it. Peace did not last long, however, and the Spanish, regretting their impulsive generosity, laid siege to the Rock with the aid of French forces in 1727. Great destruction was again suffered by the town, and the area around what is today Casemates Square was completely flattened.

It is from this point that we can trace the mixed heritage of the present population, for after the disappearance of the original Spanish inhabitants it became necessary to import a workforce from various parts of the Mediterranean, especially Genoa. The British made great use of this force to strengthen the city's defences. Ragged Staff Wharf was constructed, new barracks were built and a number of Spanish churches were turned into accommodation for the troops. New batteries were put up—Montague, Orange and King's Bastion, Devil's Tongue on the Old Mole, Grand Battery north of Grand Casemates with the adjacent Couvreport and King's Lines above, Willis', Catalan and Green's Lodge Batteries on the Upper Rock, and the Advance Batteries at Europa Point. The preparations proved justified; from 1779–83 a combined Spanish and French force staged the worst siege ever experienced by the population. Yet both fortifications and people endured, and the phrase 'safe as the Rock of Gibraltar' came into common use as a result. Modern Gibraltar's series of rock tunnels and galleries also date from this time; in 1782, in order to defend the northern end of the rock, tunnels were dug into the rock to enable guns to be placed at a commanding height halfway up. Even when the Great Siege was over, the tunnelling continued, and finally a large chamber was opened under 'The Notch', and called St George's Hall. Now there are about 48 km (30 miles) of tunnels; Gibraltar is still very well defended.

After a decade of uneasy peace the Gibraltarians were once again in the thick of things—this time at the outbreak of the Napoleonic Wars between Britain and France. For once, Spain was an ally, and it can even be assumed that the people of the Rock actively welcomed the hostilities: business perked up remarkably—repairing ships, supplying the Royal Navy with food and ammunition, and auctioning off contents of ships captured by the British fleet. On 21 October 1805, Nelson and his 27 'Wild Geese' triumphed at Trafalgar, an event still celebrated in Gibraltar, and the admiral's body was borne back to Rosia Bay in a cask of brandy (whence the naval term 'Nelson's Blood'). Ten years later, the end of the war heralded the start of a long period of peace and prosperity for Gibraltar, by which time the population was firmly established in occupations that relied not only on the military presence, but also on external trade.

1814 saw the appointment to Lieutenant Governor of Sir George Don, a man of considerable calibre. By this time the population had swelled to 10,000, and was badly in need of an efficient civil administration. The new governor embarked on an ambitious programme of improvements: building hospitals and public gardens, creating opportunities for business and trade. Life became peaceful and prosperous.

During the two World Wars Gibraltar provided a safe harbour where the Allies could repair ships and replenish stocks. In World War II many of the civilians were evacuated to safer spots on the globe, notably the UK, Madeira, Jamaica and Morocco. (Those who ended up in Morocco were forced to move on again when the Vichy government in France made it clear they were not welcome.) The airstrip was built at this time, which meant the disappearance of the cricket and football pitches, together with the race-course. The miles of tunnels under the Rock were developed further, and used for food storage, hospitals and miltary headquarters; and the invasion of Africa, 'Operation Torch' was spearheaded through Gibraltar, General Eisenhower and his advisors completing much of the planning from here.

By the time the War ended the Gibraltarians had developed an even deeper sense of their own identity, partly from being separated from 'El Penon', their homeland. In 1950 the Duke of Edinburgh inaugurated the first elected Legislative Council, and in 1969 the Gibraltar Constitution stated that Britain promised never to surrender the sovereignty of Gibraltar to another state against the wishes of the people. General Franco of course re-opened the whole issue of sovereignty, and the border was closed in 1969, not to open again until 1985. This had a profound effect on the population and in general only served to strengthen their resolve, and deepen the gulf between them and Spain. Far from being dismayed at the closure of the frontier, many older Gibraltarians were actually disappointed when it was re-opened, feeling that they had lost their safe little haven, their isolated 'English village'. They now face the future with some trepidation, always suspicious of their nextdoor neighbour; they insist on the retention of the wire fence between the two states. The present socialist government feels that a strong economy, supported by foreign investment, will allow her to exist without having to rely financially on a big brother, be it the UK or Spain. When you talk to a Gibraltarian, from any walk of life, you come away with the impression that they are more than capable of doing so.

The Future

Space is of the essence in Gibraltar, and the present government has given the go-ahead for ambitious and extensive programmes of land reclamation. Most of the prime areas in Gibraltar are owned by the Ministry of Defence, which has now agreed to confine its operational needs to smaller areas, thereby allowing the necessary expansion to take place. A large expanse of water near the airport is due to be reclaimed, on which low-cost state housing will be built. The runway itself is destined for expansion, but this is a touchy political issue at the moment, under talks between the Spanish and Gibraltar governments. As well as providing more living space, the programme includes extension of the industrial zone to the south of the peninsula, with office blocks, warehousing, light industry and ship-repair facilities to attract foreign investment—so important if Gibraltar is to be economically independent, which Gibraltarians are determined to be, without losing their strong cultural ties with Britain.

The third phase of Gibraltar's expansion caters to tourism and recreation on the open Atlantic side, at Catalan Bay. Here large hotel complexes are envisaged to promote the as yet limited tourist market. To facilitate easier access to this side of the rock means drilling a three-laned tunnel through its base, and this ambitious project should be completed by the mid-1990s.

With all the new industries and commercial enterprises that Gibraltar is trying to attract, the government's plan is to double the present population from 30,000 to 60,000; and with £500 million of actual and future investment, they are keen to co-operate with Spain, for each has what the other requires: Spain has the space to build factories, Gibraltar the potential to provide jobs for the Spanish market.

GETTING AROUND

By bus: Gibraltar town buses and taxis serve the frontier, about 0.8 km ($^{1}/_2$ mile) from the centre of town. On arrival, tiny buses holding about 15 people wait to take you into the town. If you are coming by car, leave it in La Línea, as there are frequently long delays as customs check the day-trippers' stash of goodies. The border only opened in 1985 (Franco had closed it to try and choke Gibraltar's economy, and the reopening was delayed by Spanish pique over the Falklands War), but a direct bus service now links Gibraltar with the Costa del Sol.

By air: There are at least three daily flights to London Gatwick, run by GB Airways; twice-weekly flights to Manchester, and regular flights to Casablanca and Tangier. GB Airways has check-in facilities at Victoria, meaning you don't see your luggage again till you arrive.

By sea: One ferry per day to Tangier in the summer. The fares are expensive (£19 or day-trip return £28) like everything else in Gibraltar, and you'd be slightly better off doing it from Algeciras. In summer there's a hydrofoil to Algeciras and Tangier, daily except Sunday if the weather permits.

Rock tours: Many companies offer guided tours of Gibraltar and its sights; Bland Travel, Cloister Building, Irish Town (tel 79 200) also runs a 'Trafalgar Tour' from Rosia Bay to Tarifa in Algeciras, and dolphin safaris in the bay.

The Town

Despite a certain amount of bad press, Gibraltar is still much more than just a perfect replica of an English seaside town. The town is long and narrow, strung out along **Main Street** with most of the shops and pubs. The harbour is never more than a couple of blocks away, and the old gates, bastions and walls are fun to explore.

The short tunnel at **Landport Gate** will probably be your entry point if on foot; dating from the 18th century, it was for a long time the only entrance by land. It leads to **Casemates Square**, one-time parade ground and site of public executions, now an

163

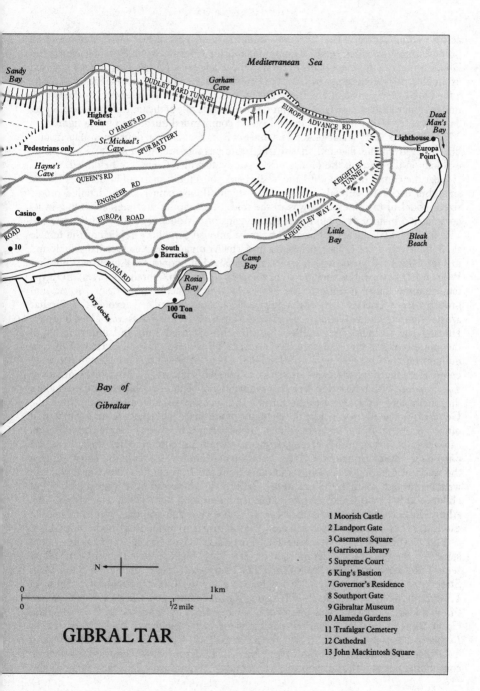

Sandy
Bay

Mediterranean Sea

Gorham
Cave

DUDLEY WARD TUNNEL

Highest
Point

O'HARE'S RD

Dead
Man's
Bay

EUROPA ADVANCE RD

Pedestrians only

St. Michael's
Cave

SPUR BATTERY
RD

Lighthouse

Europa
Point

Hayne's
Cave

QUEEN'S RD

KEIGHTLEY
TUNNEL

ENGINEER RD

EUROPA ROAD

Casino

ROAD

KEIGHTLEY WAY

Little
Bay

Bleak
Beach

10

South
Barracks

Camp
Bay

ROSIA RD

Rosia
Bay

Dry docks

100 Ton
Gun

Bay of
Gibraltar

N

0   1km
0   ½ mile

GIBRALTAR

1 Moorish Castle
2 Landport Gate
3 Casemates Square
4 Garrison Library
5 Supreme Court
6 King's Bastion
7 Governor's Residence
8 Southport Gate
9 Gibraltar Museum
10 Alameda Gardens
11 Trafalgar Cemetery
12 Cathedral
13 John Mackintosh Square

active trading centre. The Casemates building itself, part of the town's defences and barracks, now provides seedy accommodation for Gibraltar's 4000-strong Moroccan labour force, but there are plans to revamp the whole area. **King's Bastion** is now used as an electricity generating station, but probably started out as an ancient Arab Gate, added to by the Spanish in 1575, and further extended in the 18th century by the British under General Boyd. It played an important defensive role at the time of the Great Siege, and it was from this spot that General Elliott commanded during the fierce fighting in 1782. **Ragged Staff Wharf** takes its name not from the sartorial deficiency of its troops, but either from the flagstaff that marked safe passage into the harbour, or from an emblem on the arms of the House of Burgundy, to which Charles V belonged.

Near the centre of town, off Line Wall Road, you should spare a few minutes for the small but excellent **Gibraltar Museum**, which offers a painstakingly detailed room-sized model of the Rock as it was in the mid-1800s, and a thorough schooling in its complicated history. It is built over the remains of a **Moorish bath**, with Roman and Visigothic capitals on its columns. The museum also contains a replica of the female skull found in Forbes Quarry in 1848, a find which predates the Neanderthal skull found in Germany by 8 years. (Perhaps Neanderthal Man should be known as Gibraltar Woman.) Other exhibits include archaeological finds from Gibraltar's caves; an Egyptian mummy found floating in the bay by local fishermen, dating from 750 BC and probably from Thebes; a natural history collection; and a gallery devoted to Gibraltar artists—among them Gustavo Bacarisas, Mania and Olimpia Reyes (18–20 Bomb House Lane, Monday–Friday 10–6, Saturday 10–2; closed Sun). In Library Street, in the grand building that was once the Governor's Residence, is the **Garrison Library**, built during the Great Siege of 1779–83 in the hope of preventing boredom in sieges to come. Here there are extensive archives on Gibraltar's history. Nearby are the offices of *The Chronicle*, which reported Nelson's victory at Trafalgar. The **Supreme Court** looks diagonally across the street to the former 16th-century Franciscan Convent, now the **Governor's Residence**, where the changing of the guard takes place (check with tourist office for times). If it's bucketing down, an occurrence frequent in winter months, you can watch these serious proceedings from the warmth and comfort of the *Angry Friar*, the pub on the corner. **Southport Gate**, at the top of Main Street, was built in 1552, during the reign of Charles V, and has additions from the 19th century. Next to it you can wander through shady little **Trafalgar Cemetery**, where sad little inscriptions tell of children killed by disease, and of young men who met their bloody end at sea. The **Alameda Gardens**, a few yards away, are more cheerful; you can stop in to see the exotic flora before taking the **cable car** (£3.50 return trip) up the Rock to the Apes' Den.

The **Cathedral of Santa María la Coronada** (Main Street and Cannon Lane) stands on the site of the chief mosque of Gibraltar, of which some remains can still be seen. The **Anglican Cathedral of the Holy Trinity** was consecrated in 1838 (off Main Street, near the museum), and in Engineer's Lane the **Great Synagogue**, rebuilt in 1768, is attended by Gibraltar's 700-strong Jewish community. **King's Chapel**, part of the Franciscan Convent, was one of the few buildings left standing at the end of the Great Siege, and was an earlier sanctuary for those sheltering from the attack by Barbarossa and his pirates, although the place itself was looted. Today, however, legend has it that it is haunted by the Grey Nun, Alitea de Lucerna, whose family forced her into convent life because they disapproved of her lover. He, however, managed to sneak into the convent, dressed as a Franciscan friar, and the two continued their relationship until, inevitably, they were discovered. The lover drowned as they tried to escape, and poor Alitea remains to stalk the cloisters, bemoaning her lost (if not unrequited) love.

The Rock

The famous silhouette, surprisingly, does not hang over the seaward edge, but faces backwards towards La Línea. From 1400 feet (metres) up, the views from the upper part of the rock are magnificent: the Costa del Sol curves away to the east, the mountains of Morocco sit in a purple haze across the narrow straits to the south; and way below, where the Mediterranean opens out into the wide and wild Atlantic, tiny toy-like craft plough through the waters in full sail. The Rock's entire eastern face is covered by the **Water Catchment System** that supplies Gibraltar's water—an engineering marvel to equal the tunnels. The only ways to get up on to the Rock, besides taking the taxi tour (£16 for a carload is the current official rate) are either to walk or to take the cable car up from the southern end of town. Halfway up, it stops at the **Apes' Den**. Gibraltar's best-known citizens are officially Barbary apes, a species of gregarious monkey much more common on the African side of the straits. They are unique in Europe, though, and there is an old saying that as long as they're here, the British will never leave. Understandably, they're well cared for, and have been since the days of their great benefactor, Winston Churchill. The Gibraltarians are fond of them, even though (as a local guidebook solemnly notes) they 'fail to share the same respect for private property' as the rest of us. Now that most of their feeding-grounds have been built over, they are on the dole, and it's fun to watch them when the official Keeper of the Apes comes round at feeding-time. Legend has it that the apes, two packs of them numbering 60 in all, travel to and from their native Morocco by an underground tunnel in the rock (open 10–7 in summer, 10–5.30 in winter, 50p adm).

Nearby are remains of a **Moorish wall** and, a short walk to the south, **St Michael's Cave**, a huge cavern of delicate stalactites now sometimes used as an auditorium. In the 19th century wealthy merchants would rent it out for extravagant parties; it was also a favourite venue for illegal duels, away from the censorious eye of the authorities; and during World War II it was converted for use as a hospital. If you intend to come here for a concert, bring a waterproof hat—the roof leaks. (Open daily 10–7 in summer, 10–5.30 in winter; sound-and-light shows at 11 and 4, £1.50 adm.) **Gorham's Cave**, by the shore near Europa Point, was almost certainly inhabited by Neanderthal man, and is considered to have a potential wealth of finds; archaeologists from the British Museum have been carrying out extensive digs here. On the northern end of the Rock, facing Spain, the **Upper Galleries** are an extensive section of the original British tunnels, and were hacked and blown out of the rock during the Great Siege of 1779–83, the work of Sergeant-Major Ince, who was rewarded for his labours with a plot of farming land and a racehorse. (Horse-racing and hunting were extremely popular; the airport was once the site of a racecourse). Open to visitors, the Galleries have wax dummies of 18th-century British soldiers hard at work digging and blowing up Spaniards. From here it's a short walk down to the **Moorish Castle**, probably founded in the 8th century by Tarik-ibn-Zeyad, but its best-known feature, the **Tower of Homage** dates from the 14th century when Abu'l Hassan recaptured Gibraltar from the Spanish. At present Gibraltar's

167

prison is housed (and occupied) in the keep, but hopes are that this will be moved to a new military building. Unfortunately, some rather short-sighted town planning allowed a housing estate to be built within the castle's boundaries, again highlighting Gibraltar's acute need of space.

If you want to sit on a beach, Gibraltar has a few, but they're all on the eastern side, opposite from the town, and accessible by bus. **Catalan Bay** and **Sandy Bay** are both a little built-up and crowded, the former slated for even greater development in the near future. **Eastern Beach** (dubbed 'Margate' in the 19th century) is better, though unfortunately it's next to the airport. The Bay of Gibraltar is a favourite playground of schools of dolphins, who on a good day will put on a show for the camera-toting bipeds on the shore. For sports enthusiasts the waters are ideal; from windsurfing to scuba-diving. In Marina Bay you can charter yachts or cabin cruisers.

TOURIST INFORMATION
There's a booth right inside the frontier, one in the airport terminal a few hundred feet away, another at Waterport Coach Park; and offices in Cathedral Square (tel 76 400), and in the Gibraltar Museum, 18–20 Bomb House Lane (tel 75 555).

CURRENCY
These days, most shops and restaurants in Gibraltar are perfectly happy to take British, Spanish or Gibraltarian money. The enclave has its own currency and stamps—don't be stuck with any when you leave, as it's hard to get rid of anywhere else.

WHERE TO STAY   (tel prefix 350)
In La Línea, if you're on a budget. Prices in Gibraltar are twice to four times what they would be for comparable hotels in Spain. If you really want to stay on the Rock, consider the **Montarik Hotel** on Main Street, tel 77 065; good value by Gibraltar standards (£56 for a double with shower or bath, breakfast extra). Similarly, the **Bristol** is in the heart of town, with swimming pool, and TV in all rooms (£51 for double with bath, £45 with shower; 8–10 Cathedral Square, tel 76 800). In the same price range, though not quite as comfortable, the **Continental** is just off Main Street (£50; 1 Engineer Lane, tel 76 900), with a tacky fast-food restaurant on the ground floor. For the businessman the **Holiday Inn** offers sterile anonymity, along with air-conditioning, sauna and jacuzzi (£90; Governor's Parade, tel 70 500). The **Rock Hotel**, a quality resort hotel of long standing, is up on the heights—about halfway up, under the cable car and near Gibraltar's casino. Visiting dignitaries and the occasional celebrity stay here. There's a pool, beautifully landscaped gardens and rooms with sea view and balconies (£85 for a double with balcony, £70–75 without, depending on land or sea view; located on Europe Road, tel 73 000). The **Queen's Hotel**, just outside the old city walls on Boyd Street (tel 74 000) is pretty characterless but has less expensive accommodation—£28 for a double without bath, £30 with—and there are good views of the Rock and Bay. If you need a beach the other resort hotel is the very modern **Caleta Palace**, Sir Herbert Miles Rd, on Catalan Bay, tel 76 501 (£48–60 for a double, depending on the view). At Sandy Bay, the **Gibraltar Beach** has all rooms with sea view, and the option of self-catering apartments (£45 with bath; Sandy Bay, tel 76 191).

There is one opportunity for a cheap room in Gibraltar, the **Toc H Hostal** on Line Wall Rd near the harbour, tel 73 431, where they'll put you up for £6 per person. Understandably, they are usually full.

EATING OUT

This isn't such a problem. Main Street is lined with pubs, fish shops, and cafés, and there are plenty of little places around Catalan Bay and the other beaches. Nearly all the hotels have restaurants. The **Rock Hotel**, is arguably the best place for lunch; colonial decor and discreet waiters help to set the scene for Gibraltar's answer to Raffles in Singapore, and the steaks are flown in fresh from the UK daily—so there! Popular among the locals is the restaurant in the **International Casino Club** (7 Europa Rd, tel 76 666), and for five-star service you won't find a better place here. Concerned with maintaining high standards, the management has a strict ruling on dress—even local celebrities have been turned away for inappropriate attire. There's a wide range of international dishes, and the terrace has great views overlooking the bay and Algeciras—a perfect place to watch the sun go down on the Atlantic, if not the Empire. Full meal with wine runs to £25–35.

In town: **Cheers Brasserie** fills up with tourists at lunchtime and is a popular meeting place, where you can enjoy the large terrace and soak up the sun. The tasty and inexpensive snacks include club sandwiches, a variety of salads, chilli, as well as full English breakfasts (G1 Cornwall Centre, tel 79 699; snacks £3–5, full meals £8–10). **El Patio** is another good spot; even Spaniards cross the border to sample its excellent Basque cuisine and Mediterranean fish specialities—rare delights considering the British culinary traditions around here. Particularly popular with the business community, who jokingly refer to it as the 'Canteen', this place fills up at lunchtime. For a real treat telephone a day ahead and put in your order for *bacalao pil-pil*, delicious cod cooked slowly in garlic and olive oil. (About £15 per head; 54 Irish Town, tel 70 822; closed Sat lunchtime and Sun). Another restaurant that attracts business people is **The Office-Boardroom**, but don't let that put you off. The decor's plush and the menu decidedly French—oysters, French onion soup, rainbow trout, *langoustines*, lobster thermidor, *entrecôte* and Chateaubriand, *flambé*-ed desserts, and prices are not outrageous (£20–30; Cornwall's Centre, Cornwall's Lane, tel 40 078). **La Bayuca** is a long-time favourite; Gibraltar's oldest and best-loved, although hard to find. The walls are lined with photos of its more famous customers, and the decor is pleasantly rustic. The menu is limited, but first-rate: steaks, chicken, fish, and some Mediterranean dishes (£10–15; 21 Turnbulls Lane, tel 75 119; closed Tues and Sun lunch). Just of Main Street, **Bunter's** provides welcome relief from some of the noisier establishments nearby. No blaring music or sloppy pints of ale here; the company is jovial and civilised, and the bar an ideal place for a cocktail while you decide on your meal: potted shrimps, pies, fresh salmon and steaks, rack of lamb and ribs, the more exotic boned duck and monkfish kebabs, and some truly great traditional English desserts—apple pie and cream, or sherry trifle (£20–25 including wine; 1 College Lane, tel 70 482; closed lunchtime Sat and Sun, and all August). Reservations are a must at **Strings** (44 Cornwalls Lane, tel 78 800), a small and intimate restaurant serving a decent selection of international dishes: smoked salmon, *gravadlax*, shrimp in wine sauce, grilled fish and meats, cheesecake (£15–20; closed Mon). **Sax** piano bar and restaurant attracts a young crowd; expect queues at weekends. The fare is mixed—English, Mexican, Italian, and the lunchtime menu particularly recommended. Light snacks are also available, and there's live music two evenings a week (around £15 for full meal; 1st Floor, International Commercial Centre; closed Sun lunch). A little off the beaten track, **Jim's Den**, 25 Prince Edward's Rd, tel 71 289, has a simple English menu, with simple white-washed walls; it's a big hit with expats, and a popular place to drop in for a chat and bite to eat (£10–15 for a full meal). In a lane off Main Street is the quaint **Country Cottage**, 13–15 Giros Passage, tel 70 084, complete with antique furnishings and Olde Worlde atmosphere, although even the locals agree that it's a bit twee; the reliable and well-presented menu includes sole mornay, shrimp, scampi, and meat dishes from *brochettes* to Angus steaks (£20–30).

There are a handful of Indian restaurants around; the **Maharaja**, 5 Tuckey's Lane, tel 75 233, with the simplest furnishings of the lot, offers some of the best food. The service is efficient and friendly, and all the old Indian favourites can be found on the menu (£10–15).

In Marina Bay you can sit out and watch the yachts or plane spot the airstrip at **Bianca's**, which has reasonably priced fish, meat and pizza; around £12–15 for a full meal (Marina Bay, tel 73 379). Nextdoor **Da Paolo** has well prepared fish specialities, but is a little more expensive at about £15–20 (tel 76 799). The recent influx of Danish capital and business interests has meant the opening of **The Little Mermaid**, a refreshing addition to the ethnic culinary scene. The interior is sleek and modern in the Danish style, and all the usual Scandinavian specialities appear. Help your open sandwiches down with an *Aalborg Acquavit* and *Tuborg* chaser, instead of wine (£10; Marina Bay).

There are around 360 pubs in Gibraltar, many serving food in one form or another. The best are **The Clipper**, 787 Irish Town, popular with Gibraltarians and visitors alike for its good roast beef and lasagna; and **The Royal Calpe**, 176 Main Street, where the grub is authentically English and served piping hot. And as a parting memory of Gibraltar before you drive back across the border, drop into the patriotic **Old Bull and Bush**, complete with portrait of Queen Elizabeth II; drinks are chalked up on a slate as in days of yore. Pictures of England and English pubs cover the walls, and there are no *tapas* in sight, just crisps and hard-boiled eggs. Gibraltar's late-nightlife happens up at the **Casino**—dress well and take lots of cash.

SHOPPING

Expats residing in Spain flock across the border to pick up familiar brand-name groceries and household items at British prices; the real bargains are to be had in the top range of luxury goods. Remember that Gibraltar is VAT-free, and savings can be considerable. This is a selection—but shop around.

Antiques: Bensaquen Antiques, 290 Main Street.

Cashmere: Carruana, 181 Main Street (Jerseys, suits and fabrics).

Cuban cigars, and perfume: S.M. Seruya, 165 Main Street, and Stagnetto's, 56 Main Street.

Jewellery: Sakata, 92 Main St and The Red House, 66 Main Street (cultured pearls, *Cartier, Rolex*)

Menswear: Garcia, 190 Main St (*Dax, Burberry*, etc).

Porcelain: Omni, 3 Main Street.

ART AND ARCHITECTURE
AND WHERE TO SEE IT

Until the coming of the Moors, southern Spain produced little of note, or at least little that has survived. To begin at the beginning, there are the 25,000-year-old cave drawings at the Cueva de la Pileta, near **Ronda**, and Neolithic dolmens near **Antequera** and **Almería**. No significant buildings have been found from the Tartessians or the Phoenicians, though remains of a 7th-century BC temple have been dug up at Cádiz. Not surprisingly, with their great treasury of metals, the people of the region were skilled at making jewellery and figurines in silver and bronze (also ivory, traded up from North Africa where elephants were still common).

Real art begins with the arrival of the Greeks in the 600s. The famous Lady of Elche in the Madrid museum, though found in the region of Murcia, may have been typical of the Greek-influenced art of all the southern Iberians; their pottery, originally decorated in geometrical patterns, began to imitate the figurative Greek work in the 5th century. The best collection of early work is in the Archaeological Museum at **Sevilla**, also the museum at **Málaga**.

During the long period of Roman rule, Spanish art continued to follow trends from the more civilized east (ruins and amphitheatres at **Italica, Carmona, Ronda**; reconstructed temple at **Córdoba**; museums in **Sevilla, Córdoba** and **Cádiz**). Justinian's invasion in the 550s brought new influences from the Greek world, though the exhausted region by that time had little money or leisure for art. Neither was Visigothic rule ever conducive to new advances. The Visigoths were mostly interested in gaudy jewellery and trinkets (best seen not in Andalucía, but in the museums of Madrid and Toledo). Almost no building work survives; the Moors purchased and demolished all of the important churches, but made good use of one Visigothic architectural innovation, the more-than-semicircular 'horseshoe' arch.

Moorish Art

The greatest age for art in Andalucía began not immediately with the Arab conquest, but a century and a half later, with the arrival of Abd ar-Rahman and the establishment of the Umayyad Emirate. The new Emir and his followers had come from Damascus, the old capital of Islam, and they brought with them the best traditions of emerging Islamic art from Syria. 'Moorish' art, like 'Gothic', is a term of convenience that can be misleading. Along with the enlightened patronage of the Umayyads, this new art catalyzed the dormant but not entirely dead culture of Roman Spain, creating a brilliant synthesis; of this, the first and finest example is the Mezquita, the Great Mosque of **Córdoba**.

The Mezquita was recognized in its own time as one of the wonders of the world. We are fortunate it survived, and it is chilling to think of the literally thousands of mosques, palaces, public buildings, gates, cemeteries and towers destroyed by the Christians; the methodical effacement of a great culture, an act unparalleled in the history of Europe.

We can discuss this art from its finest production, and from little else. As architecture, the Mezquita is full of subtleties and surprises (see p. 75). Westerners have tended to dismiss the Moorish approach as 'decorative art', without considering the philosophical background, or the expression of ideas inherent in the decoration. Figurative art being discouraged by Islam, artists used other means: Arabic calligraphy, which soon became an Andalucían speciality; repetitive geometric patterns, mirroring a Pythagorean strain that has always been present in Islam; and a meticulously clever arrangement of forms, shapes and spaces, meant to elicit surprise and delight. The infinite elements of this decorative universe (see Topics, p. 40) come together in the most unexpected of conclusions—a reminder that the basic principle of Islam is unity.

The 'decorative' sources are wonderfully eclectic, and easy enough to discern. From Ummayad Syria, the general plan of the rectangular, many-columned mosques, along with the striped arches. From Visigothic Spain, the distinctive horseshoe arch. The floral arabesques and intricate, flowing detail, whether on a mosque window, a majolica dish or a delicately carved ivory, are the heritage of late Roman-art, as can be clearly seen on the recycled Roman capitals of the Mezquita itself. The Umayyads in Syria had been greatly impressed by Byzantine mosaics, and had copied them in their early mosques. This continued in Spain, often with artists borrowed from Constantinople. Besides architectural decoration, the same patterns and motifs appear in the minor arts of al-Andalus, in painted ceramics, textiles and in metalwork, a Spanish speciality since prehistoric times—your English baron of the time might have traded a village for a fine Andalucían dagger or brooch.

Such an art does not seek progress and development, in our sense; it shifts slowly, like a kaleidoscope, carefully and occasionally finding new and subtler patterns to captivate the eye and declare the unity of creation. It carried on, without decadence or revolutions, until the end of al-Andalus and beyond. Under the Almohads, who made their capital at **Sevilla**, it created the Tower of Gold and the Giralda, model for the great minarets of Morocco.

The Christian conquest of Córdoba, Sevilla, and most of the rest of al-Andalus (1212–80), did not put an end to Moorish art. The tradition continued intact, with its Islamic foundations, for another two centuries in the Kingdom of Granada. In the rest of Spain, Muslim artists and artisans found ready employment for nearly as long; their 'Mudejár' art briefly contended with imported styles from northern Europe to become the national art of Spain. Most of its finest productions are not in Andalucía at all—the churches of Toledo, the towers of Teruel and many other towns of Aragón. The trademarks of Mudejár building are geometrical decoration in *azulejo* tiles and brickwork, and elaborately carved wooden *artesonado* ceilings.

Granada, isolated from the rest of the Muslim world and constantly on the defensive, produced no great advances, but this golden autumn of Moorish culture brought the decorative arts to a state of serene perfection. In the Alhambra (continued throughout the 14th century), where the architecture incorporates gardens and flowing water, the emphasis is on panels of ornate plaster work, combining floral and geometric patterns with calligraphy— not only Koranic inscriptions, but the deeds of Granada's kings and much contemporary lyric poetry. Another feature is the stucco 'stalactite' ceilings, translating the Moorish passion for geometry into three dimensions.

Granada's art and that of the Mudejár cross paths at **Sevilla**'s Alcazar, expanded by Pedro the Cruel in the 1360s; artists from Granada did much of the work. Post-1492

172

Mudejár work can also be seen in some Sevilla palaces, such as the Palacio de las Dueñas or the Casa de Pilatos. The smaller delights of late Moorish decorative arts include painted majolica ware, inlaid wood chests and tables (the *taracea* work still a speciality of Granada), and exquisite silver and bronze work in everything from armour to astronomical instruments; the best collection is in the Alhambra's Museum of Hispano-Muslim Art.

Gothic and Renaissance

For art, the Reconquista and the emergence of a united Spain was a mixed blessing. The importation of foreign styles gave a new impetus to painting and architecture, but it also gradually swept away the nation's Moorish and Mudejár tradition, especially in the south, where it put an end to 800 years of artistic continuity. In the 13th century, churches in the reconquered areas were usually done in straightforward, unambitious Gothic, as with S. Ana in Sevilla, built under Pedro the Cruel, and the simple and elegant parish churches of **Córdoba**. In the next century, Gothic lingered on without noticeable inspiration; Sevilla's squat and ponderous cathedral, the largest Gothic building anywhere, was probably the work of a German or Frenchman.

The Renaissance was a latecomer to Andalucía. In 1506, when the High Renaissance had already hit Rome, the Spaniards were building a Gothic chapel in **Granada** for the tombs of Ferdinand and Isabella. This time, though, they had an architect of distinction; Enrique Egas, who had already created important works in Toledo and Santiago de Compostella, made the Capilla Real Spain's finest late-Gothic building, in the lively style called 'Isabelline Gothic' or 'plateresque', roughly corresponding to the contemporary French Flamboyant or English Perpendicular. The Plateresque in the decorative arts had already been established in **Sevilla** (the huge cathedral retablo, begun in 1482), and would continue into the next century (the cathedral's Royal Chapel and Sacristy). Other noteworthy figures of this period are the Siloes: Gil de Siloe, a talented sculptor, and his son Diego, who began the cathedrals at Granada (1526) and at Ubeda.

Genuine Renaissance architecture arrived with Pedro Machuca, who had studied in Italy. Strongly influenced by the monumental classicism of Bramante, his imposing Palace of Charles V (1527–8), in the Alhambra at **Granada**, actually antedates the celebrated Roman palaces it so closely resembles. Andalucía's Renaissance city is **Ubeda**, with an ensemble of exceptional churches and palaces; its Sacra Capilla de Salvador contains some of the finest Renaissance reliefs and sculpture in Spain. In the stern climate of the Counter-reformation, architecture turned towards a disciplined austerity, the *estilo desornimentado* introduced by Juan de Herrera at Philip II's palace-monastery of El Escorial, near Madrid. Herrera gave **Sevilla** a textbook example in his Lonja, a business exchange for the city's merchants. His most accomplished follower, Andrés de Vandelvira, brought the 'unornamented style' to a striking conclusion with his Hospital de Santiago in **Ubeda**, and other works in Ubeda and **Baeza**; he also began the ambitious cathedral at **Jaén**.

Baroque and Beyond

This style, like the Renaissance, was slow in reaching southern Spain. One of the most important projects of the 17th century, the façade for the unfinished **Granada** cathedral, wound up entrusted to a painter, Alonso Cano (1664). The idiosyncratic result, with its three gigantic arches, shows a little appreciation for the new Roman style, though it is firmly planted in the Renaissance. Real Baroque arrived 3 years later, with Eufrasio López de Rojas's façade for Jaén cathedral. The most accomplished southern architect in the decades that followed was Leonardo de Figueroa, who combined Italian styles with a native Spanish delight in colour and patterns in brickwork; he worked mostly in **Sevilla** (S. Salvador, begun 1699, Collegio S.Telmo, 1724, and the Convento de la Merced, now the *Museo de Bellas Artes*. Baroque sculpture was largely a matter of gory realism done in wood, as in the work of Juan Martinez Montañes (Sevilla cathedral) and his disciple Juan de Mena.

The 17th century has often been described as a 'golden age' of painting in Andalucía. Giving ample room for exaggeration, there is still Velázquez (1576–1656), a native Sevillian who left the region forever in 1623 when he became painter to the King. Almost none of his work remains in the south. Of those who stayed behind, there is Alonso Cano, whose work often has a careful architectonic composition that betrays his side-career as an architect, but seldom ranges above the pedestrian and devotional. Francisco Herrera of Sevilla (1576–1656) shows a little more backbone, in keeping with the dark and stormy trends of contemporary Italian painting. Best of all is an emigrant from Extremadura, Francisco de Zurbarán, who arrived in **Sevilla** in 1628. He is often called the 'Spanish Caravaggio', and though his contrasts of light and shadow are equally distinctive, this is as much a disservice as a compliment. Set in stark, bright colours, Zurbarán's world is an unearthly vision of monks and saints, with portraits of heavenly celebrities that seem painted from life, and uncanny, almost abstract scenes of monastic life like the *Miracle of Saint Hugo* in the Sevilla museum. Seeing the rest of his best work would require a long trip across two continents; the French under Maréchal Soult stole hundreds of his paintings, and there are over eighty in the Louvre alone.

In the next generation of southern painters, the worst qualities of a decaying Spain are often painfully evident. Bartolomé Estebán Murillo (1618–82), another Sevilliano, is the best of them; two centuries ago he was widely considered among the greatest painters of all time; modern eyes are often distracted by the maudlin, missal-illustration religiosity of his saints and Madonnas, neglecting to notice the exceptional talent and total sincerity that created them. Even harder to digest is Juan de Valdés Leal (1622–90), obsessed with the Hallowe'en blood-and-bones side of Counter-reformation Catholicism to an extent that will often evoke either laughter or disgust (these two artists can be compared in **Sevilla**'s museum and Hospital de la Caridad).

If any style could find a natural home in Spain, it would be the Rococo. Eventually it did, though a lack of energy and funds often delayed it. Vicente Acero introduced the tendency early on, with a striking façade for the cathedral at **Guadix**. He had a chance to repeat it on a really important building project, the new **Cádiz** cathedral, but the money ran out, and the result was a stripped-down Baroque shell—ambition without the decoration. The great tobacco factory in **Sevilla** (1725–65), the largest project of the century in Andalucía, met a similar end, leaving an austere work, an unintentional precursor of the neo-classical. Whenever the resources were there, Andalucían architects responded with a tidal wave of eccentric embellishment worthy of the Moors—or the Aztecs. Pre-Columbian architecture may have been a bigger influence on Spain than is generally credited; judge for yourself at the chapel and sacristy of the Cartuja in **Granada** (1747–62) the most blatant interior in Spain.

Elsewhere, the decorative freedom of the Rococo led to some unique and delightful buildings, essentially Spanish and often incorporating eclectic references to the styles of centuries past. Granada's church of San Juan de Dios (José de Bada 1737–59), is a fine example. In **Córdoba**, there is the elegant Convento de Merced (1745), and the choir of the Cathedral, inside the Mezquita, a 16th-century Gothic work redecorated with elaborate stucco decoration by Juan de Olive and stalls and overall design by Pedro Duque Cornejo (1748–57). **Sevilla**, in its decline, was still building palaces, blending the new style with the traditional requirements of a patio and grand staircase; the best of the century's palaces, however, is in **Ecija**, the Palacio de Peñaflor (1728). Many smaller towns, responding to the improved economic conditions under Philip V and Charles III, built impressive churches, notably **Priego de Córdoba, Lucena, Utrera, Estepa** and Ecija.

For all Andalucía's troubles, it should not be surprising that little has been produced in the last two centuries. Pablo Picasso, of Málaga, was the outstanding example of the artist who had to find his inspiration and his livelihood elsewhere. Despite the lack of significant architecture, Andalucíans hold on to the glories of their past with tenacity; splashes of *azulejo* tiles and Moorish decoration turn up in everything from bus stations and market houses to simple suburban cottages. One of the functions of a World's Fair is to catalyze new styles and ideas. In this newly prosperous and confident region, perhaps Sevilla '92 will prove an opportunity to catch up for lost time.

HISTORICAL AND ARCHITECTURAL TERMS

Ajimez: in Moorish architecture, an arched double window

Alameda: a park or promenade

Alcazaba: a Moorish fortress

Alcazar: a Moorish fortified palace

Almohads: group of puritanical Muslims, originally Berbers, who ruled Spain from about 1147 to 1213

Almoravids: fanatical people of Berber origin and Islamic faith who founded an empire in N. Africa that spread over much of Spain in the 11th century

Arrabal: quarter of a Moorish city

Artesonado: Mudejár-style carved wooden ceilings, panels or screens

Ayuntamiento: city hall

Azulejo: painted glazed tiles, popular in Mudejár work and later architecture (from the Arabic *az-zulaiy*, a piece of terracotta)

Barrio: city quarter or neighbourhood

Bóveda: vault

Capilla Mayor: seat of the high altar in a cathedral

Carmen: a Carmelite convent, or Morisco villas with pleasure gardens outside Granada

Cartuja: a Carthusian monastery

Castrum: Roman military camp

Churrigueresque: florid Baroque style of the late 17th and early 18th centuries in the style of José Chirriguera (1650–1725), Spanish architect and sculptor

Ciudadela: a citadel

Converso: a Jew who converted to Christianity

Coro: the walled-in choir in a Spanish cathedral

Corregidor: royal magistrate

Cortijo: Andalucían country house

Custodia: tabernacle, where sacramental vessels are kept

Diputacíon: seat of provincial government

Embalse: reservoir

Ermita: hermitage

Esgrafiado: style of painting, or etching designs in stucco, on a façade

Estilo Desornamentado (or *Herreran*): austere, heavy Renaissance style inaugurated by Philip II's architect, Juan de Herrera

Fandango: traditional dance and song, greatly influenced by the gypsies of Andalucía

Feria: major festival or market, often an occasion for bullfights

Finca: farm or country house

Fonda: a modest hotel, from the Arabic *fonduq*, or traders' inn

Fuero: exemptions, or privileges of a town or region under medieval Spanish law

176

Grandee: a select member of Spain's highest nobility

Hammam: Moorish bath

Hidalgo: literally 'son of somebody'—the lowest level of the nobility, just good enough for a coat-of-arms

Homage tower: the tallest tower of fortification, sometimes detached from the wall

Humilladero: calvary, or stations of the Cross along a road outside of town

Isabelline Gothic: late 15th-century style, roughly corresponding to English perpendicular

Judería: Jewish quarter

Junta: a council, or specifically, the regional government

Kufic: very angular style of Arabic calligraphy derived from the city of Kufa in Mesopotamia, often used as architectural ornamentation

Lonja: merchants' exchange

Madrassa: Moslem theological school, usually located near a mosque

Medina: walled centre of a Moorish city

Mezquita: a mosque

Mihrab: prayer niche in a mosque facing Mecca, often elaborately decorated

Mirador: a scenic overlook or belvedere

Morisco: Muslims who submitted to Christianization to remain in al-Andalus after the Reconquista

Mozaráb: Christians under Muslim rule in Moorish Spain

Mudejár: Moorish-influenced architecture, characterized by its decorative use of bricks and ceramics; Spain's 'national style' in the 12th–16th centuries

Ojival: pointed (arches)

Patio: central courtyard of a house or public building

Plateresque: heavily ornamented 16th-century Gothic style

Plaza: a town square

Plaza de Toros: bullring

Plaza Mayor: square at the centre of many Spanish cities, often totally enclosed and arcaded

Posada: inn

Pronunciamento: a military coup

Puerta: gate or portal

Reja: iron grilles, either decorative ones in churches or those covering the exterior windows of buildings

Retablo: carved or painted altarpiece

Romería: pilgrimage, usually on a saint's feast day

Sagrario: reliquary chapel

Sala Capitular: chapterhouse

Taifa: faction or division, especially the taifa kings who divided Spain after the 1031 fall of the Caliph of Córdoba

Taracea: inlaid wood in geometric patterns

Vega: a cultivated plain or fertile river valley

LANGUAGE

Castellano, as Spanish is properly called, was the first modern language to have a grammar written for it. When a copy was presented to Queen Isabella in 1492, she quite understandably asked what it was for. 'Your majesty', replied a perceptive bishop, 'language is the perfect instrument of empire'. In the centuries to come, this concise, flexible and expressive language would prove just that, an instrument that would contribute more to Spanish unity than any laws or institutions, while spreading itself effortlessly over much of the New World.

Among other European languages, Spanish is closest to Portuguese and Italian—and of course, Catalán and Gallego. Spanish, however, may have the simplest grammar of any Romance language, and if you know a little of any Romance language you will find much of the vocabulary looks familiar. It's quite easy to pick up a working knowledge of Spanish; but Spaniards speak colloquially and fast, and in Andalucía they do it with a pronounced accent, leaving out half the consonants and adding some strange sounds all their own. Expressing yourself may prove a little easier than understanding the replies. Spaniards will appreciate your efforts, and when they correct you they aren't being snooty; they simply feel it's their duty to help you learn. There are dozens of language books and tapes on the market; one particularly good one is *Teach Yourself Spanish*, by Juan Kattán-Ibarra (Hodder & Stoughton 1984). If you already speak Spanish, note the Spaniards increasingly use the familiar 'tu' instead of 'usted' when addressing even complete strangers.

Pronunciation is phonetic but somewhat difficult for English speakers:

Vowels

a   – short a as in father
e   – short e as in set
i   – long e as in complete
o   – long o as in note
u   – long u as in flute
ie   – both vowels pronounced separately
ue   – short e, the u is silent
üe   – we, as in dwell

Consonants

b   – in the middle of a word, often pronounced as v
c   – before the vowels i and e, it is a Castilian affectation to pronounce it as *th*; many Spaniards and
      all Latin Americans pronounce it in this case as an *s*
g   – before i or e, pronounced as a hard H
h   – usually silent
j   – hard H
ll   – ly or y
ñ   – ny as in canyon (the˜ is called a *tilde*)
q   – k
r   – usually rolled, which takes practice
z   – th

Stress is on the penultimate syllable if the word ends in a vowel, on the last syllable if the word ends in a consonant; exceptions are marked with an accent.

If all this seems difficult, consider that English pronunciation is even worse for Spaniards. Young people in Spain seem to be all madly learning English these days; if your Spanish friends giggle at your pronunciation, get them to try to say *squirrel*.

Practise on some of the place names:

Madrid (ma-DREED)
Sevilla (se-VEE-ah)
Cuenca (KWAYN-kah)
Sigüenza (sig-WAYN-zah)
Jerez (her-ETH)
Málaga (MAHL-ah-gah)
Valladolid (vy-ah-dol-EED)

León (lay-OHN)
Cáceres (CAH-ther-es)
Jaén (ha-AIN)
Trujillo (troo-HEE-oh)
Badajóz (ba-da-HOTH)
Alcazar (ahl-CATH-ar)
Arévalo (ahr-EV-vah-lo)

Useful Words and Phrases

yes	*sí*
no	*no*
I don't know	*No sé*
I don't understand (Spanish)	*No comprendo (Español)*
Does someone here speak English?	*¿Hay alguien que hable inglés?*
Speak slowly	*Hable despacio*
Can you assist me?	*¿Puede usted ayudarme?*
help!	*¡Soccoro!*
please	*por favor*
thank you (very much)	*(muchas) gracias*
you're welcome	*de nada*
It doesn't matter	*no importa*
all right	*está bien*
excuse me	*perdóneme*
be careful!	*¡Tenga cuidado!*
maybe	*quizás*
nothing	*nada*
It is urgent!	*¡Es urgente!*
How do you do?	*¿Cómo está usted?*
Well, and you?	*¿Bien, y usted?*
What is your name?	*¿Como se llama?*
hello	*¡Ola!*
goodbye	*Adios/Hasta luego*
good morning	*Buenos dias*
good afternoon	*Buenas tardes*
good evening	*Buenas noches*
What is that?	*¿Qué es eso?*
what	*qué*
who	*quien*
where	*dónde*
when	*cuando*
why	*por qué*
how	*cómo*
how much	*cuánto*
how many	*cuántas*
I am lost	*Me he perdido*
I am hungry	*Tengo hambre*
I am thirsty	*Tengo sed*
I am sorry	*Lo siento*
I am tired	*Estoy cansado*

I am sleepy	*Tengo sueño*
I am ill	*No siento bien*
Leave me alone	*Déjeme en paz*
good	*bueno/buena*
bad	*mal/malo*
it's all the same	*es igual*
slow	*despacio*
fast	*rápido*
big	*grande*
small	*pequeño*
hot	*caliente*
cold	*frío*
up	*arriba*
down	*abajo*

Shopping/Sightseeing

I would like ...	*quisiera ...*
where is/are ...	*dónde está/están ...*
how much is it?	*¿cuánto vale eso?*
open	*abierto*
closed	*cerrado*
cheap/expensive	*barato/caro*
bank	*banco*
beach	*playa*
bed	*cama*
church	*iglesia*
hospital	*hospital*
money	*dinero*
museum	*museo*
newspaper (foreign)	*periódico (extranjero)*
pharmacy	*farmacia*
police station	*comisaría*
policeman	*policía*
post office	*correos*
sea	*mar*
shop	*tienda*
telephone	*teléfono*
tobacco shop (subpost office)	*el estanco*
toilet/toilets	*servicios/aseos*
men	*señores/hombres/caballeros*
women	*señoras/damas*

Time

what time is it?	*qué hora es?*
month	*mes*
week	*semana*
day	*día*
morning	*mañana*
afternoon	*tarde*
evening	*noche*
today	*hoy*
yesterday	*ayer*
soon	*pronto*
tomorrow	*mañana*
now	*ahora*
later	*despues*
it is early	*está presto*
it is late	*está tarde*

180

Days

Monday	*lunes*
Tuesday	*martes*
Wednesday	*miércoles*
Thursday	*jueves*
Friday	*viernes*
Saturday	*sábado*
Sunday	*domingo*

Numbers

one	*uno/una*
two	*dos*
three	*tres*
four	*cuatro*
five	*cinco*
six	*seis*
seven	*siete*
eight	*ocho*
nine	*nueve*
ten	*diez*
eleven	*once*
twelve	*doce*
thirteen	*trece*
fourteen	*catorce*
fifteen	*quince*
sixteen	*dieciséis*
seventeen	*diecisiete*
eighteen	*dieciocho*
nineteen	*diecinueve*
twenty	*veinte*
twenty one	*veintiuno*
thirty	*treinta*
forty	*cuarenta*
fifty	*cincuenta*
sixty	*sesenta*
seventy	*setenta*
eighty	*ochenta*
ninety	*noventa*
one hundred	*cien*
one hundred and one	*ciento-uno*
five hundred	*quinientos*
one thousand	*mil*

Transport

airport	*aeropuerto*
bus stop	*parada*
bus/coach	*autobús/autocar*
railway station	*estación ferroviario*
train	*tren*
port	*puerto*
port station	*estación maritímo*
ship	*buque/barca/embarcadero*
automobile	*coche*
ticket	*billete*
customs	*aduana*
seat	*asiento*

SOUTHERN SPAIN

Travel Directions

I want to go to...	*Deseo ir a...*
How can I get to...?	*¿Como puedo llegar a...?*
Do you stop at...?	*¿Para en...?*
Where is...?	*¿Donde está...?*
When is the next...?	*¿Cuándo sale el próximo...?*
From which stop does it leave?	*¿De donde sale?*
How long does the trip take?	*¿Cuánto tiempo dura el viaje?*
How much is the fare?	*¿Cuánto vale el billete?*
Good trip!	*¡Buen viaje!*
here	*aquí*
there	*allí*
close	*cerca*
far	*lejos*
full	*lleno*
left	*izquierda*
right	*derecha*
forward	*adelante*
backward	*atrasada*
north	*norte/septentrional*
south	*sud/sur/meridional*
east	*este/oriente*
west	*oeste/occidental*
corner	*esqina*
square	*plaza*

Driving (Most signs will be in international pictographs)

rent	*aquilar*
car	*coche*
motorbike/moped	*scooter/mobylette*
bicycle	*bicicleta*
petrol	*gasolina*
garage	*garaje*
This doesn't work	*Esto no funciona*
mechanic	*mecánico*
map	*mapa*
Where is the road to?	*¿Dónde está el camino a...?*
Is the road good?	*¿Es buena la carretera?*
breakdown	*avería*
(international) Driver's licence	*carnet de conducir (internacional)*
driver	*conductor, chófer*
speed	*velocidad*
exit	*salida*
entrance	*entrada*
danger	*peligro*
no parking	*estacionamento prohibido*
narrow	*estrecha*
yield	*ceda el paso*

182

Menu and Restaurant Vocabulary

Hors d'oeuvres and Eggs	Entremesas y Huevos
artichokes with mayonnaise	*alcachofas con mahonese*
frog legs	*ancas de rana*
olives	*aceitunas*
broth	*caldo*
assorted hors d'oeuvres	*entremeses variados*
baked eggs in tomato sauce	*huevos de flamenco*
shrimp in hot garlic sauce	*gambas pil pil*
cold soup	*gazpacho*
fried eggs	*huevos al plato*
scrambled eggs	*huevos revueltos*
rice soup	*sopa de arroz*
asparagus soup	*sopa de espárragos*
garlic soup	*sopa de ajo*
noodle soup	*sopa de fideos*
chick pea soup	*sopa de garbanzos*
lentil soup	*sopa de lentejas*
vegetable soup	*sopa de verduras*
Spanish omelette (with potatoes)	*tortilla*
French omelette	*tortilla a la francésca*

Fish	Pescados
small soles	*acedías*
fish marianated in white wine	*adobo*
clams	*almejas*
anchovies	*anchoas*
eels	*anguilas*
baby eels	*angulas*
crayfish	*ástaco*
tuna fish	*atún*
codfish (usually dried)	*bacalao*
sea bream	*besugo*
tunny	*bonito*
fresh sardines	*boquerones*
mackerel	*caballa*
squid (*en su tinta*, in its own ink)	*calamares (or chiperones)*
crab	*cangrejo*
spider crab	*centollo*
whitebait	*chanquetes*
squid	*chiperones*
baby clams	*chirlas*
clams	*coquilas*
sea bass	*dorada, lubina*
pickled or marinated fish	*escabeche*
prawns	*gambas*
lobster	*langosta*
giant prawns	*langostinos*
sole	*lenguado*
shellfish	*mariscos*
mussels	*mejillones*
hake	*merluzo*
halibut	*mero*
razor-shell clams	*navajas*

oysters	*ostras*
barnacles	*percebes*
whiting	*pescadilla*
swordfish	*pez espada*
hake	*pijotas*
plaice	*platija*
octopus	*pulpo*
monkfish	*rape*
skate	*raya*
turbot	*rodaballo*
salmon	*salmon*
red mullet	*salmonete*
sardines	*sardinas*
trout	*trucha*
scallops	*veneras*
fish stew	*zarzuela*

Meat and Fowl	**Carnes y Aves**
meatballs	*albóndigas*
roast	*asada*
beefsteak	*bistek*
tripe	*callos*
pork	*cerdo*
spiced sausage	*chorizo*
chops	*chuletas*
suckling pig	*cochinillo*
rabbit	*conejo*
heart	*corazón*
lamb	*cordero*
pheasant	*faison*
cold meats	*fiambres*
fillet	*filete*
liver	*hígado*
wild boar	*jabalí*
raw cured ham	*jamón de York*
baked ham	*jamón serrano*
tongue	*lengua*
pork loin	*lomo*
blood sausage	*morcilla*
pigeon	*paloma*
duck	*pato*
turkey	*pavo*
partridge	*perdiz*
spicy mini-kebabs	*pinchitos*
chicken	*pollo*
bull's tail cooked with onions and tomatoes	*rabo/cola de toro*
kidneys	*riñones*
sausage	*salchicha*
salami	*salsichón*
brains	*sesos*
fillet steak	*solomillo*
beef	*ternera*

*Note that *potajes, cocidos, quisadas, estofados, fabadas* and *cazelas* are various kinds of stews.

Vegetables	Verduras Legumbres
artichokes	*alcachofas*
celery	*apio*
rice	*arroz*
rice with saffron and seafood	*arroz marinera*
aubergine (eggplant)	*berenjena*
onion	*cebolla*
mushrooms	*champiñones*
cabbage	*col, repollo*
cauliflower	*coliflor*
endives	*endivias*
salad	*ensalada*
asparagus	*espárragos*
spinach	*espinacas*
chickpeas	*garbanzos*
green peas	*guisantes*
French beans	*judías*
lettuce	*lechuga*
lentils	*lentejas*
potatoes (fried/baked)	*patatas (fritas/salteados)*
cucumber	*pepino*
pepper	*pimento*
leeks	*puerros*
beetroots (beets)	*remolachas*
Spanish mushrooms	*setas*
carrots	*zanahorias*

Fruits and Desserts	Frutas y Postres
apricot	*albaricoque*
almonds	*almendras*
rice pudding	*arroz con leche*
cake	*bizcocho pastel torta*
ice cream and coffee float	*blanco y negro*
cherries	*cerezas*
plums	*ciruelas*
prune	*ciruela pasa*
custard (crême caramel)	*flan*
raspberries	*frambuesas*
strawberries (with cream)	*fresas (con nata)*
biscuits (cookies)	*galletas*
slush, iced squash	*granizado*
ice creams	*helados*
figs	*higos*
apple	*manzana*
peach	*melocotón*
melon	*melón*
orange	*naranja*
flan with ice cream	*pajama*
pastries	*pasteles*
pear	*pera*
pineapple	*piña*
banana	*plátano*

cheese	*queso*
soft white cheese	*requesón*
watermelon	*sandía*
pie	*tarta*
shortcake	*torta*
nougat	*turrón*
grapes	*uvas*

Beverages	**Bebidas**
mineral water (without/with fizz)	*agua mineral (sin/con gaz)*
milkshake	*batido de leche*
beer	*cerveza*
coffee (with milk)	*café (con leche)*
Spanish champagne	*cava*
chocolate	*chocolate*
milk	*leche*
tea (with lemon)	*té (con limón)*
wine (red, rosé, white)	*vino (tinto, rosado, blanco)*

Other Words	
(olive) oil	*aceite (de oliva)*
marinade	*adobo*
garlic	*ajo*
lunch	*almuerzo/comida*
sugar	*azúcar*
sandwich	*bocadillo*
change	*cambio*
waiter	*camerero*
menu	*carta*
dinner	*cena*
spoon	*cuchara*
knife	*cuchillo*
bill	*cuenta*
breakfast	*desayuno*
meat pie	*empañados*
ice	*hielo*
lemon	*limón*
butter	*mantequilla*
marmalade	*mermelada*
table	*mesa*
honey	*miel*
bread	*pan*
roll	*panecillo*
ground pepper	*pimentón*
plate	*plata*
grapefruit	*pomelo*
(without) salt	*(sin) sal*
sauce	*salsa*
napkin	*servilleta*
cup	*taza*
fork	*tenedor*
toast	*tostada*
glass	*vaso*
vinegar	*vinegre*

FURTHER READING

General and Travel

Baird, David, *Inside Andalusia* (Lookout Publications). Background reading. Glossy, full of history and anecdote.

Borrow, George, *The Bible in Spain* (various editions, first written in 1843). A jolly travel account by a preposterous Protestant Bible salesman in 19th-century Spain.

Brenan, Gerald, *South from Granada* (1957). A sharp-eyed, evocative account of Brenan's many years in the village of Yegen.

Chetwode, Penelope, *Two Middle-Aged Ladies in Andalusia* A delightful bosom-heaving burro-back look at the region.

Ford, Richard, *Gatherings from Spain* (Everyman). A boiled-down version of the all-time classic travel-book *A Handbook for Travellers in Spain*, written in 1845. Hard to find but worth the trouble.

Hooper, John, *The Spaniards* (Viking 1986). New on the market, a comprehensive account of contemporary Spanish life and politics. Well done.

Jacobs, Michael, *A Guide to Andalusia* (Viking). Informative and well-researched volume on history, culture and sights.

Luard, Nicholas, *Andalucía* (Century). Readable chronicle of life in an Andalucían village.

Lee, Laurie, *As I Walked Out One Midsummer Morning* and *A Rose for Winter*. Very well-written adventures of a young man in Spain in 1936, and his return 20 years later.

History

Brenan, Gerald, *Spanish Labyrinth* (Cambridge, 1943). Origins of the Civil War.

Carr, Raymond, *Modern Spain 1875–1980* (Oxford, 1985). A confusing period, confusingly rendered.

Castro, Americo, *The Structure of Spanish History* (E. L. King, 1954). A remarkable interpretation of Spain's history, published in exile during the Franco years.

Elliot, J. H., *Imperial Spain 1469–1714* (Pelican, 1983). Elegant proof that much of the best writing these days is in the field of history.

Gibson, Ian, *The Assassination of Federico García Lorca* (Penguin 1984).

Kanen, Henry, *The Spanish Inquisition* (out of print). The definitive history.

Mitchell, David, *The Spanish Civil War* (Granada 1982). Anecdotal; wonderful photographs.

Thomas, Hugh, *The Spanish Civil War* (Penguin, 1977). The best general work.

Watt, W. H., and Cachia, Pierre, *A History of Islamic Spain* (Edinburgh University Press, 1977).

187

Art and Literature

Brenan, Gerald, *The Literature of the Spanish People* (Cambridge, 1951).

Burkhardt, Titus, *Moorish Culture in Spain* (Allen and Unwin). Indispensable for understanding the world of al-Andalus.

García Lorca, Federico, *Three Tragedies* and *Five Plays: Comedies and Tragicomedies* (Penguin).

Irving, Washington, *Tales of the Alhambra* (various editions) and *The Conquest of Granada*, London, 1986.

Moorish Poetry, translated by A. J. Arberry (Cambridge, 1953). A translation of a 13th-century anthology, mostly of Andalucían poets.

CHRONOLOGY

c.50,000 BC	Earliest traces of man in Andalucía
c.25,000 BC	Paleolithic Proto-Spaniards occupy and decorate region's caves
c.7000 BC	Arrival of Iberians, probably from North Africa
c.2300 BC	Bronze Age settlement at Los Millares, largest in Europe
c.1100 BC	Phoenicians found Cadiz
c.800 BC	Celts from over the Pyrenees join the Iberians; period of the kingdom of Tartessos in Andalucía
c.636 BC	Greeks found trading colony near Málaga
c.500 BC	Carthage conquers Tartessos
241 BC	Carthage loses First Punic War to Rome
227 BC	Rome and Carthage sign treaty, assigning lands south of the Ebro to Carthage
219 BC	Second Punic War breaks out when Hannibal besieges Roman ally Sagonte
218 BC	Hannibal takes his elephants and the war to Italy
211–206 BC	Romans under their Proconsul Scipio Africanus take the war back to Spain, defeating Carthage
206 BC	Founding of Italica, a Roman veterans' colony, near Sevilla
55 BC	The elder Seneca born in Córdoba
46 BC	During the ups and downs of the wars and colonizations of Spain, Caesar intervenes, riding from Rome to Obulco (60 km from Córdoba) in 27 days; founds veterans colony at Osuna
27 BC	Augustus divides Iberian peninsula into Interior Spain, Lusitania (Portugal) and Further Spain, soon better known as Bætica (Andulucía)
39 AD	Roman poet Lucan born in Córdoba
50	All of Spain finally conquered by Romans, who lay out the first road network
54	Trajan, future Roman emperor, born at Itálica
70	Romans under Titus destroy the Temple in Jerusalem; in the subsequent Diaspora thousands of Jews ended up in Spain
76	Hadrian, Trajan's successor in 117, born at Itálica
306	Council of Iliberis (Elvira, near Granada) consolidates the Christianization of Spain; votes for the celibacy of priests and bans Christians from wedding pagans
409–428	Vandals vandalize Bætica and change its name to Vandalusia
478	Visigoths, followers of the Arian heresy, control most of Spain, including Andalucía
554	Byzantine emperor Justinian sends troops to take sides in Visigoth civil war, and overstay welcome
573	King Leovigild of the Visigoths chases the Greeks out of their last footholds in Andalucía
589	Leovigild's son, Reccared, converts to orthodox Chritianity
602–35	St Isidore, Bishop of Sevilla, whose writings provide main link between the ancient and medieval worlds
711	Arabs and Berbers under Tariq defeat Roderick, the last Visigoth king
718	Pelayo, in Asturias, defeats Muslims in battle, marking the official beginning of the Reconquista
732	The Arabs reach their high-water mark at Poitiers
756	Abd ar-Rahman, of the Ummayyad dynasty, first Emir of al-Andalus; begins the Great Mosque of Córdoba
844	Abd al-Rahman II begins the Alcázar in Sevilla
880–917	Revolt against Umayyads by Ibn-Hafsun, at Bobastro
912–976	Emir Abd ar-Rahman III declares himself Caliph of Córdoba and begins the magnificent palace-city of Madinat az-Zahra
977	Last enlargements of the Great Mosque by Al-Mansur
994	Birth of Ibn-Hazm of Córdoba (Abernhazam), greatest scholar of century and author of famous treatise on love, *The Ring of the Dove* (d. 1064)
1003	Birth of love poet Ibn Zaydun in Córdoba (d. 1070)
1008	Caliphate starts to unravel
1013	Berbers destroy Madinat az-Zahra
1031	Caliphate abolished as al-Andalus dissolves into factions of the Taifa kings
1085	Alfonso VI of Castile and the Cid capture Toledo from the Muslims
1086	Taifa kings summon aid of the Berber Almoravids
1105	Birth of philosopher Ibn-Tufayl (Abubacer) in Guardix, author of charming narrative romance *Hayy ibn-Yaqzan* (The Awakening of the Soul), one of the masterworks of al-Andalus
1110	Almoravids gobble up the Taifa kingdoms

1126	Birth of Ibn-Rushd in Códoba, philosopher and commentator on Aristotle, better known in the west as Averroës (d. 1198)
1135	Alfonso VII of Castile and León takes the title of Emperor of Spain
1145	Uprisings against the Almoravids
1172	Almohads conquer Sevilla, rounding off defeat of Almoravids
1195	Completion of the Giralda in Sevilla
1212	Alfonso VII's victory at Las Navas de Tolosa opens the gate to al-Andalus
1231	Muhammad ibn-Yusuf ibn-Nasr carves out a small realm around Jaén
1236	Fernando III (the saint) captures Córdoba
1238	Muhammad ibn-Yusuf ibn-Nasr takes Granada, founding the Nasrid dynasty and beginning construction of the Alhambra
1248	Fernando III takes Sevilla with the help of his vassal, Muhammad ibn-Yusef ibn-Nasr
1262	Alfonso X (the Wise) picks up Cádiz
1292	Sancho IV takes Tarifa
1309	Guzmán el Bueno seizes Gibraltar
1333	Alfonso XI loses Gibraltar to the king of Granada
1350–69	Reign of Pedro the Cruel of Castile
1415	Ceuta captured by Portuguese, though it remained in Spanish hands after the division of the two kingdoms
1462	Enrico IV gets Gibraltar back for Castile
1479	Isabella and Ferdinand unite their kingdoms of Castile and Aragon
1480	Spanish Inquisition sets up a branch office in Sevilla
1492	Ferdinand and Isabella complete the Reconquista with the capture of Granada and expel Jews from Spain; Columbus sets off from Sevilla to discover the New World
1500	First Revolt of the Alpujarras
1516	Birth of lyric poet Luis de Góngora in Córdoba
1519	Isabella and Ferdinand's grandson becomes Emperor Charles V
1528	Sculptor Pietro Torrigiano dies in the Inquisition's prison in Sevilla
1556–98	Reign of Charles' bureaucratic son, Philip II
1568	Philip II's intolerance leads to the Second Revolt of the Alpujarras
1580	Sevilla largest city in Spain, with population of 85,000
1599	Diego Velázquez born in Sevilla (d. 1660)
1609–14	Philip III forces half a million Muslims to move to North Africa
1617	Murillo born in Sevilla (d. 1682)
1627	Birth of Sevillan libertine don Miguel de Mañara, believed to be the original Don Juan Tenorio of Tirso de Molina and the *Don Giovanni* of Mozart
1630	Madrid becomes the largest city in Spain
1649	Plague leaves one out of three people dead in Sevilla
1667–1700	Reign of Charles II, last of the Spanish Habsburgs
1700–36	Louis XIV exports his brand of Bourbon to Spain, in the form of his grandson Philip V
1704	Anglo-Dutch fleet, under the auspices of Charles of Austria, captures Gibraltar
1726	Spain tries in vain to regain the Rock
1757	Completion of Sevilla's tobacco factory, where Carmen would work
1783	Treaty of Versailles confirms British possession of Gibraltar
1788–1808	Reign of the pathetic Charles IV, caricatured by Goya
1830	So many English winter in Málaga that they need their own cemetery
1832	Washington Irving publishes *Tales of the Alhambra*
1876	Manuel de Falla born in Cádiz
1881	Pablo Picasso born in Málaga; Nobel prize-winning poet Juan Ramón Jiménez born in Moguer de la Frontera (d. 1958)
1893	Andrea Segovia born near Jaén
1898	Birth of Federico Garcia Lorca, near Granada (d. 1936)
1920	Ibero-American Exposition in Sevilla gets a disappointing turnout
1936–39	Civil War
1940	Hitler tries to get Spain to join Axis by promising to help Spain conquer Gibraltar, but Franco says no
1953	First economic-military cooperation between Spain and the USA
1956	Spain ends its protectorate in Morocco, but keeps Ceuta and Melila
1962	Franco's Minister of Tourism gives go ahead for development of the Costa del Sol
1966	An American bomber over Palomares collides with another plane and drops four nuclear bombs
1975	Death of Franco; Juan Carlos crowned King of Spain
1982	Felipe Gonzalez of Sevilla elected Prime Minister
1985	Frontier between Gibraltar and Spain opens
1986	Spain and Portugal join the EC
1992	International Exposition in Sevilla to commemmorate the 500th anniversary of Colombus' sailing

INDEX

Note: Page references in *italics* indicate illustrations; references in **bold** type indicate maps.

INDEX